AMERICA THE
BEAUTIFUL

AMERICA THE BEAUTIFUL

As Seen Through the Eyes
of Its Immigrants

BY
ROBERT POLLOCK

America the Beautiful As Seen Through the Eyes of Its Immigrants

ISBN-13: 978-1-955937-90-0 (Paperback)
ISBN-13: 978-1-955937-00-9 (eBook)

Published by Defiance Press and Publishing, LLC

Bulk orders of this book may be obtained by contacting Defiance Press and Publishing, LLC.
www.defiancepress.com.

Defiance Press & Publishing, LLC
281-581-9300
info@defiancepress.com

DEDICATED TO

My father, Robert Pollock, Sr.
and his father, Archie Pollock,
who arrived as an orphan from Ireland in 1910.

Their wisdom, guidance, and love were
an inspiration to me and all who knew them.

TABLE OF CONTENTS

An abbreviated overview of the American journey from its discovery through the Revolution, and on to it becoming one of the world's greatest and most attractive countries for immigrants.

What were the living conditions in the homelands of some of our immigrants? What was it about America that motivated those immigrants to forsake all and make their way to this land?

Once immigrants arrived in America, what paths were taken to reach their current place? How did they establish themselves and map a way forward?

Was America what they had envisioned it might be? What may have been different from their expectations, and was it all they had hoped?

INTRODUCTION

> *America—it is a fabulous country, the only fabulous country; it is the only place where miracles not only happen, but where they happen all the time.*
>
> —THOMAS WOLFE

This book is, in many ways, a love story; it is two love stories. First, it is a story of America. We discover what it is, what it's been throughout history, and what has attracted people from all corners of the planet to her shores. How has the song of America's beauty spread throughout the world? Perhaps even more important, are those same qualities of historical attraction still present today? Do today's immigrants have the same chances of success as their forefathers?

Second, it is a story of the immigrants themselves. What motivated them to come? What were their experiences once they arrived? Was this the America they envisioned; was it all they had hoped? What personal qualities and attributes do they see as essential to success? There are literally thousands upon thousands of beautiful stories surrounding America's immigrant population, but so few are ever told. In some small way, this book attempts to give voice to just some of those stories. In those few, however, let it be understood that there

1

exist many thousands of others who traveled similar paths and made similar journeys.

This work began with one such story. It came about, as is so often the case, quite by accident. I was placed at a table with a salesperson by the name of Said, who was originally from Morocco and then living in Florida. In our conversation, he spoke at length about his homeland, what life was like as he was growing up, how he came to be in America, and his experiences up to that time. It was a fascinating tale of a young man from unimaginable poverty who came to America with no money and no English skills, only hope. His exuberance and love of America pervaded his entire conversation, and it was inspiring to hear of these feelings for his adopted country.

Thinking about Said's story in the days to come, I wondered just how many others had their own story waiting to be told. How many other immigrants have also come to realize and appreciate the beauty of America? As I continued my time in Florida, I began to take note of the many immigrants I met along the way; there were maître d's, waiters, shuttle drivers, counter people, men and women from all walks of life. During each meeting, I took the time to ask about their stories and what they now thought of America. I was gladdened and amazed to hear how many of them had come to love this country. Not everyone was wealthy or notably successful; in fact, most were not. But almost all spoke of worthwhile lives that offered value to their communities and a hope for an even better future. These were stories I recognized should be told, not hidden in the shadows. These were perspectives waiting for a voice, and I felt compelled to bring at least a few to light. I ask myself, through the sharing of these stories and ideas, might we not *all* find a greater appreciation for the beautiful country in which we live?

In an act of full disclosure, I readily admit I come to this work with some distinct biases. The most important of these is an unflagging love for this country. The chosen stories are those related by migrants who came from other places but found America's promise. In selecting interviewees, several criteria were essential. First, their presence had to have legal status. They did not have to be citizens or even in the process of obtaining citizenship; they simply needed to be here legally. There were many reasons for this requirement, not the least of which was I did not want to unintentionally expose anyone to subsequent risks.

Second, they had to have been in the United States sufficiently long enough to experience its realities; they had to have sufficient time to encounter the full spectrum of life's victories and trials. Priority was given to narratives that were unique or contained uplifting qualities such that readers could share in their sense of hopefulness and success. These stories do not accrue overnight; they do not evolve without their own sense of drama. In them, however, we are provided a window through which we can see the face of America's dream through an outsider's eyes—the eyes of our immigrants.

Last, I wanted to relate stories from those who harbored a genuine love and appreciation for America. This is not to say there might not have been concerns or there were not aspects of the country they at some point found unattractive; of course, there were occasional misgivings. If we are to have any balance, we must be mindful to confront those things where continued effort must be made; we must acknowledge there are still blemishes to be healed. Understand, too, we can love our spouse and children while continuing to recognize our own imperfections.

The presentation of the book is a narrated collection of stories, anecdotes, observations, and quotes provided by America's immigrants. These stories and commentaries come from a wide variety of sources. Published biographies or autobiographies were especially useful in describing stories from earlier periods in our history. Compendiums of short biographical sketches from other references helped round out specific points. Articles, editorials, and speeches written by immigrants provided important insights that only an immigrant might supply. Finally, there are the numerous personal interviews conducted over more than two years to add more contemporary contexts. To avoid unnecessary redundancy, I selected those experiences and narratives that were unique or interesting, and coupled them with historic voices and quotes to capture the important ideas reflected in each chapter. Italics are used to distinguish the comments of other speakers. A final note is that, in telling these stories, the aim was to maintain the contributor's voice as much as clarity and accuracy would permit.

Efforts were made to find immigrants from a variety of countries. The relative level of personal success or station in life was not a factor. Although there was insufficient space to tell everyone's story in full, I made a sincere effort to include any thoughts interviewees identified as central to their experience.

The organization of the book does not simply recount one immigrant story after another or allow their words to stand without a necessary framework. It is not intended to be just a set of rambling biographies. Each chapter has a specific theme designed to focus on a fundamental aspect of the immigrant experience and how specific experiences might have shaped their view of America. For that reason, the reader is likely to encounter anecdotes and quotes from the same person in various segments of the book.

Writing is, at best, a solitary business. The work involves only two people: they are the author and the audience. My primary audience in this work includes those with a love of America. That said, the unfortunate reality is that the people of America have now become polarized into two disparate and sometimes strident camps. First are those who love our founding, revere our beautiful Constitution, and cherish the historical images and traditions the country has presented for almost 250 years. The second includes those who now see America as highly flawed, founded by slave owners and others of low moral value, and a country unworthy of its place in the world as an economic and cultural leader. This book is for those in the former category. I make no apology.

A second and equally important audience is America's immigrants themselves. This book speaks to the many millions who have come to this land and now call America home. They are now Americans, and it is critically important they understand how much we value their presence, and how much their contributions add to this country. By telling some of their stories, perhaps we, too, can share the beauty of their lives and how this country speaks to the world.

Finally, the book is meant to address those who might be considering America as a place to which they might someday come. Stories of their fellow travelers can provide necessary insights that will never be contained in travel books, brochures, or other media that depict American life. There are specific chapters that outline the kinds of hurdles a newly arrived individual might face and what previous immigrants have done to address them. There is guidance and insight to hopefully provide the hope, courage, and inspiration required to make informed decisions. America is not for everyone. We know that. But we also know America's voice continues to call across the continents to people of all nationalities. Some are right now considering options as to their future course. I hope the pages of this book will provide a clearer picture.

There are millions of potential future immigrants from other nations "yearning to be free;" they are the restless who are seeking an opportunity to come embrace this new land. There are stories from more than two centuries telling of travelers who have already come and made this country their own. There will be many more in the future. Will yours be one? America will always need good people with talents to offer and dreams to build. After all, this is, and intends to stay, *America the Beautiful!*

Robert Pollock

CHAPTER 1

BECOMING AMERICA

> And if ever there was a just war since the world
> began, it is this with which America is now
> engaged...We fight not to enslave, but to set a
> country free, and to make room on the earth for
> honest men to live in.
>
> —THOMAS PAINE, *The American Crisis*

AMERICA! How many times over the last two-and-a-half centuries has that one word been exclaimed to represent a hope for the future, a destination with the promise of a better life? From countries all over the world, men and women have looked to America and seen a future brimming with possibilities. It has been a place that people have endured every hardship to reach. There are countless pictures of immigrants passing the Statue of Liberty with their eyes gazing up in wonderment and their hearts full of hope. "AMERICA!" They had arrived. New and glorious opportunities must surely await. Their souls could soar with prospects of a new life.

Yes, America has almost always represented that one place where a person with a longing to be better and, armed with a desire to provide a life of happiness for his or her family, could come and make it all come true. That dream is as real today as it has been throughout history. Understand, however, a country with that kind of promise did not happen by chance, and it did not arrive overnight. No. The birth of the America that has stirred the imagination of so many was created from great trial, sacrifice, and hardship. It was forged from the flames of revolution, the acrimony of debate, and the lives of almost 20,000 patriots. In so many ways, it is only a matter of divine providence that she is here at all.

If we are to fully understand how America has attracted so many to its shores, we must first understand the true history of her birth. It is in that history that the true beauty and magnificence of this dream called America took shape and was given life. It took nothing short of a miracle to become America.

America's First Immigrants

The vision of this country began as a simple desire to be free, but the America we became took more than 100 additional years to evolve and transform itself into the beautiful ideologies of its founding. The path from Pilgrim settlers to the America of today has been in no small way a measure of God's grace; it is a miraculous rise of the Republic that has been the envy of peoples and countries the world over. The evidence for divine intervention strongly suggests that America is no accident. An isolated incidence or two of fortunate events may be simply good luck. But an extended chain of such occurrences spanning numerous years suggests something entirely different...a design!¹ It is this story of America's birth that is of *critical importance* to how America ultimately evolved; it provides vital insight as to the real reason it has been such an attraction to the immigrants who would flood her shores over the next century and a half.

The original settlers, not totally unlike the immigrants of today, arrived with the hope of starting a new life, a life free of tyranny, a life without the menacing hand of government persecution. The religious intolerance of the early 1600s grew progressively worse until, in 1629, King Charles I dissolved Parliament and initiated what would become known as the Eleven Years' Tyranny. He went so far as to declare Puritans' exercise of their faith treasonous, and conviction of such a crime carried with it the death penalty. The Puritans rightly saw these hostile actions toward their religious practice as dangerous and intolerable. As a result, many decided there was no choice but to leave England for other countries or the Americas where they could be free!

A principal individual in the early establishment of what would ultimately become America was religious separatist William Bradford, who had fled England for Holland in 1609. After eleven years in Holland, Bradford was still not satisfied, and he, along with 40 others, decided to make their way to the New World. Even though it was a perilous journey into the unknown, Bradford and the others considered it worth the risk to be able to worship their God and practice their religion however they wished. On August 1, 1620, they embarked on the *Mayflower* with 102 passengers. Within this group, about 37 were members of a separatist group known as the Leidens. The others were simply fellow travelers who also wished for a new life.

As the voyage progressed, it was determined there would need to be an understanding among everyone as to how they would govern themselves once they reached land. The document created to establish those governing rules became known as the *Mayflower Compact*. This compact was deeply steeped in scriptural teachings and the Bible. As such, all were confident that their endeavor would be consecrated by God and blessed by His hand of grace. Their journey covered a grueling 66 days and was filled with sickness, personal disagreements, sanitary issues, and almost every imaginable hardship. Yet, they made it!

When they reached land in November of 1620, they were met with nothing but rocks, forest, and increasingly harsh weather. There were no houses, no trade stores, no cleared land, and no visible means of supporting themselves through the coming winter. Bradford detailed in his journal:

> ...there was nothing but a cold, barren, desolate, unsettled, wilderness." Being thus passed the vast ocean, and a sea of troubles before in their preparation (as may be remembered by that which went before), they had now no friends to welcome them nor inns to entertain or refresh their weather-beaten bodies; no houses or much less town to repair to, to seek for succor.[2]

Enduring those extreme circumstances was such that, during their first winter, more than half of the original 102 perished of starvation, sickness, or exposure.

How were these Pilgrim settlers to organize themselves and survive this foreboding land? Originally, their contract called for everything they produced to go into a general storage. Each member of the community was to receive one common share in a way where every person got exactly the same as every other person. Equality. Whatever land was cleared, houses built, or crops grown, all was to be distributed equally. The proceeds of all work and harvest belonged to everyone in such a way that no individual would have "ownership" of anything. It was in every sense what we now might call a "commune."

Although things began in satisfactory manner, over the first three years, problems gradually set in and the settlement began to stagnate. Because everyone received an equal share no matter how much they individually contributed or how little they worked, jealousies, envy, and sometimes violent arguments began to emerge. The creative, more industrious people began to reduce their efforts. With no incentive to work harder, their motivation to produce was severely weakened. Bradford saw the flaw in this system and wrote about it in his journal.

> The experience that we had in this common course and condition, tried sundry years...that by taking away property, and bringing community into a common wealth, would make them happy and flourishing — as if they were wiser than God....

> For this community was found to breed much confusion and discontent and retard much employment that would have been to their benefit and comfort. For young men that were most able and fit for "labor and service" didn't. They waited. They didn't want to produce for other men's wives and children what other men should have been providing, and eventually this "was thought injustice." Why should

you work for other people when you can't work for yourself?[3]

William Bradford, 1623

The question then became, what could be done to solve this dilemma? What could Bradford do that would re-energize this fledgling community and insert new life? What he decided was to release the power of the individual; he would remove the shackles dictated by "common ownership," and allow every person to reap the full harvest of his or her own labor. In more contemporary language, he instituted a system of "free enterprise." This new approach allotted to every person a plot of land to do with exactly as he saw fit. Whatever he produced, whatever he created, it was his own and that of his family. *It was in that moment that the core seed of America's greatness was planted; her cornerstone was laid!* It was then that our basic belief in the life-giving force of the individual was born. Empowering each man to make of himself whatever his industriousness and vision would allow set the stage not only for the Pilgrims, but for every immigrant who would ever follow...*and follow they did!*

From 1630-1640, a period known as the "Great Migration" took place. During that time, more than 80,000 Puritans, religious separatists, and freedom seekers left England and Europe for the distant shores of this New World. The majority of these immigrants were clergy or tradesmen who came either alone or with small families. One such person, John Winthrop, assembled a fleet of 11 ships with nearly 700 people and fled to America where he landed in what would later be called Massachusetts.

One must bear in mind just how difficult a decision it was for someone to undertake such a journey in that day. Since the arrival of those first Pilgrims at Plymouth in 1620, all that was known came by way of personal anecdotes and secondhand accounts of the freedom and success others were said to have realized. Yet even those small amounts of information provided such a level of enthusiasm that people were willing to sacrifice all to make the dangerous, arduous journey across an entire ocean and face the uncertain fate that awaited them in what would be America.

Rutman describes the deep misgivings that besieged those making their decisions to come to this unknown land. He writes:

> Winthrop was one with all the others who left Europe for America, the great and the small, who at some point prior to the actual sailing had to make a private decision to abandon the relative security of established ways for the relative insecurity of something new, to give up all he had and truly knew for something he could only imagine, to hazard a dangerous journey and divide his family without real assurance that the family would ever be together again. For each individual this private decision was truly awesome, and the sum of which decisions peopled America.[4]

Winthrop's group reached Massachusetts in 1630, but establishing a new settlement was not easy. Winthrop was determined to settle this new land and establish his new Puritan "City Upon a Hill," a place that would epitomize love and freedom. He sermonized to the people and wrote in his diary:

> For we must consider that we shall be as a city upon a hill. The eyes of all people are upon us. So that if we shall deal

falsely with our God in this work we have undertaken, and so cause Him to withdraw His present help from us, we shall be made a story and a by-word through the world.

He later continued:

Liberty is the proper end and object of authority and cannot subsist without it; and it is liberty to that which is good, just, and honest. Love is the bond of perfection.[5]

John Winthrop, 1630

Liberty! That was Winthrop's vision. If there was a singular enduring virtue by which this new America would prosper, liberty would certainly be its foundation stone. But lofty ideals are not sufficient in and of themselves to engender a country as great as America was to become. It was still the people who would have to bring such ideas to fulfillment and give them life. It was the people who had to throw off the manacles of old ideas so as to establish this new, more lasting framework where liberty might flourish. That was not easy, nor was it fast. Like Plymouth before it, by the end of the first year, 30 percent of Winthrop's new arrivals had died, and an additional 10 percent had returned to England.[6] The winter had been harsh. Life had been full of adversity. But sufficient members remained to gain a foothold such that, over the coming years, a self-sustaining society began to emerge. Through these first two settlements of fearless Pilgrims, America had the beginning upon which its future would take shape.

The Rise of Colonial America

The true beginning of our American journey began to take place in the early 1700s. It would develop along two major fronts: the south, which began in Jamestown, Virginia, and the north, which had Boston at its center. The southern economy was primarily based upon agriculture, while the northeast emerged as a center for business, trade, and mercantilism, although there was a good deal of agriculture there as well. The development of these two areas and their economic prosperity gave America its initial grip on an ability to stand independently. Major cities like Richmond, Williamsburg, New York, Philadelphia, and Boston grew to lead America into a new era.

As new immigrants arrived, they began to disperse. Territories founded by different trading groups and individuals began to define themselves. These differing regions ultimately became separate, distinct colonies. Virginia, founded by John Smith, was the first. Massachusetts, founded by John Winthrop, was the second. Subsequently there was New York, Pennsylvania, Maryland, and so forth. The process continued until there were 13 individual colonies, each with its own economy and lifestyle. In time, each of these colonies evolved into an independent state with its own system of government, laws, and social foundation. These arrangements served the new country well and, for the most part, people were content with the arrangement.

Through the early to mid-eighteenth century, the individual states and England became closely aligned. Colonists generally saw themselves as endowed with the same liberties and benefits enjoyed by their peers in England.

Citizens proudly called themselves "Englishmen," and continued to see themselves as British citizens, albeit on the other side of the Atlantic. But European wars, economic difficulties, diplomatic entanglements, and an ever-increasing reach by Parliament into the pockets and lifestyle of Americans would soon change all that loyalty.

The Rise of Dissent and Call for Independence

The roots of American dissent with England can be traced all the way back to the French and Indian War. This conflict originally arose over a dispute between American trading companies and French traders from the north as to who had rights in what is now the Ohio Valley. This gradually escalated to a point where England feared it was losing control of the Americas. France was claiming larger and larger segments of land in the New World. Armed conflicts broke out as France began building forts around what is now Detroit, Pittsburgh, and all along the Mississippi River as far down as New Orleans. In response, England sent large armies and supplies to America to secure its position.

Of note, a most famous American was at the center of this conflict. What was his name? George Washington. Perhaps contrary to contemporary images, Washington's participation in this conflict was not well received by his family. His recently widowed mother, Mary Ball Washington, had pleaded with him not to take this command and venture into what was then a total wilderness fraught with uncertainty and danger. She had ridden two days from Fredericksburg, Virginia to beg her son to stay at Mount Vernon. But Washington, already steeped in his strong faith of divine protection, responded to her by saying:

> *The God to whom you commended me, madam, when I set out upon this most perilous errand, defended me from all harm, and I trust he will do so now. Do not you?*[7]

Initially, Washington was not to enjoy much military success. Facing the skill of experienced French regular troops, his raw militias had been no match. On a number of occasions, he had been forced to surrender his positions and withdraw, sometimes barely escaping with his life. In one perilous instance, a fatally wounded American General Braddock would rely on Washington to ride and bring back reinforcements for his scattered, wounded, and disheartened army. While desperately riding almost 40 miles through the night, Washington had two mounts shot from under him and several bullets pierced his clothes, one narrowly missing his head and piercing his hat. It was in the aftermath of these experiences that Washington himself came to reflect on this question as to why he had survived when so many others had not. He even wrote of his answer to this question to his brother, John Augustine Washington. To Washington, it was none other than the miraculous hand of Providence!

> *Dear Jack: As I have heard since my arrival at this place, a circumstantial acct. of my death and dying speech, I take this early opportunity of contradicting both, and of assuring you that I now exist and appear in the land of the living by the miraculous care of Providence, that protected me beyond all human expectation; I had 4 bullets through my Coat, two Horses shot under me, and yet escaped unhurt. We have been most scandalously*

beaten by a trifling body of men; but fatigue and want of time prevents me from giving any of the details till I have the happiness of seeing you at home; which I now most ardently wish for...[8]

George Washington, 1755

In these few lines penned to his brother, Washington provides compelling evidence of his deep religiosity and reliance on his God. This solid belief in God and His divine guidance was to persist with Washington throughout the war, and this sense of protection by the Almighty would again color his judgment when he was offered the full command of the Revolutionary Army some years later.

When Washington returned to General Braddock's side, after being unable to secure the necessary reinforcements, he found Braddock in grave condition. The general's last words were reported to have been, *"We shall know better how to deal with them another time."* Washington was indeed preparing himself to "know better" how to lead and perform in battle at a later time; these would be the battles that would lay the foundation for America's success in the war to come.

As the conflict between England and France continued, command of the sea by the English navy became increasingly successful in blocking France from reinforcing or supplying its armies. This, along with the growing proficiency of the colonial militias, introduction of English regular troops, and an almost unlimited ability of the colonists to reinforce its numbers and supplies, would prove too much for France. Ultimately, she was forced to surrender the entire Ohio Valley, along with the vast territories of the north, now known as Canada. Washington had established himself as an exceptional military commander of impeccable bravery. At the time, this might have seemed a somewhat small event, but it was later to become a major influence on just how American independence was to be won. Knowing what we now know, who can deny that perhaps it was indeed the hand of divine providence that intervened to direct these events and keep America's Washington safe. Most assuredly, Washington himself believed that to be the case.

In the immediate aftermath of this victory over the French, the costs began to exercise their role in the ultimate fight for independence. England had spent a great deal of money and resources to secure these lands for America and was itself now in serious financial difficulty. As a result, England began to impose taxes and regulations on the American states in order to replenish its depleted treasury. These new laws and taxes led many colonists to become angry and resentful of what they saw as English intrusion into their lives. Most of all, people feared the loss of that most precious commodity, the one element they had risked all to achieve...liberty!

To pay for the French and Indian War, England imposed harsh taxes on many of the imported goods the colonists relied on from England. Taxes on sugar, tea, and a number of other essential items were widely held as an improper infringement on the liberties of the American people. Without representatives in Parliament to advance the causes of American interests, the citizenry strongly objected to such government interventions, and thus were sown the initial seeds of rebellion.

The match that seemed to irretrievably light the fires of angry discontent was perhaps the *Stamp Act of 1765*. This act imposed a duty on newspapers, legal documents, and almost any form of paper transaction. Opposition to these "taxes" was widespread, intense, and violent. Indeed, it was so violent that many of the men appointed to collect those taxes were dragged from their homes and beaten. Buildings were set ablaze, and it was difficult to even find people willing to be tax collectors. To underscore the point, Benjamin Franklin, who was out of the country at the time as America's agent in the English court, had left his wife Deborah at home in Philadelphia. Not long after passage of the Stamp Act, it was rumored that Franklin had endorsed passage of the act in the English Parliament, and an angry mob formed intent on burning Franklin's home to the ground in retaliation. Deborah, not one to be intimidated, sent her daughter to safety in New Jersey but beseeched her cousin and some friends to arm themselves and come help defend the home. *"Fetch a gun or two,"* she said in defiance, and she was able to save the home by confronting the mob with arms.[9] Ultimately, there had arisen so much unrest and violence that the Stamp Act had to be repealed.

The English Parliament, however, had no intention of allowing the matter of repayment for the expense of the French and Indian War to drop. The next proposal of Parliament to tax the colonies was passage of an entire series of taxes called The Townsend Revenue Acts. These taxes included a number of new impositions, including the Tea Act that placed a duty on all imported tea. This resulted in the first significantly overt act against the British government, known as the Boston Tea Party. A group of men calling themselves the Sons of Liberty disguised themselves as Indians and threw 342 chests of tea from a British merchant ship into Boston Harbor. News of this act of defiance spread through the colonies and served to further stoke the fires of patriotic discontent.

The Townsend Acts included other highly unpopular components such as the Quartering Act, which required citizens to board and feed British troops stationed in America. As with the Stamp Act, the collection of these taxes set off a firestorm of further resentment, public demonstrations, and outrage. It also added a number of influential voices, not the least of whom were John Hancock and Patrick Henry, calling for definitive actions to be taken against England. Hancock, one of Boston's leading merchants, was particularly angry at the intrusive way the goods from his supplier, already in short supply, were being limited and taxed.

Virginia's George Washington agreed and complained to one of his British merchantmen: "I think the Parliament of Great Britain hath no more right to put their hands in my pocket, without my consent, than I have to put my hands into yours for money..."[10]

This was followed by a Letter from a Farmer in Pennsylvania, widely published in newspapers of the day. Among other things, it labeled the taxes unconstitutional and bordering on extortion. This was followed by the Dickenson Letters, which further inflamed the population with its anti-Parliament rhetoric.

Is it possible to form an idea of slavery more complete, more miserable, and more disgraceful than that of a people where justice is administered, government exercised...AT THE EXPENSE OF THE PEOPLE... IF we can find no relief from this infamous situation...we may bow down our necks, and with all the stupid serenity of servitude, to any drudgery which our lords and masters shall please to command.[11]

The discontent and rebelliousness of the citizens of Boston was not confined to the northeast. Virginia, the largest and most wealthy of the colonies, was equally vocal in its call for the repeal of the Townsend Acts. The Virginia Resolutions in support of the actions taken in Boston so outraged the royal governor of Virginia that he summarily dissolved the House of Burgesses and dismissed them from the State House. This only served to make matters worse, and patriots like Patrick Henry and George Washington both spoke out in violent opposition to the heavy-handed treatment being imposed.[12]

Indeed, the colonies were not about to take these intolerable acts without a fight. Something had to be done! The colonies elected and sent delegates to attend the First Continental Congress to be convened in Philadelphia. Business leaders and patriots were united in their resolution. They declared the time had come where all the colonies would need to stand together against the actions of the British government. A continental union was formed, which adopted a document called the Suffolk Resolves. These articles declared the Townsend Acts null and void, and further urged Massachusetts to form a "free government." The Resolves, on being presented to the British Parliament, were *not* well received.

There had been action on the other side of the Atlantic as well. With Benjamin Franklin present in court, William Pitt, now known as Lord Chatham, urged Parliament to repeal the Townsend duties and seek "an amicable solution to the difficulties now present in the colonies." He was shouted down, and his motion soundly rejected. Even the highly regarded

Edmund Burke had risen to beseech Parliament to find conciliation with America. He warned that Americans would never be subdued by force, but his voice too went unheeded. This ultimately proved one of the most unwise courses of action to ever take place in the British Parliament.[13] American tempers had been rising by the day, and surely these actions of Parliament only served to solidify *"...the good reason for which America must now not waiver."*

As these tensions began to mount in the days after the defeat of the Chatham motions, a Second Virginia Convention met at St. John's Church in Richmond, Virginia. This convention was convened to determine how Virginia would ultimately deal with the English crown and these matters of taxation. Many colonial leaders of the day were in attendance, including Washington, Jefferson, and the firebrand, Patrick Henry. Henry had developed a well-earned reputation for his eloquence and steadfast opposition to the numerous laws of taxation the British crown had imposed. It was at this Virginia Convention that Patrick Henry made one of the most famous and inspiring speeches in American history as he rose to rally a nation:

> *I have but one lamp by which my feet are guided, and that is the lamp of experience. I know of no way of judging the future but by the past. And judging by the past, I wish to know what there has been in the conduct of the British ministry for the last ten years to solace themselves and the House?*
>
> *Our petitions have been slighted, our remonstrances have produced additional violence and insult; our supplications have been disregarded; and we have been spurned,*

*with contempt from the foot of the throne...we must fight! I
repeat it, sir, we must fight! An appeal to arms and to the
God of Hosts is all that is left us!*[14]

Never one to fail to appeal to the dramatic, Henry paused
at this point and gazed about the chamber to allow his words
to hang heavily in the air, allow his countrymen to take in their
gravity. When he resumed his oratory, he did so in a
thunderously loud voice such that the walls of the chamber
were near vibrating. Everyone in attendance was riveted on
Henry's every word and leaning forward in their seat so as not
to miss even one. They were not to be disappointed!

*The war is actually begun! The next gale that sweeps from
the north will bring to our ears the clash of resounding
arms. Our brethren are already in the field! Why stand we
here idle? What is it that gentlemen wish? What would
they have? Is life so dear, or peace so sweet, as to be
purchased at the price of chains of slavery? Forbid it,
Almighty God! I know not what course others may take;
but as for me, give me liberty, or give me death!*[15]

Patrick Henry, March 23, 1775

At this last declaration, and for added effect, Henry flew
his arms apart as if breaking out of chains, took hold of an
ivory letter opener, and plunged it toward his chest. The
audience of attendees, as well as those gathered outside the
church listening and watching through windows, sat in dazed
silence. No one was daring enough to even speak in the
aftermath of those stunning words.

This speech was indeed one that has long been assumed to
have tipped the scales in favor of armed action. In its wake, a
Virginia militia was approved for combat with Patrick Henry

at its head. Less than one month later, colonial militiamen confronted British regulars at Lexington and Concord in what is now known as *"The shot heard round the world."*

As the spring of 1775 approached, Massachusetts' tensions had been reaching the breaking point. Various local militias had begun arming themselves and stockpiling munitions. The voices advocating action against British forces in the colony were gaining widespread support. General Gage, commanding the British garrison in Boston, was ordered to seize the American arsenal at Concord. He was also ordered to capture American leaders Samuel Adams and John Hancock, who were thought to be hiding in Lexington. Paul Revere and William Dawes rode out of Boston, taking different routes so as to avoid capture, to warn the colonists of the imminent British attack. The British had split their force and sent a small group to find Adams and Hancock at Lexington, while the main army of more than 700 marched on to Concord. By day's end, the colonial militia, which began at a mere 77 at Lexington, had swelled to more than 4,000 covering the entire British return route to Boston. Firing at the retiring redcoats from every town and behind every tree or wall along the way, they exacted a fearsome toll. By the time the British forces reached Boston again, 73 British soldiers had been killed and an additional 174 wounded. The colonial militia had suffered 49 dead and 42 wounded. Armed resistance had begun![16]

The American Dream is Born

It can be said that the true beauty of our American dream began here in the aftermath of Lexington and Concord.

Previously, it had been merely an idea, a loosely held vision by some of the patriots of the day. In those early days, there was no fully described outline or thought as to what America might ultimately become. Those times were more consumed with the desire for freedom—the yearning that every man should have the liberty to live as he chose without the strong hand of British tyranny reaching across the ocean to exercise its oppression. It was a dream that was to take nearly another full year to take shape but would then extend nearly 250 years into the future.

By May 1775, the Second Continental Congress had been convened in Philadelphia, and times were much different. With the stationing of troops, attempts to attack colonial munitions, and orders to capture patriots, England had presented itself as a military threat. The questions in this Second Congress centered on how to deal with England's outright aggression, not simply how to deal with a few unwanted taxes. This Congress acted! Its first response was to establish a Continental Army to be headed by none other than George Washington. They additionally authorized the printing of money to pay for what many saw as the coming war. Congress appointed committees to establish international relationships and enter negotiations with foreign governments on behalf of the colonies. In so doing, the Continental Congress had taken onto itself the new role as a *governing body*. It was no longer merely a convocation of concerned patriots. The lines were drawn, and the stage set for America to declare her independence.

This last step toward self-governance was not done in haste or without reservation. England was recognized as a formidable power that would not sit idly by when news of these latest actions became known. Establishment of an independent army was a brave undertaking that concerned many. Washington himself was not anxious to assume command. He was reluctant to even make himself a candidate. He wrote to John Hancock, president of the Continental Congress:

> *"Mr. President, Though I am truly sensible of the high honor done me in this appointment, yet I feel great distress from a consciousness that my abilities and military experience may not be equal to the extensive and important trust. However, as the Congress desire it, I will enter upon the momentous duty and exert every power I possess in the service and for support of the glorious cause.*[17]

George Washington, June 16, 1775

Washington was not in the least convinced that a Continental Army led by him would be in a position to successfully confront British might. On the contrary, he saw little ultimate hope. In speaking to his time-honored friend, Patrick Henry, he extolled: *Remember, Mr. Henry, what I now tell you: from the day I enter upon the command of the American armies, I date my fall, and the ruin of my reputation.*[18]

Numerous others were also hesitant on these first steps and continued in the hope that all might yet be set right with Mother England. John Adams, perhaps the most vocal and ardent supporter of confrontation with England, was questioned on his position by many. *"Why all this haste? Why all this driving?"* James Duane demanded to know. James Wilson then stood to exclaim, *"Before we are prepared to build a new house, why should we pull down the old one, and expose ourselves to all the inclemencies of the season?"*[19] Yet, through the great oratory of Adams and several others, Congress became convinced that no other course of action would suffice. England would surely bend America to its tyrannical will if left unchallenged.

As the Congress continued into the warmer days of summer, someone who would be a major figure in America's ultimate design arrived in Philadelphia. Thomas Jefferson, who had for some time been at home in Virginia and played a small role in the previous meetings of Congress, moved into a residence on Philadelphia's Market Street. Having been out of politics for some time, he did not arrive full of confidence and anticipation. He expressed his state of apprehension when he wrote: *"I am here in the same uneasy anxious state in which I was the last fall without Mrs. Jefferson who would not come with me."*[20] This sense of alienation and distance would dramatically change in the coming weeks.

A historic event took place on June 7, 1776, when Virginia's Richard Henry Lee introduced into the Congress a motion that read in part: *"...that these United Colonies are, and of right ought to be, Free and Independent States."*[21] The motion was passed and a committee of five was selected to draft *A Declaration of Independence.* The five men included John Adams, Benjamin Franklin, Thomas Jefferson, Robert Livingston, and Roger Sherman. It occurred in the making of this decision that an interesting exchange took place between the outspoken and tempestuous John Adams and the William and Mary-educated, less-confrontational Thomas Jefferson. Adams recorded in his diary the following conversation when Jefferson suggested he write the draft

"I will not," Adams said.

"You should do it," Jefferson said.

"Oh! No."

"Why will you not? You ought to do it."

"I will not."

"Why?"

"Reasons enough."

"What can be your reasons?"

"Reason the first, you are a Virginian, and a Virginian ought to appear at the head of this business. Reason second, I am obnoxious, suspected, and unpopular. You are very much otherwise. Reason third, you can write ten times better than I can."

"Well, if you are decided, I will do as well as I can."

"Very well. When you have drawn it up, we will have a meeting."[22]

And so it was, along with Franklin's consent and urging, Jefferson was chosen to actually write the words of the *Declaration.* From here there was no way back; there was no retreat. To use Jefferson's own words, *"We were decided!"*[23]

Jefferson and the committee concluded early on that they must rely on the great philosophers and thinkers of the time; it was to be those who understood the concept of liberty and were given to the idea that men had a God-given right to be free. Of those men, perhaps the most influential was the great John Locke in his *Second Treatise.*[24] Although certainly not the only thinker of the day used in constructing the initial draft, it was Locke from whom Jefferson derived many of the key ideas and magnificent phrasing included in America's *Declaration of Independence.* Locke's concepts, such as the rights of men, are derived from the law of nature and the will of God, the requirement that power be derived from the consent of the governed, the necessity of a people to disobey and throw off a government should it indulge in tyranny, and the unalienable rights of life, liberty, and the pursuit of happiness were instrumental.

Of course, as Rubenstein uncovers in his interview of Franklin's biographer, Walter Isaacson, although Jefferson was the primary writer of the document, he had some important help from both Franklin and Adams.[25] Franklin, with his background in editing and printing newspapers, was asked by Jefferson to look over and edit his first draft of the *Declaration*. *"Would the good Dr. Franklin, in all of his wisdom, please look over this draft?"* Franklin looks at Jefferson's work and comes upon that absolutely stunning second paragraph, but Franklin makes a key editorial suggestion. Jefferson had written, *"We hold these truths to be sacred and undeniable."* Ever the editor, Franklin suggests, *"Sacred and undeniable is three words, let's make it, 'self-evident.'"*[26] His reason for this change was not simply to reduce the phrase from three words to two, but to make it clear that we were forging a new nation built on reason and not simply the dictates of religious doctrine. The devoutly Christian Adams is also thought by most historians to have been the author of the inserted lines, *"They are endowed by their Creator with certain unalienable rights."*[27] In the final analysis, much of this cooperative effort was based on the Virginia Declaration of Rights, the words and thoughts of John Locke, and those refashioned by Jefferson, Franklin, and Adams to create one of the greatest documents in the history of man!

> *We hold these truths to be self-evident, that all men are created equal, that they are endowed by their Creator with certain unalienable Rights, that among these are Life, Liberty and the pursuit of Happiness – That to secure these rights, governments are instituted among Men,*

deriving their just powers from the consent of the governed...[28]

It is on this foundation that the greatness and beauty of America rests; it is that understanding that we are free men as endowed by our Maker. We are a people who hold in our own hands the greatness that God gave us, and the ability to determine our own future without restraint. In this single paragraph is embodied all the reason in the world for people from all nations to seek comfort in America's arms.

But that was merely the first step. The second was perhaps even more difficult; it was necessary to gain the required unanimous support from all the member colonies. The vote was close. Men knew that in signing this *Declaration*, they were also signing their own death warrants should America not succeed. John Hancock, who so famously signed the *Declaration* in large enough letters, "*...that the king would not need to put on his reading glasses to read the name...,*" repeatedly insisted: "*We must be unanimous. There must be no pulling different ways, we must all hang together.*" A statement to which Benjamin Franklin then cheerfully responded, "*Yes, we must indeed all hang together, or most assuredly we shall all hang separately.*"[29]

Guiding all of these deliberations was a near-universal sense that there was perhaps a divine intervention, that there was guidance from beyond the hand of man. Even given the vast differences in religious belief between many of the members of that Congress, there was a universal feeling of God's forbearance. This general understanding is even written into the document itself in its concluding paragraph.

"*And for the support of this Declaration, with a firm reliance on the protection of divine Providence, we mutually pledge to each other our Lives, our Fortunes and our Sacred Honor."*[30]

And, with that pledge, each stepped forward and signed his name to America's *Declaration of Independence!*

War!

The road forward was a perilous, near impossible journey. A line in the sand had just been drawn against perhaps the most powerful military nation in the world. America had no trained army or navy, it had no alliances or international relationships, it had no established monetary system to pay its bills, and it had no legitimate experience as an independent government. England was preeminent in all of those things. To make matters even more hazardous, the man appointed to command their armies came to find his inherited situation as commanding general far worse than he had even imagined. He wrote:

> *Could I have foreseen what I have, and am likely to experience, no consideration upon earth should have induced me to take this command.*[31]

> *George Washington, June 1775*

The soldiers were at best an untrained, undisciplined militia with limited or no fighting experience. To compound matters, many enlistments were to end within a year and desertions had already begun to take their toll. The men were poorly dressed, undersupplied in almost every way, and their morale could not have been lower.

At its height, Washington commanded approximately 35,000 men with which to advance the cause of the Revolution against what was universally agreed to be the greatest military in the world. In November of 1776, the British began what they believed would be a quick campaign to squash the American uprising in a single blow. Their mighty navy already commanded the seas surrounding New York. A fighting force of more than 36,000 men, including a large contingent of highly trained Hessian mercenaries, had been landed. In a series of battles, one after another, Washington's troops had been defeated and forced to retreat to avoid annihilation. The last remaining bastion was Fort Washington on the north end of Manhattan. Washington's officers assured him it could be held and defended for months, but once the British attacked, it fell in a matter of hours.[32] With losses now totaling nearly 4,000 men from an army already disintegrating from sickness and desertion, this was at best a catastrophe. Washington was devastated and, with the less than 6,000 men and officers remaining, he began his retreat across New Jersey in hopes of reaching Pennsylvania on the other side of the Delaware River.

In this moment, it might have appeared to an ordinary commander that the war for America's independence might well end in a matter of months, perhaps even weeks. It was, without question, one of the darkest hours of the Revolution. Many were despondently of the mind that all was lost. But Washington was no ordinary commander. He was a proud, resolute, and experienced fighter who refused to recognize any defeat as final. He was determined to take what was left of his army and hold firm until such time as the tides of fortune could be turned into victory.

Fortunately, Washington was not alone in his determination to fight on, to turn this dark hour into light. American patriot Thomas Paine, in his pamphlet entitled *The American Crisis*, wrote inspiring words to help stay the tide of despair that so many of the day might have felt.

> *I call not upon a few, but upon all: not on this state or that state, but on every state; up and help us; lay your shoulders to the wheel; better have too much force than too little when so great an object is at stake. Let it be told to the future world, that in the depths of winter, when nothing but hope and virtue could survive, that the city and the country, alarmed at one common danger, came forth to meet and repulse it.*[33]

> *Thomas Paine, December 23, 1776*

Washington read these lines to his crestfallen troops in an effort to bolster their spirits. He knew that the longer the war went on, the greater the chances an ultimate American victory might be. It would be difficult for Britain to maintain supplies and support its troops in a land 3,000 miles away. Moreover, the possibility of enlisting the assistance of France increased with each passing month. If America could but hold on in this gloomy hour, she might yet gain her independence.

Washington's army was now being driven south through New Jersey with General Cornwallis in close pursuit. As hoped, some protection was gained when Washington crossed the Delaware into Pennsylvania, yet an even more distressing reality of the New York debacle now faced Washington. Of the army that had fought in the Battle of Long Island, nearly half had either deserted or left during the retreat across New Jersey. Washington was now commanding a force in no way fit to stand against the highly trained British regiments. The outlook had become beyond grim. Only "God's Providence" or a miracle would serve to turn this tide. That was exactly what was to happen!

Encamped across the Delaware River in that winter of 1776, Washington knew his army was desperate for a victory. *He* was desperate for a victory. He was holding on to the slim hope that General Charles Lee with his army of 3,000 men, camped only five miles away, might join his rapidly diminishing force. General Lee was unfortunately no fan of Washington and in no hurry to join his forces. He had already blatantly ignored several earlier pleas for help.

As Washington patiently waited for word on that bitter cold, frost-bitten December morning, a fast-galloping dispatch rider approached with news...*devastating news*. General Lee, having decided to avail himself of "paid female company," had spent the previous night in a tavern operated by a Widow White. He had risen late and was in the process of preparing for the day when his aide, a Major Wilkinson, ran in to announce the building was surrounded by British soldiers. With his small guard already having been killed or fled, General Lee gave up without a fight. *This* was the news now delivered to a crestfallen Washington. He dejectedly took pen in hand and wrote these few words to his brother Jack in Virginia, "*The game is pretty near up.*"[34] Could Providence one last time intervene in this bleakest hour of America's struggle for its independence? Could Washington somehow gather sufficient strength to mount one last thrust and change the winds of fortune into America's favor?

A significant event was soon to take place that would literally change the course of the war. As is often the case, it came from a most unlikely source. At an earlier time, Washington had appointed 31 officers to his military staff, including an adjutant general by the name of Joseph Reed. Reed had had an unfortunate falling out with Washington regarding a piece of correspondence between himself and General Lee, where he had agreed Lee might be a better replacement for Washington as commander of America's forces. Washington was severely disappointed by that occurrence; however, he still respected Reed's military judgment. In fact, it had been Reed who had provided much of the intelligence on the British military activity in Trenton. Ultimately, it was Reed from whom Washington was to receive a most significant communication dated December 22nd; it was a letter of such import that history will record that it might well have been instrumental in altering the course of the war. In his letter, realizing the perilous condition of the army and progress of the war, Reed communicated his judgment that something significant had to be done on an immediate basis. He was convinced even failure would be superior to doing nothing![35]

> Will it not be possible, my dear General, for our troops or such part of them as can act with advantage to make a diversion or something more at or about Trenton? The greater the alarm, the more likely success will attend the attacks....
>
> I will not disguise my own sentiments that our cause is desperate and hopeless if we do not take the opportunity of the collection of troops at present to strike some stroke. Our affairs are hastening fast to ruin if we do not retrieve

them by some happy event. Delay with us is now equal to defeat.[36]

Joseph Reed, General Pennsylvania Militia

This letter from his former adjutant was exactly what Washington himself had been thinking. It validated a plan that had for many days been taking place in his mind. Now he needed a means to take this bold step, and he needed it fast.

Eventually the remains of Lee's army, now down to less than 2,000 men, arrived to shore up the frozen, beleaguered forces of Washington. Although near desperation, Washington knew this was not the time for indecision or half-hearted measures. This was a time for boldness. He devised a plan to move his army across the ice-filled Delaware in the dark of Christmas Eve to stage a surprise attack on the Hessian stronghold at Trenton the following morning. Christmas was not to be a joyous occasion filled with gaiety and merriment; this time it was to be a day filled with bloodshed, carnage, and cruel death.[37]

First, however, Washington had to rejuvenate these tired, beaten-down forces into one last fighting unit that could surprise the Hessians at Trenton. It was a risky business at best, but to rally and energize the flagging spirits of his remaining men, Washington yet again read aloud to them from the Thomas Paine pamphlet, *The American Crisis*:

> *These are the times that try men's souls; the summer soldier and the sunshine patriot will, in this crisis, shrink from the service of his country; but he that stands it now, deserves the love and thanks of man and woman. Tyranny, like hell, is not easily conquered; yet we have this*

consolation with us, that the harder the conflict, the more glorious the triumph.[38]

As in so many times before, it was the sound of liberty over tyranny that was used to raise the spirits of an otherwise downhearted army; the idea that freedom was worth the fight, was worth the sacrifice, even to the point of giving all, was paramount. On these words, the password for the attack became the illuminating: *"victory or death!"*

The brutal weather and icy waters of that Christmas night were such that two detachments were unable to cross. Washington was left with only 2,400 soldiers—3,000 less than originally hoped—to attack a garrison of professionally trained Hessian soldiers. Once again, however, the hand of Providence seemed to intervene on America's behalf. Luckily, because it was Christmas and bitter cold, most of the Hessians were remaining warm while recovering from parties the previous night, and there were no perimeter guards. Of even greater benefit, General Rahl, the Hessian commanding officer, was so disdainful of Washington and his near-beaten forces that he dismissed intelligence he had received that Washington was preparing to attack. It was a mistake the general would pay for with his life. The Hessian garrison was ill-prepared and poorly defended. *Washington struck with force!*

Washington split the Americans into two attack units—one under his and General Greene's command, and a second under General Sullivan's command. His unit would attack from the north and General Sullivan's second wave from the south. Washington and Greene attacked without warning in a fierce frontal assault that drove the dismantled and unprepared Hessians back toward higher ground. General Sullivan then launched his army from the south, forcing the Hessians into full retreat.

A fusillade of cannon fire was then unleashed under the battlefield command of 18-year-old Lieutenant James Monroe (who would later become America's fifth president) that exacted a further brutal toll on the garrison. Monroe shouted and exhorted his men to "take up the cannon" and loudly reminded them yet again of General Washington's countersign for the engagement: *"Victory or Death!"* Surrounded and defeated, the entire remaining Hessian army of more than 1,100 men surrendered to Washington. Washington's forces had suffered only two dead and five wounded. It was a crucially needed, stunning victory. It was a victory that inspired one British historian to offer the following observation:

> *It may be doubted whether so small a number of men ever employed so short a space of time with greater and more lasting effects upon the history of the world.*[39]

> *George Otto Trevelyan*

As history has recorded, this almost impossible victory was to be a tipping point in America's quest for freedom. God in His hand had shone forth a dearly needed ray of light onto that most coveted of all commodities—*hope!* But the war was not over, not by any means.

After a further victory at Princeton, the Continental army was defeated at Brandywine, and then all but defeated again at Germantown, Pennsylvania. Throughout the months ahead, the British were building and supplying their forces at an alarming rate. New York had already fallen, and the British were advancing on Philadelphia to take the American capital. Fear gripped the entire city and perhaps the whole country.

In the late summer of 1777, Washington had been informed that 250 British ships with as many as 18,000 troops were on their way to Philadelphia. The outlook was terrifying, but Washington still had an army and, in his view, all was not yet lost. America needed to hold the line, continue to fight, and just delay any surrender. Washington was determined.

Battles also raged in other parts of the northeast, and a stunning victory by the forces of General Horatio Gates at Saratoga, New York supplied a vitally important ray of promise. It was upon this Saratoga victory that America would build an important, war-changing alliance. From nearly the beginning, as a result of the work of Benjamin Franklin, foreign governments such as France and Spain had been secretly supporting the American efforts with money and supplies. In the aftermath of the Saratoga victory, belief among these powers that America might yet prevail began to grow. France now saw an opportunity to inflict a blow against its mortal enemy England. She began to openly use both her naval and military might to support America.

Europe also sent a number of military officers, although most not especially their best, to assist Washington in conducting the war. Two who proved to be well above the others were of inestimable help. The first was a young 19-year-old Frenchman, the Marquis de Lafayette. Initially, because of his youth and inexperience, he was anything but well received. Washington wondered what he might do with someone of such youth and sparse military experience. Could he responsibly place such a person in a command position? In presenting his credentials, Congress had to inform the young officer they did not even have money to pay him! But, because Lafayette had defied the king in even coming to America, he offered to serve without pay. Initially, Lafayette was only an advisor to Washington, although his courage and battlefield skill grew with each encounter. More important, Lafayette was able to continue inducing the French government to send supplies, uniforms, and support for the Revolution. As the record informs us, Lafayette eventually became an outstanding field officer and ultimately instrumental in America's decisive victory at Yorktown.

The second transformational figure was the Prussian-born nobleman, Baron Friedrich von Steuben. It was von Steuben who converted the relatively unskilled Continental army into a professional fighting force. Upon his arrival and review of the American army, von Steuben was astounded by the lack of battle discipline and field organization. Although speaking no English other than one swear word and "halt," he immediately took command and began teaching the essential elements of military field organization, tactics, and orderly combat. He unceasingly taught, drilled, and molded his new army into tight fighting units. His influence and expertise transformed a collection of semi-trained soldiers into a legitimate Continental army.

As the war moved forward from 1777, American forces in the north and middle Atlantic became more and more formidable in the field. The English, hoping to bring an end to the war, sent General Cornwallis with a large force to overtake the south and cripple the American resistance. Initially, Cornwallis was able to exact one victory after another throughout Virginia and the Carolinas. After these initial victories, however, the British were met by smaller American militia forces under the leadership of Nathanial Greene and the Swamp Fox, Francis Marion. Although the British won the day in these confrontations, their victories came at a cost. Attacking from concealed positions and constantly using their knowledge of local geography, Greene and Marion were often able to strategically prevail and gradually draw down the strength of the British army. This was perhaps one of the earliest versions of what today is called "asymmetrical warfare," and it was highly effective against the rigid European military field style.

Disobeying orders, a frustrated General Cornwallis unwisely retreated into Yorktown, Virginia, where he believed he could resupply and regroup. His letter to Sir Henry Clinton in New York underscored the relative lack of success Cornwallis' southern campaign had achieved. He wrote, *"I am quite tired of marching about the country... If we mean an offensive war in America, we must abandon New York and bring our whole force into Virginia."*[40] These were not the words of a confident or victorious commander. Indeed, it was here at Yorktown that the final blow of the war was to be administered by George Washington, the young French general, the Marquis de Lafayette, and the French navy.

The outcome at Yorktown was in itself a miraculous turn of events; was it perhaps even another act of Providence? By 1781, the war was in dire straits, and America was again at the very precipice of defeat. After five years of war and long after the euphoria of the victory at Saratoga had died, American forces had suffered numerous deadly losses. Even the pledge of help from France had not renewed the spirits of a population weary of war, and seemingly scant hope of a final victory. However, unforeseen events were to occur that would restore the dream that was to be America.

At his headquarters in New York, America's commander, General Washington, had been daily watching this crisis unfold and woefully observed, "*We are at the end of our tether, and now or never our deliverance must come.*"[41] That deliverance was once again to come in an unexpected way. At a small house in Connecticut, Washington was to meet with French commander Le Compte de Rochambeau to discuss the next steps their combined armies were to take. For three years, Washington had been intent on retaking New York and bringing about an end to the war. Unfortunately, this had also been sufficient time for General Clinton to make his positions virtually impregnable.[42]

Washington knew Clinton had already sent a large portion of his army south to reinforce Cornwallis. He now argued in favor of utilizing the French naval fleet by sailing them from the West Indies to engage in a combined attack on New York. *Rochambeau did not agree.* He had a different idea. Calculating the geography and military positions of New York, he felt it would be far too difficult to attack and secure the necessary decisive win. Rochambeau was fully convinced the only path was to march south and brutally attack Cornwallis at Yorktown. Upon learning that Rochambeau had *already* directed the French fleet under De Grasse to sail to Virginia, Washington was now in turmoil. He had almost no options and realized at this point that he was in an all-or-nothing position. He wrote in his diary, "*Matters have now come to a crisis; stay the course for the attack on New York, or gamble all for this new opportunity in Virginia.*"

Despite his great concern regarding moving the entire Continental and French armies of more than 8,000 men south, and giving up his idea of ever retaking New York, he informed

Rochambeau that he decided to accept his plan and attack at Yorktown. The die had been cast!

Cornwallis, with his army of 7,200 men, made a strategic decision that his Virginia base would be at Yorktown because it was located on high ground along the York River that could be easily supplied and where reinforcements could be landed. Surrounded by marshes and difficult terrain, it could be easily defended. All of these considerations were true...so long as the British fleet controlled the surrounding sea. That assumption proved to be a disastrous miscalculation.

On September 5, Admiral de Grasse's French fleet took control of the sea and the York River, thereby cutting Cornwallis off from both supply *and* retreat. After a grueling march from New York, the combined French and American armies arrived on September 28. Washington's army secured the right flank, while the French secured the left flank. Washington ordered an unrelenting bombardment of Yorktown that was to continue both day and night. Gradually, the two armies moved closer until Cornwallis was surrounded and receiving a withering artillery bombardment from three sides. In desperation, Cornwallis launched one final counterattack, but it failed miserably. Divine destiny had once again smiled on America, and Cornwallis ordered his army to lay down its arms in surrender. *America had won a smashing victory, and with it its independence!*

From a Constitutional Convention to the Birth of America

America had miraculously won its war for independence from England, but could it also win a united country? It still faced the daunting task of pulling all these different states together to forge a nation. What would be the new system of government? How would this collection of 13 colonies ever agree to just one unifying system of government? Who would lead this new nation forward and be its voice? The task of becoming one country under God was nearly as overwhelming a task as winning the Revolution itself. Yet, this was the commission facing our Founders as they searched for a constitution to guide America.

In defeating England and gaining its independence, America had changed overnight from a monarchy to a republic. As pointed out by South Carolina physician and historian, David Ramsay, its people had moved from subjects to citizens, and the difference between the two could not be greater. Subjects look to a monarch or government for protection and direction. Citizens of a republic, however, must look to one another for leadership, direction, and sustenance. They are equal, and none have hereditary rights over another.[43]

Such equality and reliance on the populace placed unique strains on this fledgling nation. It required a worthy citizenry prepared to engage in self-sacrifice. It needed virtuous and intelligent people who would be willing to accept the responsibilities of civic engagement and sacrifice.

The need for such men was an agreed-upon necessity by nearly, if not all, the Founders. They were united in their

45

conviction that a nation like America could only survive if led by men of high character, those who would serve under the blessings of God. They saw Christian faith and the teachings of the Bible as critical foundations to guide future leaders. Their reasoning was simple. The required good character for leadership would depend upon the moral compass such teachings provided, and it would take men of great character to guide and hold this frail nation to the high standards of its founding.

Patrick Henry, known best for his fiery, patriotic oratory was one most notably guided by such beliefs and strengthened with biblical reflection.[44] On the back of a paper written sometime after the Revolution, he provided a note outlining his thoughts on the war, and in its last sentences what he saw as the required place for virtue if we were to have a nation that would survive the test of time.

> *This brought on the war which finally separated the two countries and gave independence to ours. Whether this will prove a blessing or a curse, will depend upon the use our people make of the blessings, which a gracious God hath bestowed on us.*
>
> *If they are wise, they will be great and happy. If they are of a contrary character, they will be miserable.*
>
> *Righteousness alone can exalt them as a nation. Reader! Whoever thou art, remember this, and in thy sphere practice virtue thyself, and encourage it in others.*[45]
>
> *Patrick Henry*

Madison himself further observed and added in his own writings, that ordinary people would need, "...*sufficient virtue and intelligence to select men of virtue and wisdom.*"[46] As Madison saw our responsibilities, he declared it would not be enough to simply have leaders of high virtue; the men and women of the population must be virtuous themselves! It is *they* who must use such wisdom to "*select*" men of high character and virtue to lead the nation forward. That very dilemma has now rippled through nearly two-and-a-half centuries to vex us still.

The newly won Republic set out to establish a government that would maximize individual liberty, limit the power of the federal government, and sufficiently maintain the rights of each state. The last thing the new nation wanted to do was to create another powerful central government that might fall into the ways of the English monarchy.

The country had been operating under the Articles of Confederation drafted just after the Declaration of Independence. Although the Articles served a purpose, they had a number of significant shortcomings. These original Articles had been created as strictly a war-time measure. They had only granted sufficient power to a central authority to control and fund the armies, achieve sufficient recognition from foreign governments to negotiate alliances, and claim independent status. The shortcomings of this arrangement were several.

- The Articles granted complete sovereignty to the states, and the central government had no power to compel anything should a state not wish to comply. As a result, there was no mechanism to resolve disputes between states.

- As there was no central or recognized executive office, the states were at a severe disadvantage in dealing with foreign governments, establishing trading alliances, or funding a longer lasting military presence for its defense.

- Finally, as there were competing claims to the significant land portions to the west, there was no mechanism by which such disputes between states or foreign governments could be resolved.

Compounding all these shortcomings was the overwhelming debt the young country had amassed as a result of the war, nor was there a discernable means to raise the money to satisfy such debts. Initially, there was a proposal to impose a five percent import tax on all goods, but this was rebuffed by a number of states asserting it would be a violation of states' rights, and would it not be more appropriate for each state to simply continue to bear a portion of that debt according to its ability?

Alexander Hamilton stood and, in a lengthy speech of nearly an hour and a half on the House floor, made an impassioned plea to address this issue. He lashed out at Congress' reliance upon 13 states for essentially "voluntary payments." He pointed his finger and noted that there were "stingy states" that paid only a fraction of their quota or nothing at all![47] In this regard, he correctly alerted all present that, whereas domestic creditors might be patient, foreign creditors would *not* be so patient.

> *They have the power to enforce their demands, and sooner or later they may be expected to do so! If these states are not united under a federal government, they will infallibly have wars with each other, and their divisions will subject*

them to all the mischiefs of foreign influence and intrigue.[48]

Alexander Hamilton

The infighting between strong personalities in Congress and individual states made this a perilous time. Thoughtful voices became the order of the day. In addition to Hamilton, Madison and others were also convinced that, if our newly won nation were to survive, a unified nation of states was needed. Leaders would have to step forward to craft such a document. This was to be no easy task.

A constitutional convention was convened in Philadelphia in May 1787, understood by some to only "revise the original Articles of Confederation." It quickly became clear, however, that this new convention had taken onto itself the task of totally abandoning the original Articles to supplant them with a completely new system of government. The gathered representatives of each state had seemingly set themselves the task to formulate a government strong enough to remain above the states when necessary, yet grant the states sufficient sovereignty to protect their liberty and rights. Over this issue, the initial battle lines were drawn.

During this fragile and dangerous time, Madison and Hamilton stepped forward to champion the formation of a new national government. It might be rightfully argued that, although Washington and the Revolutionary patriots had won our independence, it was Hamilton and Madison who won us a nation. Hamilton, a highly controversial and polarizing figure throughout his political life, was fully convinced that, without a strong central government to bring needed oversight and governance to the conduct of commerce, defense, and financial support of the new country, it would decay into endless interstate squabbles and financial ruin. He eloquently argued that far too many of those in the Constitutional Congress were too little invested in "nationhood" and too highly invested in maintaining their own power and influence through the sovereignty of states' rights. Hamilton, along with Jay and Madison, penned more than 80 powerful essays explaining and supporting the newly evolving Constitution in what came to be known as *"The Federalist Papers."* In one of those initial five essays, Hamilton succinctly laid out the decision to be made if we were to make our way toward a unified country.

> *"We have a choice before us. We can forge a noble and magnificent federal Republic...closely linked in the pursuit of a common interest or be a number of petty states with the appearance of union."*[49]

As the country tenuously looked for its way forward in building this new nation, 55 delegates from 12 of the 13 colonies convened in Pennsylvania's State House. Heated debate around Hamilton's ideas preceded and extended all through the convention. There were Federalists such as Alexander Hamilton, James Madison, John Jay, and John Adams who strongly advocated a powerful centralized government to oversee the general conduct of the states. But just as vocal and immovable were the anti-Federalists led by George Mason, Patrick Henry, and others who advocated an extremely limited central government and powerful states' rights. Patrick Henry was so vehemently set against the institution of a federal authority that might dictate to the states how to run their affairs that he refused to even attend the convention. Madison reported to Washington, *"Mr. Henry's disgust exceeds all measure.*"[50] Even more to the point, Madison was further concerned that, by remaining aloof, Henry might "...*later combat and sabotage the entire effort.*"[51]

Within the general population, some had become so disgusted and frustrated that they even suggested establishment of a monarchy to end these disputes. Madison could hardly believe what he was hearing, and remarked, *"Even respectable citizens speak of monarchy without horror."* Washington, who had been desperately trying to stay out of these debates, prodded Madison when he wrote:

> *No morn ever dawned more favorably than ours did; and no day was ever more clouded than the present! Wisdom and good examples are necessary to rescue the political machine from the impending storm.*[52]

For these new states, there was one issue that stood out above all others as an impediment to the ratification of a new constitution: *Slavery.* This seminal question vexed the founders in such a way as to threaten the very existence of the newly formed country; many might today suggest properly so. But, in telling this story of America, it is essential that we understand the sentiments and concerns that were under debate at the time.

There were two central questions bitterly debated among the Founders. First was the question surrounding the phrase, *"All men are created equal."* Did the general population and governing officials take this to mean it purposely freed all the slaves? The second involved how slaves would be counted as part of the population. Would they be equally counted as part of a state's population and determine that state's representation in government? Would equal citizenship also determine how the state might be taxed? Moreover, if the slaves were to be considered "free men" upon ratification of this new constitution, would such not severely compromise the economic stability of the southern states, where agriculture and slaves represented major components of their economies? South Carolina and Georgia were adamant that they would neither sign nor approve a constitution that addressed or mentioned slavery. Such defections would eliminate any possibility of ratification.

America, as it is today, had a variety of groups with vested interests that could not be ignored. There were many who detested slavery and demanded the practice be remedied. On the other hand, there were states with significant economic interests that could not haphazardly be ignored. The unfortunate fact was that, in 1787, slavery had become so enmeshed in the fabric of our country and economics that no universal solution presented itself. It is still today an anathema as to how a country based on liberty and justice for all could proffer a new constitution so deafeningly silent on this question of basic human rights. How indeed could such enlightened men of the day, even though some themselves owned slaves, such as George Washington and Thomas Jefferson, stand silent regarding a practice so contradictory to the very principles on which they repeatedly said they stood?

Wilfred McClay in his book, *Land of Hope: An Invitation to the Great American Story*, perhaps offers a few clarifying words:

> *There is no easy answer to such questions. But surely a part of the answer is that each of us is born into a world that we did not make, and it is only with the greatest effort, and often at very great cost, that we are ever able to change that world for the better. Moral sensibilities are*

not static; they develop and deepen over time, and general moral progress is very slow. Part of the study of history involves a training of the imagination, learning to see historical actors as speaking and acting in their own times rather than ours; and learning to see even our heroes as an all too human mixture of admirable and unadmirable qualities, people who like us who may, like us, be constrained by circumstances beyond their control.

The ambivalences regarding slavery built into the structure of the Constitution were almost certainly unavoidable in the short term, in order to achieve an effective political union of the nation...We live today on the other side of a great transformation in moral sensibility, a transformation that was taking place but was not yet completed in the very years the United States was being formed.[53]

Wilfred M. McClay, 2019

All these vital questions and concerns of the times were swirling about, yet a new nation depended on those humanly frail voices of the day to bring enlightenment to the task. To that end, James Madison of Virginia had come prepared to forward his proposals for a well thought out central government that would be sufficient to establish reasonable laws and unite the states together as one body. Madison had gathered many of his ideas from some of the greatest minds and had come to the convention with ideas that would brand themselves into the fabric of the new nation for many years to come.

On the first day of the convention, Madison had his close friend Edmund Randolph offer his framework for the new government. Madison's outline, known as the Virginia Plan, proposed three separate branches of government that would exercise checks and balances on one another. The legislative body would have its membership based on the population of the states, something the smaller states greatly feared would disadvantage them. Most important, the new national government would exercise power even over those decisions made by the states. Such ideas for a central government with that level of power were immediately and loudly challenged.

Delaware's Gunning Bedford may well have capsulated the concern of many when he rose to rage forth, "[*The large states*] *...insist they will never hurt or injure the lesser states. I do not, gentlemen, trust you!*"[54] Bedford's concern and reservation in this regard was shared by members of nearly all the smaller states, in particular, Patrick Henry. These rancorous debates over states' rights versus a strong central government would continue for more than four months. Delegates struggled mightily to find a governmental system that might reach consensus.[55]

The summer of June and July was one of the most sweltering hot months on record, and the conditions for debate and dialog were at best miserable. A French visitor complained of the incessant heat and humidity:

> *At each inhaling of air, one worries about the next one. The slightest movement is painful. A veritable torture during the Philadelphia hot season is the innumerable flies which constantly light on the face and hands, stinging*

everywhere and turning everything black because of the filth they leave wherever they light.[56]

But perhaps divine Providence was again to intervene. On Saturday, July 13, there was a change when *"the Lord of Winds displayed his mercy with a brisk cleansing breeze from the northwest."* Then people of good will and mountainous responsibility had the opportunity to rest and sleep. A ratification vote was to be taken on that next Monday, July 15, and delegates would vote their final approval to the committee's solution to their most stubbornly argued positions. The fate of a new nation was to hang in the balance of those arguments. But make no mistake: The divine break in the weather had played a role. Catherine Drinker Bowen in her diary wrote, *"...perhaps the delegates would never have reached agreement had not the heat broken."*[57]

Over the next month, the work was polished and improved, but never again endangered by the acrimonious division that had been the case only weeks before. Madison had insisted that *"it be the scholarly Gouverneur Morris who should be credited for the finish given the style and arrangement of the Constitution."* Thus we know it was Gouverneur Morris who penned the elegant preamble:

> *We the people of the United States, in order to form a more perfect union, establish justice, ensure domestic tranquility, provide for the common defense, promote the general welfare, and secure the blessings of liberty to ourselves and our posterity, do ordain and establish this Constitution for the United States of America.*[58]

In this important opening of the Constitution is the urgently important craft of words Morris penned for a specific reason. He had accurately predicted that a constitution would be created and set into motion and, since all the delegates had been sent "by the people" of their state, this document would no longer be the creation of the individual delegates, but the decree of "We the People." Although Madison continued to have his concerns regarding final ratification of this document, his spirits were buoyed by a conversation with Franklin and the wisdom provided by that senior statesman.

> When you assemble a number of men to have the advantage of their joint wisdom, you inevitably assemble with those men, all their prejudices, their passions, their errors of opinion, their local interests, and their selfish views. From such an assembly can a perfect production be expected? It therefore astonishes me, Sir, to find this system approaching so near to perfection as it does...Thus I consent, Sir, to this Constitution because I expect no better, and because I am not sure, that it is not the best.[59]
>
> Ben Franklin

Finally, on July 16, the body came together to consider a compromise document. The tension in the air could not have been greater. It was ultimately proposed that the legislative branch would separate the two houses of Congress into a lower and upper chamber. The lower House would base its membership on each state's population, while the upper Senate would have equal representation from each state. This somewhat addressed the concern that the larger states could run roughshod over the smaller states and dictate their states' policies.

There were other issues as well, not the least of which was the continuing question of slavery. Although a temporary solution was found with the remainder to be addressed at a later date, this omission of specific language removing slavery from the American landscape was to be a continuing matter of bitter division in America. Correcting this omission would result in the deaths of more than 620,000 (the equivalent of six million today) men and women, and the near-dissolution of the nation less than 100 years later in the Civil War. By no means was this newly proposed Constitution widely and universally accepted by the delegates. The final draft of the document was the result of numerous compromises that left many of the men who drafted it dissatisfied. Of the 55 delegates, just 39 were willing to pen their names to the document. Be that as it may, these were surely some of the most important signatures in the history of America!

Even then, the framers of the Constitution realized the significance of what they had accomplished. This Constitution was the vital structure of an enduring America. It was not written to satisfy the political needs of the moment; it was written to ensure a prosperous and free America for ages to come. James Wilson, the faithful colleague of Benjamin Franklin and often his spokesperson, even though he himself was not in full agreement with all of its provisions, had stood to offer this concluding counsel on behalf of the ailing Mr. Franklin:

> We should consider that we are providing a Constitution for future generations and not just for the circumstances of the moment. I cannot help expressing a wish that every member of this Convention who may still have objections to it, would with me, on this occasion doubt a little of his

> *own infallibility—and to make manifest our unanimity,*
> *put his name to this instrument.*[60]
>
> James Wilson (speaking for Benjamin Franklin)

Although delivered by his friend James Wilson, almost all delegates honored Dr. Franklin's plea with the exception of three very prominent and influential voices, Eldridge Gerry of Massachusetts, and George Mason and Governor Edmond Randolph, both of Virginia. Because each of the thirteen states had to likewise consider endorsing this Constitution in their own legislatures, this lack of endorsement was a problem. Randolph was troubled by a number of the provisions and predicted that as many as nine states would fail to ratify the document as it was currently written. Ultimately, and after further discussion and continued argument, signers rose to add their names to the beautifully written Constitution. Franklin, very feeble in his older years, unsteadily rose to add his hand and is reported to have openly wept as he added his signature.[61]

As the convention concluded and the delegates began leaving, a woman otherwise identified as a Mrs. Powell, confronted Franklin and asked, *"Well, Doctor, what have we got, a republic or a monarchy?"* Franklin barely hesitated before responding, *"A republic, if you can keep it."*[62] And indeed, over the last almost 250 years, that challenge even today continues to be the task: *if you can keep it!*

All was not yet done. There was still the daunting and seemingly almost impossible task of gaining full ratification from at least nine of the thirteen states. Prospects for this task were by no means bright. Of the 55 men who had convened in Philadelphia, only 39 were willing to put their names to the final draft. It must have taken courage for those who did not sign "to face the stern, disapproving stare of George Washington" being cast in their direction.[63] But could divine wisdom once again win out and give birth to this dream called America? Nothing was assured.

Ratification Sets America's Course

Ironically, almost none of these prominent founders fully and wholeheartedly believed in the compromise settlement that had been agreed to in 1787. That document, the one before them now, was the result of painful compromise and deft improvisation rather than a full representation of anyone's full political ideology. It had emerged from the combination of political positions that embodied Federalist, European, and uniquely Virginian thought.[64] Yet now, each state had upon it the awesome burden of responsibility to choose whether to ratify and submit to the provisions of this new Constitution, or to reject it and look for some other means of government. Was there to even be a nation?

Individual state disagreement abounded, and it was feared the Constitution might ultimately fail in this ratification process. At the heart of almost every individual and state objection was the fear that this Constitution granted too much power to a central government. Patrick Henry, who had famously refused to attend the Convention in Philadelphia did so because, as he put it, *"he smelt a rat!"* Having waged the costly and near-disastrous Revolutionary War, Henry—along with many others—rightly feared the creation of an all-powerful government bureaucracy that could dictate laws and regulations to the states. He must certainly have wondered, why would we struggle so mightily and risk so much to free ourselves of one tyranny only to institute another? Madison tried to allay these fears by explaining the federal government had only "certain enumerated" powers and the states retained "residuary and inviolable sovereignty" over all else.[65] George Mason was also not convinced. In Mason's view, this new Constitution did not fully reduce the concern of an overreaching government that could mitigate the freedoms so dearly gained and reserved to the "individual."

It seemed many were not persuaded, and this argument continued to grow in the state legislatures. There appeared to be little room for agreement until James Madison once again stepped forward with a compromise solution. Even though he was convinced there were sufficient restrictions upon government to restrain it from overstepping its bounds and infringing upon the individual rights of the people, he suggested an initial group of constitutional amendments called *The Bill of Rights.* These rights would clearly set forth those individual rights that the government could not infringe. This *Bill of Rights* was the final step and paved the way for full ratification of the Constitution.

Although nine states had already ratified the new Constitution, Virginia would be the tenth and stood as a final major hurdle. Those favoring adoption, led by James Madison, were intent on gaining Virginia's acceptance. But there were powerful voices like Patrick Henry equally intent on defeating the ratification vote. The Virginia Ratifying Convention then was where the full debate between the two sides was to take place. Because Virginia had so many powerful voices and members of government, it was considered essential for

Virginia to also cast its vote in favor of ratification if it were to have any lasting value. Arguably it was here where the entire Constitution of United States was to either survive or be cast out and forever lost.

Madison and Henry heatedly debated the proposed document point by point for days. Madison, who had been taken ill with one of the seizures from which he sometimes suffered, was growing weary and worn down, sometimes speaking in a voice that was barely audible. Yet he pressed on. He wrote to Hamilton, "*My health is not good, and the business is wearisome beyond expression.*" Madison was eloquent in his defense. One supporter wrote to a friend, "*...notwithstanding Mr. Henry's declamatory powers, they are being vastly overpowered by the deep reasoning of our glorious little Madison.*" His sense was that, although close, "*they might still win the day.*"[66]

The ratification was hanging by a thread at this time; the fate of a "United States" hung with it. No one could reasonably predict the outcome. Henry, concerned that the Constitution might have sufficient votes, stepped forward to advance a series of amendments to the proposed documents that would limit its power and insure both state autonomy and individual freedoms. Madison could not fully agree to all of these amendments as he was convinced they held many unseen dangers. It was here that Henry waged his final battle against ratification of this Constitution should it not embody his proposed amendments. Lynne Cheney, in her book on Madison, describes it perfectly.[67]

Henry exploded:

"I see the awful immensity of the dangers with which it is pregnant. I see it—I feel it. I see beings of a higher order, anxious concerning our decision."[68]

Archibald Stuart then describes what happened next:

"A storm suddenly rose. It grew dark. The doors came to with a rebound like a peal of musketry. The windows rattled; the huge wooden structure rocked; the rain fell from the eaves in torrents, which were dashed against the glass; the thunder roared."

Stuart reports Henry relentlessly spoke on:

"Rising on the wings of the tempest, he seized upon the artillery of heaven and directed its fiercest thunders against the heads of his adversaries."[69]

It was a powerful address, and many in attendance could not help but be influenced by its passion. In the end, Madison recognized the critical balance that would need to be struck if this Constitution were to receive Virginia's assent. Some compromise would be essential. On the next day, Madison conceded that he would not oppose added amendments except where any might pose a danger. When the full vote was taken, Virginia had ratified the Constitution by a vote of 89-79, and to further recommend any needed amendments to Congress for their consideration. The Constitution, along with Madison, had won the day. In many ways, it was no small miracle. It was nearly beyond the simple comprehension of man to see this country's foundation established in such a way. Once again, the fate of a new nation had survived by the narrowest of margins. Madison wrote of it in this regard:

It is impossible for the man of pious reflection not to perceive in it a finger of the Almighty hand which has so frequently and signally extended to our relief in the critical stages of the revolution.[70]

James Madison

America had her new government. She had a Constitution that would become the envy of countries all over the world. In its magnificent design were the seeds on which America would grow to become the greatest economic power the world has ever seen. It was also the country that would embody the greatest level of individual freedom in Western civilization. The doors to unlimited growth were open, and freedom-loving people from all over the globe flocked to her shores to help build a nation.

Over the next centuries of America's growth, immigrants came from every corner of the earth. Their contributions helped staff our factories, build our railroads, develop our farms, and increase both the economic and human value of the new country. Entrepreneurs, inventors, craftsmen, and laborers all made America one of the leading nations of the world.

John F. Kennedy, in his book, *A Nation of Immigrants*, eloquently sums up the contributions and importance of the American immigrant to the development of our American dream.

The continuous immigration of the nineteenth and early twentieth centuries was thus central to the whole American faith. It gave every old American a standard by which to judge how far he had come and every new American a realization of how far he might go. It reminded every American, old and new, that change is the essence of life, and that American society is a process, not a conclusion... The abundant resources of this land provided the foundation for a great nation. But only people could make the opportunity a reality.[71]

John F. Kennedy

Kennedy's observation of America brings us up to today. It brings us to the questions that only immigrants can answer. What has made this country attractive to so many, and what have been the paths of their journeys? What is their view of this America they have found? We must recognize that the stories here represent only the tiniest fraction of the millions of similar stories that now populate the vast and varied lands of this country. Yet, it is through these stories and what they tell us that provides our history such power. Through hearing these immigrant voices, we may get a better glimpse of what the phrase *"America the Beautiful"* might actually mean.

CHAPTER 2

Coming to America

Leaving one's homeland to begin anew in another country perhaps halfway around the world can be a daunting, heart-wrenching decision. It rarely comes easily or without great contemplation and some degree of pain. One's existing community, culture, and lifestyle are well known, but what to expect in a new land is unfamiliar, filled with questions, and possibly even worrisome. There may be a family you leave behind, in some cases with the risk of never seeing them again. The mother who brought you into this world and provided you her unconditional love will often not be with you on this journey. A father who may have provided his guidance and support through every endeavor might no longer be there. Then there is the extended family that provided a network of relationships who will now be irreplaceable. Such considerations can weigh heavily on the heart of anyone considering America as a new home. For every person, the determining factor in their ultimate decision is based on his or her individual circumstances. For that reason, the story surrounding each decision is varied and unique. One such story from Saritha Prabhu of India appeared on the Opinion Page of the Knoxville News Sentinel, July 15, 2019:

> I immigrated here 27 years ago in 1992 at the age of 27. Every immigrant's experiences of immigrating and assimilating are personal and at the same time universal.
>
> Some things are common: the act of uprooting and transplanting can be life-altering and character-building. There is gratitude for the blessings of your new land, accompanied by an ineffable feeling of loss of the often-mythical place in your heart called "home."
>
> And so it was for me too, a sort-of-born-again experience—leaving the comforting cocoon of my extended family in India, coming here with the proverbial four suitcases with my newly-wed husband, assimilating into a radically different culture from the one I grew up in, and gradually transforming into a hybrid citizen who straddles two cultures, two worldviews.[1]
>
> Saritha Prabhu, India, 2019

For each immigrant seeking to re-establish his or her life, like Saritha, there is a transformation that, over time, inevitably takes place. Indeed, it is a "hybrid citizen who straddles two cultures, two worldviews." A more descriptive term might be someone's "Americanization." It is not an easy or rapid process. It requires not only an awareness but an adoption of new customs, new modes of behavior, and new ways of thinking. These new ways of life often come at the expense of former customs and understandings. It can be a troublesome price to pay. Marcus Ravage, whose more complete story we will hear later, passionately describes the realities of adapting to the new ways of life in America. Having come from a Jewish upbringing in the small working-class Romanian village of Vaslui in 1909, he had set himself no easy task.

> For I hardly need tell you that becoming an American is a spiritual adventure of the most volcanic variety. I am not talking of taking out citizens' papers. It cannot be too often repeated that the shedding of one's nationality and the assumption of another is something more than a matter of perfunctory formalities and solemn oaths to a flag or Constitution. I mean allegiance to the state is one thing, but renouncing your priceless inherited identity, and blending your individual soul with the soul of an alien people is quite another affair. It is this staggering experience of the spirit, this slipping of his ancient ground from under the immigrant's feet, this commingling of souls toward a new birth, that I have in mind when I speak of becoming an American. To be born in one world and grow to manhood there, to then be thrust into the midst of another with all one's racial heritage, with one's likes and dislikes, aspirations and prejudices, and to be abandoned to the task of adjusting within one's own being the clash of opposed systems of culture, tradition, and social

convention; if that is not heroic tragedy, I should like to be told what it is![2]

Marcus Ravage, Romania

Unaware of the difficulties of such a cultural transformation as a young man, Marcus had decided he had to set his eyes on reinventing himself in a new land. But attempting to leave one's home for a different country in the early 20th century was quite different from those who might make that transition today. In 1900 Romania, it was absolutely required that he have the blessing of his father to leave for America. Marcus, however, viewed his prospects for a better life in Vaslui as extraordinarily limited. The exaggerated stories of his uncle had led him to become convinced that his future, if he were to have one, was in America. Disappointingly, his father had already forbidden him once to leave with an earlier group that had departed on foot. Glowing reports of their travels and successes along their journey only added fire to his dream to make his own way. Marcus approached his father again with renewed enthusiasm.

> *I asked him, after all the rebuffs his efforts had met, whether he could still hope to make anything of me in Vaslui. Just what did he expect to turn me into? I painted a gloomy picture of life in Romania—the poverty, the absence of every variety of opportunity, the discriminations of Government against us. Whichever way one turned there were prohibitions and repressions.*[3]

But even this was insufficient to gain the required consent. It was not until he confronted his father with the grim prospect that he would likely be conscripted into the army like his older brother that things began to change. Chronicled in his autobiography, *The Making of an American*, Marcus pleadingly conveyed his concerns to his father with near desperation.

> And when at last he [his brother Paul] had become master of his calling and was about to become independent, "...along came the scarlet monster and packed him off to its musty barracks, to be fed on black bread and cabbage, to learn senseless tricks with his feet and a gun, to spend days and whole weeks in prison cells, as if he were a criminal, to be slapped in the face like a bad boy, and to live in constant terror of war. If this is the sort of future you want for me," I concluded, dramatically, "you are right in trying to keep me here."[4]

This remonstrance finally convinced his father to allow his son to leave home and make his way to that largely unknown place called the United States. His father continued to have grave concerns, and somewhat secretly envisioned that, once in America, his son would become disenchanted and return home. As it turned out, the initial disenchantment came, but the return home did not. A determined spirit is difficult to deny.

There are countless other stories of those who stubbornly set their minds to come to the United States. They dream of a better future, and they are convinced this is where they can bring that dream to life. For Said Fadloullah, a small boy living in a tiny Moroccan village, he had made up his mind early in life. In his interview, he describes how and why he decided America was the place he would one day live.

> Home for me was a very small town in Morocco called Shima. It was an extremely small place with maybe only

1,000-2,000 *people. As you can imagine, there was really nothing there except the houses, such as they were. There were no convenience-type things like in America; basically you had to go somewhere else to get almost anything. Of course, we had school but that was really about it. We would walk to school and come home. There were no toys or things you could buy to play with. If you wanted some kind of toy, you just had to make it yourself. As far as living conditions were concerned, our house had my older brother with his wife and two children. Then there was my mother, me, and my sister, too, all living in this maybe two-bedroom type home. And not a two-bedroom home like you would see here in America. No, it was a Moroccan type of home that didn't really have the kinds of rooves or walls like here. It was just a really small house and living there with that size family was hard on everyone. When it would rain, there was just so much mud and water, and you had to still live in this and walk in it. As I told you, it was a difficult life, and everyone just did the best they could.*

Financially it was hard, too. We really didn't have any money or consistent way to make a living so that maybe we could do something better. My brother finally got a small job, so that was really how we lived. When I was 10, I would go around and try to sell plastic bags to neighbors that perhaps they could use when they went to the flea market. I also sold cigarettes one at a time; you know, I did whatever I could do to make just a little money. We lived day to day. Every little bit helped, but nothing was assured. It was in those days that I really made up my mind that I had to somehow find a way to come to America. My father died when I was only 13, and that made things even more difficult, but it also seemed to make me even more determined to come.

During these days, I would see TV or pictures of America and I would tell everyone, "One day I am going to go there." I had to go there. They would all laugh or just say, "Yes, OK, you will go there." Of course, I don't think anyone really believed me or even believed such a thing was possible. It just wasn't done. If you were from Morocco, there was just no way you were going to America; NO WAY. It wasn't done.

Once I saw this television show that had Miami in it, and it looked so beautiful with nice cars and trees, and beaches with great looking people. I would dream about it. I even got a picture to put up in my room, and said, "That is where I am going to go one day, and when I get there, I am going to take a picture and send it back to you so you can see for yourself!" It was my dream from when I was little. Everyone would smile and say, "OK, Said, one day you will go there." No, I knew that was not going to be easy. A U.S. visa was almost impossible to get. Still, I knew somehow, it would happen. I knew.

When my brother got older, he got into a college. He came to America, and because he was here, after 10 years he could bring me over to be with him. Still, it was not easy, but he arranged all the papers and permits. Although he couldn't send me anything to help with the trip, I finally had a means for entering and a way to come. In 1986 some people helped me, I got my visa and came to the United States. Yes, I made it. I was here; I was finally in the United

States! And you know what? I did go to Miami and take that picture.

Said Fadloullah, Shima, Morocco

When living in difficult circumstances, a future unlikely to improve is a strong motivation for change. It is understandable then, when one hears numerous stories or sees pictures and movies of what life might be like in the United States, whether accurate or not, relocating becomes a strong goal. That was clearly the case for both Marcus and Said. There are many others.

Vincent Diaz, an immigrant from Honduras, likewise determined at a fairly young age that his circumstances were unlikely to change unless he left to begin anew in America. For so many, a family history of poverty and difficult living circumstances would perpetuate from one generation to the next. Vincent decided that would not be his future.

My path to America actually started when I was very young. In my country, when you finish sixth grade and go to seventh, you have to begin paying for your supplies. So, I went to my father and asked if I could go on to seventh grade. He said, "Well, I can't do that, we don't have the money. But you can come work on the farm where I work." I didn't even go to 7th grade. I had to begin working with my father on the farm.

After three years, when I was sixteen and had been working on this farm all that time, I began thinking to myself, "If I have children, they are not going to live like this and do this kind of work. I am going to give them a better life than this." But I knew the only way to change this life situation was to get out of Honduras; I had to go somewhere else.

At that time, I already had a brother who was here in the United States. So I called him, and we made arrangements that, if I came, I would be able to live with him and go find work. Of course, I didn't speak English, not a word. I came across and went to live with my brother anyway. I have always been a good worker, and I found a job fairly fast at a Chinese restaurant. That was my beginning here.

Vincent Diaz, Santa Lucia, Honduras

For Vincent, he had the good fortune to have a brother already in America. He had a place to stay and someone to help him get a start. For someone who spoke no English, that was a significant advantage. The next steps, however, would determine if that initial advantage could be turned into something special.

Greg Lhamon, in his 2015 blog post, tells of a particularly interesting exchange with an Albanian immigrant by the name of Bledi. Greg was taking a shuttle van to LAX, and the two began having a conversation about the differences between Bledi's European culture and what he had found here in America. Their brief encounter was a familiar example of what it is in America that attracts so many immigrants. The conversation is recounted by Greg as follows.

We talked for two hours. Bledi spoke reverentially about George Kastrioti Skanderbeg, the 15th century Albanian national hero who led his people against the Ottomans for two decades. He told me why most Eastern European countries claim the Great Alexander as a native son even though he was Macedonian.

Eventually, I asked Bledi the question I always ask an immigrant:

"So, why did you come to America?"

"To escape socialism. I was in Albania when it was still communist. Communism collapsed in the early '90s and that's when socialism took over."

"What was it like living under communism?"

"Horrible. Just horrible." He looked away.

"Was it better under socialism?" I asked.

"Better than communism, but still not good. No one worked hard."

"Why not?"

"Why would you?" he said. "I was an engineer. I made $64 a month...same as everyone else. It didn't matter how much education I had or how hard I worked. I always got paid the same."

"So, you like it here?" I asked.

He laughed. "Of course! I can get ahead here. I make more here driving this shuttle than I ever did back in Albania."

He paused.

"But I won't drive this shuttle forever. I've got plans."[5]

As related by Greg Lhamon

Bledi escaped communism and socialism to come to a country where he could earn a better living and be free. But it was more than that. His true dream is embodied by his last statement. *"But I won't drive this shuttle forever. I've got plans."* Unlike his situation under Albanian communism and socialism, Bledi saw a brighter future now that he was here in America. Bledi had become convinced that, through hard work, he could realize even larger aspirations; that was his real objective, and it would come true. He knew it. After all, he was an American.

A second account of such a transition is related by Myo Thwe Linn, who immigrated as a refugee from Myanmar (formerly Burma) in 2010. He, too, saw the situation in his homeland as limited and unattractive. He related his own journey in coming to America in an interview during the summer of 2020. He was asked if he had felt mired in a bad place. Did he see his future as unlikely to improve?

> *Oh, especially before I came to the United States, I was nothing. In Myanmar, once I became an adult I was in the militia, and I thought I would always have to stay in the militia. There seemed no way out to make a different living. I am just me, and who am I to rise above such a life? I lived in the military almost eight years. You should know that in Myanmar one does not have what you here describe as a regular life. Even after many years of growing up, we frankly didn't know anything of the real world. You can't travel or learn much of other countries other than stories or what you might read. The government doesn't let you have anything like a passport or even something for your own identity. There is nothing like that for people like me. You have nothing to even prove you are*

a real person. That is not a concern of the government. Everyone is basically the same except them.

Over time I decided that kind of life was not for me, not for my future. I began to think about trying to come here. As I got older, my situation grew even worse. It became dangerous. I was afraid of the police because they could come at any time and just arrest you. There didn't need to be a particular charge, and you wouldn't even know what crime you were being arrested for. I saw this happen so often to others, and I was very afraid that one day it could be me.

I was fortunate. As a result of an assignment in the militia, I met someone from the American government and got the chance to apply for a visa to the United States. I was placed on the Health and Human Resources list as a possible refugee. This was a ray of light for me, my dreamed-of opportunity! At the time, however, I was constantly afraid someone would come and require me to stay. I was certain that, if such a thing happened, I would ultimately find myself in prison. There wasn't any kind of life for me where I was, and I desperately needed to get out. I had been determined to go for some time, and with this piece of luck, I now had the prospect for a new life. I wanted that chance to prove my productivity, my worth, and perhaps be allowed to enter in the United States as a refugee.

Myo Thwe Linn, Myanmar

Myo did achieve his refugee status and received sanctuary in the United States. He was relocated to Michigan where there was a substantial Myanmar community. He is now in the cleaning industry, married, working a full-time job, and also driving an Uber to earn extra money. He is forever grateful for his opportunity to enter the country and see the fulfillment of his dream. Like so many immigrants, he is still struggling to realize his full potential. He spoke of his path forward and how his faith in God and personal determination would set his course.

> *To be honest, my determination is certainly still burning. But as to my future, it is also in God's hands. He will take me wherever. That's my faith at this time. If I saw I had a chance or opportunity to learn at a college or university, I will certainly take advantage of that and go. For me to move ahead, I cannot stop learning. Right now, a college level education might be too expensive and difficult to afford. I will need to work hard and eventually make a better income, but I am not afraid of hard work. I will need to take advantage of whatever opportunities I can because I have a family now, and I need to take care of them.*

Myo Thwe Linn, Myanmar

For Ingrid Kliefoth, growing up in post-WWII Germany was beyond an appalling experience, and one she is so happy her children did not have to endure. At the age of seven, she was separated from her parents; an aunt was forced to come pick her up and care for her. During that period, refugees were often sent in freight cars to some minimalist dumping ground. Eventually they found themselves placed in a refugee camp on a peninsula in northern Germany. At the one end was the sea, and at the other end the Russian army. Living conditions were deplorable by almost any standard. The aunt had to peel potatoes all day to help feed the Russian army. Ingrid describes her time growing up in these post-war years, and how she ultimately came to the United States.

> In that time, people who already lived on the peninsula were required to provide a room to refugees if it was needed. Understandably, they hated us. We were not clean, we smelled, and we represented a totally unwanted burden to the family. Common necessities like bathrooms, cooking or meal preparation, and even sleeping were nearly non-existent. You went outside to use the bathroom, often slept on the ground or floor, and prepared whatever little you had to eat with limited facilities at best. Even though we had ration cards, there really wasn't much food, and anyway, as I said, we had no kitchen to prepare it. One person was allowed only a half a pound of meat per week, so some families pooled their efforts and could make a stew or something like that, but meals were very, very skimpy. It was tough.

> After we were reunited and my mother had met my stepfather, we were able to move to a town nearer to Stuttgart. We moved in with my grandparents, who had two rooms. We lived in one room and they lived in the other. Later, as I got older, I was finally able to attend school where I studied secretarial work. This provided the initial access to job openings as an executive secretary. I was hired at this company, but things did not go fast. I had to work my way up through every department so that I was aware of what went on at all levels of the company. Ultimately, I found a job as an executive secretary with a

company that would later become affiliated with Electrolux.

It was during this time in my life where I met a friend who had a job with a family in Sweden. She told me, "Oh, it's just great to be in Sweden. Life is so different and so much better; you should come here." She convinced me, and life was better. It was like night and day. It was just wonderful. I had my own room, and I had my freedom, and when I had free time, it was so great to just do what I wanted. I first worked for a nice family. but then later I worked for a very well-known professor of architecture and his family. I took care of their two children as well as everything around the house. This family happened to also be friends with an ambassador. When that ambassador's family was going to Britain for two weeks, they needed someone to stay with their teenage daughters. I was really ready for something different in my life; oh, I was ready to fly. I interviewed and got the job. It was a wonderful situation, and everyone got along well. When the Swedish Ambassador was assigned to Washington and asked if I would like to come work in America, I was beyond excited. Everything was arranged for me, I had not one difficulty, and here I came to America.

I had always been a little enamored of America. The area in which I lived when I was going to school had a number of American military facilities surrounding it. It always seemed that the people on those bases were so friendly and happy; they were nice to be around. Of course, I knew a little of America from numerous other sources as well. I don't know, it just looked like a nice country that I would *really like. So, when the opportunity presented itself, I was more than happy to come with the Swedish ambassador. I will also just admit that when I got here, I intended to stay right from the start. Today I have realized everything I ever wanted here, and in my blood, I am red, white, and blue.*

Ingrid Kliefoth, Germany

Likewise, Gunta Krasts-Voutyras of Latvia was a product of immigration in the immediate aftermath of World War II. Part of her story was provided in July of 2020 by Post-Star editor, Kenneth Tingley, in "FLASHBACK: *An American Journey.*"[6]

Gunta endured a childhood that few of us today could appreciate. When she was only five, she recounts how curious she was as to why her father was digging an underground trench. He knew the war was coming and worked day and night to provide a place where the family could hide. The family lived in a region of Latvia that was directly between the Soviets in the north and the Germans arriving from the south. There would be no escape from the ravages of a war that was certain to come. She learned her survival skills quickly and the value of that mysterious bunker her father had built. *"When the moon was out, we knew the bombers were coming. When it was overcast, we knew we were safe."*

Gunta also has a vivid memory of the night a Nazi officer appeared at the door in 1942. She described his polished uniform, blond hair, and youthful face with terrifying blue eyes. He was there to inform the family that their father had been arrested in town by the Germans, and they were only there to allow some last good-byes. It was, as anyone might imagine, a heart-wrenching moment that devastated the family! When after three months her father had still not returned, she remembers her grandmother pleading with her mother to just move on; her husband was not coming back. There was no hope of a reunion.

Shortly after this incident, the family was rounded up and put into cattle cars where they were transported for days back to Germany for defense work. Here they were placed in a factory that made airplane parts. The days were filled with hopelessness and despair.

But the war did end. Lives were once again being repaired and put back together. In these latter days, Gunta would go out onto the autobahn to show people a picture of her father and ask if they had seen him. There was no success. Then, by some miracle, Gunta's father found his way back from his forced labor camp in Italy. The family was united once more. To Gunta's mind, it was a million-to-one chance of such a thing happening, yet it did. Four years later, the entire family immigrated to the United States. Providence reigned, as their departure took place only days before a mass deportation of Latvians to Siberia began.[7]

Gunta provided a short memoir of her reflections on this time, beginning with her first contact with a strange "care package" she had received as an elementary school child. The following account was excerpted from her memoir, and offered in a book edited by Hugh Downs, *My America: What My Country Means to Me* (2002).[8]

> A very, very long time ago, in another time, another culture, another country, I received the care package. All the other elementary school children in my class did, too. I, however, had a photograph in my package: a picture of the little girl,

my age, who had packed that gift. I no longer remember what wonderful goodies were in this delight from Heaven, but I do remember the photograph: a girl, my age, about 12 years, sitting on the bottom step of her porch. She had long, beautifully curled hair and a marvelous dress. Everything surrounding her looked so clean and well taken care of, the shrubs, the path leading from the sidewalk up to the house. She was looking into the camera and smiling.

For a child who had endured detention camps, cold water cascading onto her emaciated body in mass shower rooms, had her hair "shampooed" with gasoline, been yelled at and pushed around by armed guards, this photo was surely a place in Heaven.

In due time, I, together with my family, immigrated to the United States. Late in the evening in the spring of 1949, the SS Laplanda dropped anchor outside Boston Harbor. Several hundred of us, the former refugees, stood around on the deck in a combined feeling of anxiety and fascination. The lights of Boston seemed dreamlike, like a Christmas gift wrapped in sparkling paper. Most of us, young and old, stayed up all night, milling about, fantasizing, worrying about how it would be. Will our parents find a job? What kind of job? How will we learn English? Who will teach us? What about school? To get good grades one needs to understand the teacher's instructions, a very worrying point.

All of this imminent new life we were all embarking upon became more spirited as the ship slowly chugged into port. We disembarked into a huge terminal. Long tables placed end to end stood across the width of the Great Hall. Each table above it had a letter from the alphabet. We understood this type of processing; we had been through this dozens of times before. The difference was that this particular one was taking place on the soil of the free world. Therefore, we knew, once we walked out the door, we were truly in America and free.

On the outer perimeters of the terminal, I noticed some very gracious ladies standing by tables laden with boxes of something edible. At closer look, the boxes contained something round and fluffy-looking. These ladies were exquisitely dressed in bright colors of green, blue, red, and pink, and all had on their arm a white band with a Red Cross on it. They had beautiful shoes and stockings, and their hair looked like they had never slept on it.

I noticed when someone took one of these round things, their fingers got white powder on them. I could see the disapproving look of my grandmother's eyes; she had brought me up to never accept anything from a stranger, and definitely never, ever in public.

Being the willful, independent child I had always been, I took a round thing from the box as the lady came by. It melted in my mouth, white sugar flying all over my face. And strangely it had a hole in the middle. This was my first introduction to American generosity and kindness, and I can never pass a display of white sugar donuts without remembering that day in March of 1949.

To be an American is an incredible privilege. This means pride in my country as I present my American passport at an airport check-in. This means intellectual freedom. This means the ability to obtain an education. This means *freedom from persecution, the privilege to own property, to speak up when a wrong is done without fear of being shot. This also means religious freedom by having the privilege to worship in the church of one's choice. My America means walking on a street without being accosted with a demand for ID. It means freely buying food in a store.*

This is my America. This is where my family came to for freedom. I hold my America in the greatest respect and will never, ever allow anyone to hurt this nation.[9]

Gunta Krasts-Voutyras, Liepja, Latvia

For Gunta, like so many who escaped communism, socialism, Nazi occupation, or some other repressive and dangerous government, America has been a life-saving refuge; it has been a place that offered safety and a level of freedom that would have been hard to imagine in earlier times. Perhaps it is that singular sense of salvation that affords each of them such a sincere level of love for America. It is born from an appreciation unlike any other.

Maximo Alvarez escaped Cuba with his family when he was only 13 years old. As he describes his experience, his father was desperate to get out from under the communist regime of Fidel Castro. The family came as part of Operation Pedro Pan, which was a mass exodus of more than 14,000 Cuban children to the United States between 1960 and 1962. Although the father's original intent was to take the family to Spain, once they arrived on American soil, they remained to build their life here. Maximo went on to college, then opened his own gasoline distribution business in south Florida for the Citgo Corporation. He ultimately became so successful that he was invited to participate in an economic council with the president of the United States. His love of this country and the opportunities it afforded him permeate his words.[10]

> *Imagine that in 1961, as a 13-year-old, by myself, on my way to Spain, I was not even coming here, I arrive in this great country. Almost 60 years later I'm sitting next to the President of the United States! You talk about the American dream. This is the only country in the world, no other country, you can start a business in the trunk of your car, and in a very few years, with hard work, commitment, and all the core values that we learn from this very culture of ours, we can become very important to our future. We can become those people who make the next generation better than the one before. Why do you think you had to close the borders? Because everybody in the world wants to come here. No one is ever forced to come here. We come here because, in my case, my parents chose that I would not be indoctrinated by a communist country.*
>
> Maximo Alvarez, Havana, Cuba

Even for those who may have never set foot on American soil or even been acquainted with an American, there is an almost universal understanding that America offers its people freedom. To someone who has lived in tyranny, as did Maximo and his family, the sweet smell of liberty often holds an attractiveness like no other.

A Russian teenager, Ilya Somin, who had immigrated out of the Soviet Union to Israel with his parents in 1979, tells of an exchange with the Russian chessmaster, Boris Gulko, in 2010. Ilya was curious as to the reasons such a famous person would defect when he was clearly one of Russia's more privileged and elite citizens. His response revealed just how valued that personal safety and independence might be to the oppressed.[11]

In January 2010, my father went to hear a talk by Boris Gulko, a Jewish Russian chess grandmaster who had won the USSR championship in 1977, then later emigrated to the United States. Eventually, he had won the U.S. championship as well. Knowing my interest in chess history, my father asked whether I had any questions I wanted him to pose to Gulko. I told my father to ask why Gulko had decided to leave the Soviet Union. My father said that this was a stupid question. The answer was too obvious. Nonetheless, I persisted in urging him to ask it. After all, Gulko had been a privileged member of the Soviet elite who had every reason not to risk those privileges.

Gulko's answer to my question was a telling one. He said that he did not want to be a "slave" anymore. Despite his relatively privileged status, he could no longer tolerate life under the control of a totalitarian state that, among other things, could take away all his privileges at any time.

Like most Soviet Jews, Gulko had experienced plenty of anti-Semitism. But it was not so much the special oppression of the Jews that led him to emigrate, but the generalized oppression he endured along with all the other citizens of Lenin's Workers' Paradise. My parents' motives for leaving were in many ways similar to Gulko's. They too were fleeing communism as much or more than *anti-Semitism. Only their decision was easier than his since they didn't have as much to lose.*[12]

Ilya Somin, from his personal memoir,
"The Road to Freedom," 2010

For Ilya and his parents, their decision to emigrate to America was similar to Gulko's, although somewhat different in that his family had less to give up. They were not privileged, and their lives were fraught with hardships from which they were unlikely to escape had they stayed in Russia. Their story of coming to America was further told by Ilya in that same 2010 memoir.

Why did my parents become disillusioned with communism and the USSR? For many Soviet Jewish emigrants, the crucial factor was anti-Semitism. My parents had experienced this form of prejudice all their lives. All Soviet citizens were required to carry an internal passport that included a line denoting their "nationality." The passport was a requirement for applying to college, getting a job, moving into a new apartment, or almost any important transaction. If the nationality line said "Jew," it was a ticket to discrimination in hiring, college admissions, and elsewhere.

My father had finished first in his class in one of Leningrad's best high schools. But the "Jew" in his passport made it highly unlikely that he could be admitted to any of the top universities. When he and my mother graduated from the second-tier school they went to (my father was again the No. 1 student), they knew that the same passport line would close off many of the best job opportunities. Back in the 1950s, my grandmother had been fired from a research job during Stalin's purge of "rootless cosmopolitans"—a code word for Jews.

In the end, however, anti-Semitism was not the only reason for my parents' decision to emigrate, and perhaps not the most important. Their most fundamental concern was the much broader lack of freedom of which anti-Semitism was just one manifestation. They had grown tired of the constant lies and censorship, and the need to carefully watch everything they said.

Furthermore, my father was an avid student of foreign languages. He yearned to use his linguistic talents and see the world beyond the USSR—something forbidden to all but a tiny minority of Soviet citizens. For her part, my mother wanted to have her own apartment, a life free of constant control by the official bureaucracy, and greater freedom to make her own decisions.

Beginning in the early 1970s, some Soviet Jews had been allowed to leave for the United States and Israel. These pioneers sent back word that life in the West was different, better and, most of all, freer. Like many Russians, my parents also secretly listened to Western radio broadcasts from the BBC and Voice of America. Despite strict official censorship, some books and magazines also occasionally made their way through the Iron Curtain. For example, my father recalls reading a smuggled copy of New York Times reporter Hedrick Smith's classic 1976 book, The Russians.

If a Jew applied for permission to emigrate, it was by no means certain that it would be granted. Rejection could mean years of penury and official harassment as a "refusenik." Refuseniks were excluded from most jobs (even many of those otherwise available to Jews) and from many educational opportunities. Still, being Jews meant that we at least had a chance to leave. Most other inmates of Lenin's prison house were not so fortunate.

Despite the risks, my parents chose to exercise the one special privilege granted to Soviet Jews and applied to emigrate. It was the best decision they ever made, and certainly the best thing that ever happened to me.

My parents and I left the Soviet Union in early 1979. The timing was perfect. Just a few months later, the Soviet government ended nearly all Jewish emigration, and many "refuseniks" were left to wither on the vine for eight long years until Mikhail Gorbachev's Perestroika opened the gates once again.

My parents and grandparents believed that they were probably parting forever. Their willingness to endure such a separation in order to escape the Soviet Union is yet another measure of how awful life under communism was.

In the 1970s, Jews who left the Soviet Union did so under the legal pretense of "returning" to Israel, their "historic homeland," and "reuniting" with their families there. Since the USSR and Israel had no diplomatic relations, Jewish emigrants first went to Austria and then Italy, from whence some went straight to Israel while others, like my parents, waited to get refugee visas to come to the U.S. Even before leaving the Soviet Union, my parents had already chosen America over Israel. They believed— correctly—that the U.S. offered greater freedom and opportunity and had heard good things about it from *friends and acquaintances who had come to the U.S. earlier.*

We eventually got our American visas and arrived in the United States on June 6, 1979. It was the 35th anniversary of D-Day, and the day before my sixth birthday. Our refugee visas had been arranged by the Hebrew Immigrant Aid Society (HIAS), which had also arranged a host community for us. Many Russian Jewish immigrants ended up in New York City living among other Russians. But HIAS placed us in the affluent town of Westport, Connecticut, where there were few if any other Russian speakers. We were here.[13]

Ilya Somin, Leningrad, Former Soviet Union

The repressive circumstances and bureaucracies of communism was certainly one reason many saw the West as more desirable. Sometimes, however, other issues weighed equally as much. Decisions that require you to transplant yourself from the foundational roots of your home country to an entirely new one can be immensely difficult to make. Sly Dumitru of Romania found this to be the case where he described it in his interview.

A great deal of my early life was spent under communism, then in 1989 communism fell and things began to improve for us as a family. The transition from communism to so-called democracy was pretty much a growing process. It was a little better from an economical point of view, and living conditions were slowly improving. There were still the breadlines, unstable electricity where sometimes you had electricity and other times not, and sometimes there was water, but rarely hot water. Heating was not something you could count on either. It was harsh. As I said, these things were getting better, but nothing close to the kinds of services we have here.

When I was younger and growing up, I lived with my mom, and we stayed with my aunt and uncle. We had five people in a very small apartment, and there never seemed enough money to provide for all that was needed. When I could, I would try to help my uncle by working during the summers when school was closed. I went to my grandparents who lived in the country where I could work on their farm. Every little bit helped.

Eventually I finished regular school and began college where I studied in the computer field; it was something similar to what we now might call robotics. During that second year, my mother and I began thinking about coming to America. My stepfather had come over here eleven years earlier and we really wanted to reunite as a family...you know, be all together again. As I said, I hadn't seen him in eleven years at that point. Of course, there was also the other side of this idea, which was that I was in college and doing well. Should I give that up? I had friends and there was still other family I would have to leave. I was torn in that respect, and at times felt like I didn't want to leave all that behind. Eventually I decided to just give it a try. I thought, "Well, I will just go and see how things are once I get there." I really had no idea how things would really be, so it was a bit of a risk. Also, there were a few political issues taking place at the time that made my decision even more complicated. This was right after the war in Yugoslavia, and so many of us were unhappy with *the intervention actions of the United States in that conflict. In the end, I said, "Well, I'll just go now, and if it doesn't work, I'll come home." Because my stepfather was already in America, we were able to get our visas and make the trip, which ultimately landed us in Florida...quite a different place than Romania, I'll assure you!*

Sly Silviu-Cristian Dumitru, Bucharest, Romania

Family can be a strong influence in making our choices in life. Sly and his mother were anxious to reunite with the father in America, yet there were friends and other family who would be left behind in Romania. There was also the concern for his own educational plans. Would he be able to pursue that aspect of his future in a new and unfamiliar country? As we will see when his story continues, that concern was not unjustified. But make the move he did. Like so many others, he took a chance.

There are many immigrants who have come to America because of marriage. This is particularly true where one of the partners was in military service stationed in a foreign land. Such was the case for a young Korean girl, Kim Oksun-Comazzi. Living in the small town of Suwon, Korea, she was working on an American military base where she was to meet her future husband. Life in Suwon was good in many ways. She had six sisters, a good family, and they were reasonably happy even though they were living in a mud brick home with a straw roof. Things had not always been easy, but they managed. Having gone through a prior occupation by Japan as well as the Korean war, the family had stayed intact and lived a relatively stable life. For Kim and her family, the decision for her to marry and leave for America was beset with emotional and heart-searching challenges. To complicate matters further, by virtue of her position at the military base, Kim had also become a primary source of income for the family. This loss of income was no small matter. Although Kim knew a little of America from stories and various other sources, relocating to the United States was not a move she had ever fully intended. Love changed that.

> I was, of course, in love with my husband, but I don't know that I ever thought I was going to come to America when I was small. As a child, I often heard the adults and my parents talking about how in the west they had more freedom. It was a place where there wasn't hunger and plenty to eat. I was little, so I really didn't know what they meant when they said, "freedom." On the other hand, "hunger" was a word I did understand. With such a large family, there was always food, but perhaps rarely all we wanted.

> I had a good job on the military base, and I was really the bread winner for our family. If you worked in the town, you might have to work seven days a week, 12-15 hours a day to earn the income I had in the base store. Base jobs were almost impossible to get, and I was so lucky to have it.

> I married Bob; in fact, I married him twice. The first time was a local marriage and celebration where we had to go all over town to fill out papers and do the things required to make a marriage in Korea. Then in December, we got married at the base chapel. Then it was official, and I was going to come to America. To be honest, though, I don't think I was ever 100% certain this was going to happen. I

even kept my job at the base until the very last day when I was supposed to get on the plane. If somehow this didn't happen, I did not want to lose that position. It was not replaceable.

I can remember being on that plane as it left Korea and I was so sad. I was already so homesick I just cried and cried. We stopped in Anchorage for a while and then I flew on to New York where my husband and his family were waiting for me. I was so nervous that I would do something wrong. I remember when I first met my mother-in-law, I kept my head down so as to not look in her face. I thought that would be too disrespectful. I kept my head facing down whenever I was with her for several weeks because I thought that was etiquette. But mom would say, "That face. Lift it up. You're a beautiful girl." I learned that the proper etiquette was actually to face the person and not bring down my face. I had so much to learn in this country.

Kim Oksun-Comazzi, Seoul, Korea

For other immigrants, the decision to come to America was not theirs at all. That decision had been made by their parents, and they arrived as young adults or children. The experiences as children may have been different than they might have been had they arrived as adults, but their road has often been filled with obstacles and unanticipated twists of fate, too.

In 1959, tragedy struck the DiMauro family when the mother, Sophia died leaving nine-year-old Joe, his older brother Vincenzo, and his older sister, Vincenza, in the care of their grandmother in Sortino, Sicily. Their father, Cesare, had already left the family and traveled to America in 1955. Wishing to reunite the family, he began the task of bringing the children to America. As is the case with all immigrants, that task began with securing the necessary visas, organizing travel plans, and making the arrangements regarding what would happen once the children arrived in the United States. It was a massive family effort, and things did not move quickly.

> As part of the legal process to come to America I, my older brother, and older sister had to travel to Messina, Sicily and the American consulate where we could get the needed papers to come to America. This was obviously an all-day affair, and part of the process once we got there, besides all the paperwork and legal baptism certificates or birth certificates and everything else, is that we had to go through an extensive physical exam. There seemed to be countless questions and checks that seemed to be unending. Unfortunately, my brother, because he had had a touch of tuberculosis earlier in his life, was denied permission to come to America with my sister and me. It would not be until two years later he was healthy enough where they would give him approval to come here and join us in America.

> I came to America with my older sister in late October of 1960. We had to travel to the capital of Sicily, Palermo, where we caught a Greek liner, The Queen Frederica, bound for New York. For a nine-year-old this was exciting; it was to be a great adventure. We were traveling to places we'd never been, riding on a huge ocean liner, and going to America! We boarded with our big steamer trunks full of clothes and were out at sea. It was a journey that took us through the Mediterranean and the North Atlantic

Ocean for the next seven days until we finally reached a dock in New York. Ellis Island was closed by then, so it was somewhere on the west side of New York City. Unfortunately, that trip for my sister and me was not the best. The North Atlantic had been filled with rough seas and huge waves; both my sister and I were so seasick we spent almost the entire time lying in our beds. But eventually we made it. We were in America. My aunt was waiting for us at the dock and took us to her house, which was on the northeast side of the Bronx. That was where we lived for the next fourteen years.

Joseph DiMauro, Sortino, Sicily

But this is not the whole story. The important question to be answered is *why* had Joseph's father, Cesare, decided to come to America? As a roadbuilder who was responsible to break up and move rock, it was a hard job, but steady work. As such, he had already experienced some success and was living a middle-class life in Sicily. How is it that America held such an attraction? Moreover, how did that decision ultimately play out, and was the promise of America all he had hoped? Joe describes his father's reasoning:

My father had decided to come to America by himself in 1955 to live with his sister. This meant he had to leave my mother in Sicily with me and the other two children. I really don't know what kind of conversations took place between my parents about this decision; I was only nine at the time. I'm sure it must have been hard on my mother. My father had been talking with my aunt in America for some time and I'm sure he had heard many stories and reports before making the decision to move. What I also remember is that, in his mind, even though we were middle class in Sicily, he believed America was going to afford his children and family the opportunities for a better life, a more complete life than we would have if we remained in Sicily. Unfortunately, my mother died just four years after Dad left for the United States. We had to move in with my grandmother and aunt who owned the house next to my mother and father's. That event led the family to decide the children needed to go to America to be with their father.

In looking back, all the reasons our father gave as to why he came to this country have been fulfilled. For us, America has truly been a land where we've been blessed beyond all my father's expectations. We have all worked hard our entire lives, and we have managed to be successful. This country has been wonderful to us, and we enjoy great lives. We are grateful to live here where we were all able to achieve our goals and more.

Joseph DiMauro, Sortino, Sicily

Some who came did not come by a direct route, nor did they even arrive with the United States having been their primary destination. They came by way of other countries and perhaps over a number of transitional years. In some cases, the road to America included uncertainty and even danger. In spite of such trials, and no matter what the cost, some risked everything to reach this country. Such was the case for Sorin Ranghuic, from Galti, Romania.

Sorin had enjoyed solid employment working in a laboratory that produced motherboards for a foreign-based computer company. Living under communist rule at the time, Sorin became convinced it was unlikely he would move to a higher position in the company. Neither did he see other employment opportunities for which he could apply. Under communism, to get good quality work, one needed to be a member of the Communist Party, and Sorin was not a member. He felt locked in place and convinced that, if he were to have a better future, it would have to be somewhere other than Romania. That realization sent him on a multi-year journey involving five countries. In an interview in the fall of 2020, Sorin described his thinking and the harrowing route he traveled.

> *What had made me decide to come to the West was I saw more opportunity, a chance for a better life. In Romania, like I said, you could not do anything unless you were a member of the Communist Party, and even then, they controlled everything. They basically told you what you could do and what you couldn't do. If you wanted to get a promotion or move to a better job, the first question was always, "Are you a member of the Party?" If you said, "No," then that pretty much meant you would not get that promotion or new job. So, I thought, in the West, there is much more opportunity and a better chance for success. That was my thinking. In the West, I could do whatever made me happy and enjoy life. A person has to do what he is happy doing; it must be something he enjoys and can be proud. If I stayed in Romania, nothing would have changed. Here I could do whatever I wanted. Why, because here there is liberty! You are free. You can do whatever you want. Also, here you do not have to be afraid. There is no one who can intimidate or threaten you. I wanted that freedom. That was my goal, and I could not do that in Romania. Here I can do everything I enjoy and not have to*

ask if it is OK or have permission. Freedom is so important to me.

But getting from Romania to where I am today, well, that was not easy either. After I decided to leave Romania, two friends and I decided to make our way to Germany. We crossed over into Poland and traveled back areas until we came through a cornfield just before the Polish/German border. On the other side of the cornfield, we came to a big bog, or maybe even a swamp, that we had to cross. We would have to cross about 400 feet of mainly mud and a foot of water before we would actually reach the border. The bog was up to our chest and completely covered us in mud. We just had to slog through as best we could and as quietly as we could. We were constantly afraid we might alert border guards.

When we reached the border itself, there were two fences; there was the Polish fence that was about eight foot tall and had barbed wire on top. There was a similar fence on the German border. There was also nearly twenty feet of "no man's land" between the two fences. The borders were patrolled by both soldiers and guard dogs that we could hear from where we were hiding. It was really tense. We had each brought a little luggage of clothes, but we soon realized there would be no way to carry any luggage across the fences. We had to leave the bags and just take what minimum clothes we could put over the barbed wire and protect ourselves. It was a dark night, so we hoped we could get over quickly and not be noticed. We threw our clothes over the wire and helped each other over the top. We didn't come across any Polish guards that night, but on the German side, the guards and their dogs were a big concern. The entire nightmare made us really nervous. I think the mud from the bog helped us because perhaps it may have kept the dogs from getting our scent. Whatever the case, it didn't seem the dogs knew we were there.

Once across the two fences, we laid on the ground and feared that perhaps one of the guards saw us, or at least knew someone was there. If so, he chose to not do anything because he just kept walking. Once in Germany, we crossed a cornfield and happened onto a house where we were able to get some water and clean ourselves. Once we were in Germany, we decided to go our separate ways. I never saw those people again.

After about a year in Germany, I decided to go to Canada and crossed into Belgium where they had international shipping. I spent the next month looking for a way to get onto one of those ships going to the west. I met several friends who also wanted to go to Canada, and we ultimately stowed away on a container ship full of beer. We hid in a small compartment deep inside the ship having just what little food and water we could carry with us. The crossing took a little longer than five days, but when we reached the port, we found we were locked inside this compartment. We had to use a hammer and chisel to make a hole just large enough to crawl out and get ashore.

Once I got into Canada, I was able to apply for asylum. In Canada, once they give you temporary asylum, you can get your work card and enough benefits to live. To get citizenship, however, you had to learn French and then reapply. For me, I couldn't master it, and so I wasn't *accepted. I realized Canada was not going to work out for me and decided to try America.*

I got a lawyer and he helped me apply to the United States as a political refugee. This required an interview where I blended the experiences of both me and my sister in order to make my story as convincing as possible. My lawyer told me what I would need to say and assured me there was about a 90% chance I would get accepted. Maybe so, but I think the experiences with so many dangerous people and perhaps the overall story made a difference as well. I received my political asylum and, shortly after the interview, I was issued a green card. Now, here I am in the United States where I now have my own business, enjoy a good life, and am having dinner with you. It was maybe a little bit of a long road, but I'm happy.

Sorin Ranghuic, Galti, Romania.

As aptly noted, Sorin came to realize that vision of being his own master, having his own business. He currently lives near Nashville, Tennessee with his Romanian wife and children, and for him, the chances he took became worth it. The United States is also a fortunate benefactor in that it has yet another decent, hard-working immigrant who loves this country.

As these stories have amply shown, there are many reasons and many roads that led people to this country. Whatever the circumstances, their stories are testaments to the triumph of the human spirit and its ability to shape a better future. Never underestimate what can be accomplished by a resolute mind and sufficient opportunity.

CHAPTER 3

Journeys in America

The thing about time is that it steals things; it steals your youth, your health, your loved ones, relationships, and so much more. It never gives them back so, at the end of the day, all we have left are the memories—the stories of our journeys. For the immigrant, those stories are unique. They are full of twists and unexpected turns, and yes, marbled with human interest. They are stories complete with sacrifice, setbacks, obstacles, courage, and wonderful breakthroughs. That is the subject here; it will be a view into a few of those American journeys.

America has millions of such stories to tell, and those presented here represent only the smallest fraction of that total. Their narratives have been gleaned from personal interviews, biographies, written articles, or other works. Each account provides but a small window into the decision-making, experiences, and reflections of that immigrant's personal path, but their words will punctuate the power of the American dream as realized by those who lived it as new arrivals to these shores.

Unlike most native-born Americans, the immigrant faces somewhat more numerous barriers and concerns to make his or her path forward more challenging. There are issues of language, isolation, uncertainty, assimilation, discrimination, finances, and the ever present "nay-sayers" who constantly stand in the way of personal dreams. For some immigrants, it was a matter of survival to even make their way to America. Success in their struggle to reach America was a marvel in itself.

For Said Fadloullah of Morocco, coming to America was something he had thought about from when he was a young child. He didn't have any thoughts of becoming something special or living a luxurious life. For Said, America simply offered a way of life that far exceeded what he was living in his little village of Shima. Although one's initial vision might not fully foresee all that a new homeland's future might hold, as pleasant as that might be, early dreams can often be exceeded by reality. This was certainly the case for Said who was, in many ways, the inspiration for this book. He has a beautiful American journey to share.

> *After my brother helped me come to America, I found myself in Orlando, Florida and unable to speak a word of English. I wasn't really worried all that much as I knew I was willing to work hard and pretty certain I would find*

a job of some kind. The main thing was, I was here. The first job I found was at Wendy's flipping burgers. I went there and my brother helped me to talk to the manager. He just told him that I didn't speak English, but it was just a grill job, and it wouldn't be so important. I worked there for almost eight months before a friend of my brother asked if I wanted to work as a busboy in one of the hotels near Universal Studios. He told me I could make one hundred dollars a day there. "What?! A hundred dollars for just one day?" I am immediately recalculating that amount of money into Moroccan money. No, that can't be right, I thought. Of course, it never really reached a hundred dollars for a day; maybe it was forty or sixty, but at that time there is no $100 in this kind of work.

On one day the hotel was so busy with people coming and going, there was chaos at the check-in, and I see this guy and he has so much money he is putting into his pocket. I was thinking, that's a LOT of money. I went to him and said, what job do you do for a living? He said he was a bellman. I said, "OK. What do I have to do to become a bellman?" He asked, "Do you speak English? Do you have any experience?" I told him, no, not really. He just laughed and said, "Well, you can't get this kind of job then. You have to speak English." But I see he had already made $350 for that day, and I am thinking, I have to get that kind of job. I looked at him and said, "I swear to you, my friend, I'm going to be a bellman." He laughed and laughed. I asked him to show me to the place where the boss who hired the bellmen was. He told me, but also added, "Well, *he's not going to talk to you." But I said, "Just show me anyway."*

This was really my next step; I needed to finally have someone say, "yes." I thought if I could just talk to him, I could convince him I could do the work. When I got to his office, he wasn't there, but I just sat and waited until he got in. When I finally spoke to him, I told him I worked as a busboy in this hotel, and I wanted to be a bellman. He said "no." So, I thought, well, I will ask someone else. I said, "Could I speak to the person in charge of you?" He laughed and said I could try, but I still wasn't going to get that job. But I didn't give up. I went upstairs to talk to the Human Resources manager, but she already had his email that said I couldn't speak English and couldn't do the job. So again, I didn't get the job. I left, but I didn't take this well. I couldn't accept it. After two more weeks, I went up to the hotel's general manager in his office. His secretary said he is far too busy and wouldn't be able to see me. I wasn't going to go away that easy. I told her, "Well, I have nothing to do anyway; I will just wait until he is not so busy." I sat down and waited...and waited. I was there for well over forty-five minutes, and I guess they concluded I wasn't going away. She told me she thought I was wasting my time because my English was just not good enough. No, I was going to talk to him anyway. Finally, he let me in and after just a few minutes he said, "This is probably not the job for you." I begged him, "Just give me a chance. Give me one month, and if I don't do well, you just fire me. But I will do well, and you won't fire me. Just give me this one chance." He finally gave in and said, "OK, I give you one month."

I don't know how this happened, but in perhaps my first or second week, I took this family to their room and helped them get settled in. We talked a little while I straightened everything for them and put things away. When I was coming back down, I saw that he had given me $100! But that was not the end. I know God must have been there for me. The man came down and found that his car wouldn't start. I saw he was having this problem and said, "Perhaps it's the battery. I will help you." I went in and got a battery charger to start the engine, but once it was running, I said, "Let me take it to the auto place and get you a new battery so this doesn't happen to you again." He was so happy with me. He wrote a letter to the owner of the Loew's Hotels telling him how well he had been treated and what a great hotel staff he had. I knew I now had a job there forever. Nobody was going to fire me.

After a couple of years in that job, another chance meeting happened. I went out with this friend, and he was telling me how his brother was making twenty, thirty, even forty thousand dollars selling timeshares. They were paying bonuses of twenty and thirty thousand on top of that. Oh, my God, I thought. I need to go do this job. I went and applied, and even though I am still struggling a little with my English, the people knew my brother and gave me just a floor job. I didn't do well, and after eight months, I think well, I need to do something else, this isn't working. I didn't much like the company as well. My wife told me to be patient, but I wanted to work in a better company where I could make something of myself.

One day I was driving down International Boulevard, and I saw there was this sign by the Sheraton saying they were hiring. When I applied, they began by giving you this huge psychology exam. Oh, I tell you this, it was a nightmare. They are asking questions in the English way, and I am trying to quickly answer in the Moroccan way. It didn't turn out well. Fortunately, someone I knew who was already in the company called the director and suggested, "Just let him come in and talk to you. I think he will be fine." The director saw me, then put me in the training class where right away they gave me this huge thousand-page manual you have to memorize. I knew right away I wasn't going to pass that either. After a week, I went to the manager and said, "Just give me a chance. Put me on the floor. I will do well, I promise." I went on, "What is your number one salesperson doing?" He told me this fantastic number, but I just blurted, "I will do better. I will be your number one, and if, after a month, I'm not, I will just leave, and you will never have to see me again. You won't have to fire me. I will just go on my own." After that first month, guess what? I was number one! I did over $250,000!

Eventually, the company asked me to become the manager, then they moved me to senior manager, then I became the director of sales. Now I am a project director and in charge of the entire resort right here in Orlando! I know...this is amazing. I am just so blessed by all this. You *know, nowhere else could I do this. Who would have ever thought I would do this?*

Said Fadloullah, Shima, Morocco

If there is an American story more reflective of what might happen with perseverance, courage, and a work ethic sufficient to overcome all, you will be hard pressed to find it. One can only imagine what colleagues, prospective bosses, and hiring managers must have thought about this young Moroccan who was unable to understand the English word "no." Nay-sayers, doubters, and hesitant human resource directors notwithstanding, Said was never one to allow their lack of confidence in him to dissuade his ambition. If you meet Said, you will sense those defining characteristics that helped him reach his current status...a love of people, a joy in his work, and a sincerity that permeates his every conversation. His American story must surely serve as an inspiration to all.

Vincent Diaz of Honduras also came to America by way of a brother who had traveled here earlier. Although he also arrived with no command of English, he was able to find an initial job in a Chinese restaurant as a cook. From that inauspicious beginning, his journey in America took him in a direction he could never have foreseen when he decided at age sixteen to change the direction of his life.

I found my first job fairly fast in a local Chinese restaurant. A Hispanic in a Chinese restaurant. Anyway, I was there for only two weeks when they let me do prep-work and become a cook. Of course, everything was in Chinese, so I had to learn to read the orders in Chinese. When I was nineteen, I spoke English a little better, I became a server in the daytime but moved up to manager at night. In time I had saved a little money and asked if I could be a partner. The owner said that could never happen. No Chinese restaurant would have a Hispanic as a part owner. I knew then that I had to do something else. This would not be what I do for life,

You know, whatever I do in life, it is my life, I have to decide what it will be. And whatever it is, I have to be willing to put everything I have into it; I can't just be working for somebody else. I am what I do, and life needs leaders! The more leaders we have, the stronger we are. Limits don't work for me. I don't have limits. I grow every day. I learn something else to be better every day.

So, as I said, I saw this position as the end of the Chinese business, and I quit. From there I went to work in a local Mexican restaurant. They had what they called an "Open Door Policy." That meant if you worked hard and learned the business, it was possible for you to become a partner. You show what you can do, and you move ahead. I worked for sixteen years as a manager. My first three months was just as a waiter, but then they moved me right up to an assistant manager. I have to tell you that at first, I didn't want to take the assistant manager's job. I didn't think I knew enough yet and maybe I wouldn't be good. Let me tell you a story about that because it was what made me take that job. At that time, there was another person in the restaurant who, for whatever reason, didn't like me. He kept making comments and was pushing me. I was afraid this was going to be a problem if I became the manager. I mentioned this to the man offering me the manager's position, and he said, "Fine, so tomorrow you are the manager, and you just fire him." I said, OK, and I took the job. The next day, when this other worker found out I was the manager, he comes to me and says he is sorry, he made a mistake, and please don't fire me. I said, "I am not here to fire you, I just want to work with you so we can do well, but if you don't think you can do that, then just walk out that door and save me a lot of trouble." He stayed and everything worked out.

After I worked in manager positions at all their restaurants, I got a call when I was home visiting in Honduras. The caller said they wanted to sell me the two restaurants. I thought about this and said to myself, why? Maybe something was wrong, and they want to get out from under and just get rid of it. I was cautious, and I told them, I don't have that much money. They told me it could all be worked out, don't worry. I asked God, if He gives me the chance, I want to do it right. God, please don't give me this if it is not right. I was happy at this point and making money, so if this isn't what He wants, then take it away. But these two men, one was a big doctor, they talked to me. They are going to buy a building that would be suitable for a restaurant in [a neighboring town], and this would be the start. I drove out and looked at the cars and other businesses in this town. I realized this location would be good, and the restaurant would have a good chance to be successful. They had given me this yellow envelope a number of weeks earlier, and that envelope had been sitting on my desk unopened all that time. I was actually going to throw it out, but just as I was about to do that, I was called to the door to talk to a customer. When I came back, that envelope was in the middle of the desk, so I opened it. To me, it was a message. It described the details *for this possible business. I called realtor. I did my math, and they gave me a lease which I signed. I prayed on this a lot, but in the end, I just felt it was going to be OK. There is just so much opportunity here in America if you will just be determined to take it.*

Vincent Diaz, Honduras

For a young Ethiopian woman, Shegitu Kebede, the road to America was fraught with almost unimaginable dangers. Having lost her parents at the age of five, she spent most of her childhood in an orphanage run by Catholic missionaries. Once war arrived, the orphanage closed, and she was abandoned to find her own way. Her journey, as described in her personal interview and also by her book, *Visible Strengths, Hidden Scars*, is one of remarkable perseverance and an unconquerable will to survive.[1] Fleeing a socialist/communist, repressive, and dangerous regime to come to America proved a blessing she never imagined when she was a young woman. Her American story is one worth reading.

I was born and raised in the world where I lost my parents at the age of five and taken to an orphanage. There, it was a family atmosphere and a lot of children. The missionaries were very nice to us, and we had loving, caring times. Our days were filled with gardening, knitting, crocheting, basketball, volleyball, and board games. But then the war came; our missionaries were told to leave the country, so they had to flee and left us behind.

The government became desperate to get soldiers in the army. Of course, no one wanted to go. Their way of making people go was to comb the rural areas and kidnap boys or any men they could find. Anyone who didn't have money or someone to speak on their behalf, they became soldiers. My younger brothers were twelve and thirteen, and I was so worried that they're going to take them, too. If that should happen, then I would have nobody left as a family. I took it as my duty to protect my brothers.

I first decided that I would need to get married and make a home, that didn't work either. My husband was soon forced to leave, and we became separated. Even though I was three months pregnant and only eighteen, I decided I had to make my way out of the country and get to a refugee camp in Kenya. During the day I would hide, and then during the night I walked barefoot. It took me about three months, but I was almost immediately thrown in jail. Once I got out, I finally made it to the refugee camp in Nairobi. I had my daughter in the camp, then after three-and-a-half years finally got my refugee status. You had no choice regarding what country you would go to; the UN decided that for everyone. I was given my asylum in the United States. Once you were assigned, the way things worked was the airlines would place a refugee in whatever seat that was not sold. You just sat in the airport and waited for whatever flight they put you on. It seemed I was waiting and waiting and just not getting my flight. Then finally I was put on a plane and flown out to, of all places, North Dakota! It was probably the whitest of white places in America.

In North Dakota, I happened to meet another black woman with a little girl about the same age as my daughter. We became friends and the two girls became friends as well. I laugh, but perhaps we were the only colored people in all of North Dakota. My friends decided to go to Minneapolis, and because I did not want to break up our friendship, I also moved to Minnesota. This was another big change for us.

But here is the thing. There were so many times in my life I wanted to commit suicide. I almost killed myself on a number of occasions, but when I look back today, I'm an incredibly lucky and successful person. I have had so much good fortune that I never could have even imagined. But I would not measure my success by currency; rather it is by just still having a sound mind.

I am a mother and grandmother. Who might have thought that, after all I went through, I could have this success? I didn't give up my life. I thank God, I didn't give up. I remember those days being a refugee. I just sat and ate a little. No running water or shower. No school. Nothing. Now, I'm eating, and I support myself. I was picked from a refugee camp back in 1989, and then assigned to go to America.

In America, I started by having a cleaning business. I also owned and ran a second business, the Flamingo Restaurant. Many businesspeople and friends helped me, and I am so fortunate in that respect. Business is in the culture of America. It brings people together and allows them to grow and flourish. I was so blessed. My daughter is in college in California. I have many friends. I am so fortunate to be in America now. I find it hard to get all the words to describe it.

Shegitu Kebede, Ethiopia

Know too, Shegitu's journey did not end here with only her successes in the business world. There are many immigrants who have come to America and become mentors to others traveling similar paths. After she moved to Minneapolis, she established both a business and then an outreach program to help other immigrant women struggling just to survive. Certainly, America is a land full of opportunity, but when newly arrived immigrants find themselves suddenly transplanted from a different part of the world, possessing limited English skills, and knowing nothing of how this new world works, it can be simply overwhelming. Shegitu had learned this, and she understood the challenges. Her journey continues now as one woman from Ethiopia reaching out her hand to help others address the stark realities of life in a new and unfamiliar country. This is where her story continues.

Getting started in Minnesota was a challenging time, but at the same time a learning process for me. I had just divorced and been going through some financial difficulties prior to arriving. Initially, I began working for a nonprofit organization where I had the chance to interact with a lot of immigrant women. I heard their stories and what they were going through to get their lives together. I understood their difficulties. I said to myself, you know, I have the ability to access information, and now I speak the language. I thought, if I was having difficulty, imagine what it looks like for those who do not even have the advantages I have. In that moment, I said to myself, I can't just see this go on. I quit my job, and I went to my boss who was very high up and I told him I have this idea in my head. "It may sound crazy, but I want to start a cleaning business where I can hire and help others. I've worked in that business for a while, and I know how it works. Also, I can understand what it looks like for other immigrant women who are not able to speak English, and who go out and try to find a job to support their children." To my mind, it was also possible they may even be living in a domestic abuse situation with no way out. He listened to me and said, "Yes, I think it's wonderful. I will do everything I can." He did, and he was wonderful. He wrote letters to the presidents of local apartments or office buildings explaining what I wanted to do and helped get my first contracts. So many of these owners tried to help me.

Once I got things going, I began to take in those less fortunate immigrant women and train them. It wasn't just the cleaning, but I also provided language and computer classes. I added a work readiness program that partnered with the other institutions like the University of Minnesota, Minneapolis Technical College, and Augsburg College. I recruited college students and trained them so they would know the best ways to help these immigrant women. Each day, I would take these immigrant women out to teach them how to do the actual cleaning tasks that were necessary. When they would come back, we had their other classes. Those with English problems, we helped with their English. Those who had enough language ability or had a high school diploma, we focused on such things as operating a computerized cash register so they could be cashiers or work in places like cafeterias, restaurants, or hospitals. Basically, we were training for work readiness. I also taught life-skills such as how to get along with your co-workers, deal with your boss, and the importance of being on time and at work every day. Beyond all of this, our women also had to learn things like how you take care of your personal hygiene, handle cultural differences, and basically get accustomed to the way things were done in America. All this could take five or six months, but once I felt a person was ready, I took them out to look for a job. I created a resume for them, drove them to prospective employment opportunities, and became their reference. I also talked with community people to ask for work clothes or supply other services like transportation or housing. I didn't want the person to have to remain only within the immigrant community. You need to interact and know your entire community.

Later we also started a quilt program. For this I recruited white American women from the neighborhood, especially those who were retired and sitting at home. I brought them together, and we cooked food together, did potluck suppers, and talked. It was a mutual exchange of cultures and ideas where the ladies learned how to cook African food, and we learned how to cook American food. The first year I believe I had about 38 women who graduated from that program and who are right now working somewhere in the Twin Cities.

I didn't stop there. I also thought about their children because I was a single mom with two children of my own. I knew how hard it was when you're working all day to *come home and then be a mother to your children. Their education is so important. We started an after-school program to help them with homework and socialize. I also partnered with the local 4-H program, which has now expanded to be an extension program with the University of Minnesota. It brings a variety of activities such as science and math programs in such a way that the kids hardly know they're working and learning those things. We partnered with others to take them to neighborhoods and places where successful people lived and enjoyed life. I wanted the kids to see and realize there are many life rewards when you apply yourself and do well at school. Pay attention, don't just sit around with nothing to do. Live a clean life and stay away from gangs and drugs. We wanted each one to realize that they have to study and work hard, but there is a good life waiting if you do those things. Most of all, your life has worth! This is my American life now, and these are my passions.*

Shegitu Kebede, Ethiopia

Yosel Epelbaum, who later became Joseph Pell, was an immigrant born in Poland in 1924, but then moved to the Ukraine in later youth. His is a story of his father and brother being killed by the Nazis, harrowing personal escapes, and a treacherous path that ultimately led to America. Barely escaping capture by the Nazis in 1942, he made his way to a nearby wood where he joined a group of partisans. While serving with these partisans against the German military, his very life was at risk every day. His specialty was blowing up trains. In the years after the war, having no trade or specific skill, he went from country to country making a living in the black market. About this time, his friend, Paul Sade, convinced him to move to America.[2]

In 1947 he arrived, and his American journey began. His early experiences as an American immigrant are reflective of what mid-twentieth century Jewish immigrants encountered and how America, personal venture, and fate can combine to shape a life. A small part of his story is recounted here in three excerpts from his 2011 autobiography, *Taking Risks*.

> *Stepping off the ferry from Ellis Island and setting foot in Manhattan, I saw other immigrants meet with the excited shouts and warm embraces of relatives. Laughter, cries of joy, and prayers of thanksgiving filled the air. There was no one there waiting for Yosel Epelbaum. Of the hundred fifty million people in America, I knew only one, Paul Sade, and he was not about to leave his job in Baltimore and come up to New York just to hug me when I arrived.*
>
> *Alone and with no place to go, I led an aimless existence. I had not come as a tourist with a list of sights to see, and anyway I had no one to show me around. Even more limiting was my lack of English, causing problems as soon as I left the hotel room. That's why I ate most of my meals at the Horn and Hardart Automat where what you saw was what you got. But at a regular restaurant, some advance planning was required to ensure there would be no surprises. Trying hard not to be rude, I would walk through the place and glance around at the other diners until I saw someone eating a dish I thought I'd like. Then*

I would sit at a table nearby so when the waiter came over,
I could order just by pointing at the other person's plate.[3]

Yosel decided to make a visit to a support group, the Biala Podlaska Society. His visit was anything but successful. The men he met were somewhat standoffish and uninviting even though they had probably been immigrants themselves at an earlier time. They offered him some food during which time he told them his life story and current circumstance. After eating, the men huddled, and then gave Yosel a check for twenty-five dollars, which he immediately returned. He had not come for money! As he put it:

"They had all the compassion of government bureaucrats." Their behavior was typical of the arrogance and insensitivity I encountered from many American Jews in these postwar years, especially those who had been immigrants themselves and tended to look down their noses at newcomers.

Yet, I was anything but depressed as I moved through the bustling midtown streets near my hotel. It was a time of being in limbo and yet one of intense anticipation because I had the feeling that, after a short period of waiting, I would get a fast start in the Golden Land. Through the windows of delicatessens, I saw cooks and I knew I could be one. I saw grocers and butchers and I thought I could do that kind of work, too. And then I'd move up the ladder from there. I'm a quick study, I told myself. I'll learn on the job and perform as well as the Americans themselves.

After reuniting and living with his friend, Paul Sade, the two looked for work in New York and found themselves working in lower tier sweat shops with long hours and poor pay. Yosel talks about his decision to make his way west. A brief conversation, perhaps of seemingly only passing importance at the time, became a turning point in Yosel's life. It provided that all important light on the road forward.

Paul was in the back of the hot, noisy factory, pressing pants with an industrial-strength iron. He told me to wait for him until his shift ended, in the comfortable home of one of his uncles where he occupied the guestroom. When he returned that evening, we began a serious discussion about the future.

First, I asked him how much he was getting paid, "Seventy-five cents," he answered. "This is why you came to America? To press pants for seventy-five cents an hour?" After talking it over for a couple of days, we decided to hit the road, head west, and see what opportunities were out there. I was more than ready to end my stay in New York. We went back to Manhattan long enough to pick up some belongings and boarded a train for Chicago.

I don't remember putting a lot of thought into our destination. It was a city known for commerce and seemed to be the most logical next step. "Chicago" had the right ring to it. On a raw October day, with the wind blowing off the lake, I noticed a large, inviting poster in the window beckoning people to San Francisco. It featured, of course, a magnificent birds-eye photo of the Golden Gate Bridge. It's the longest suspension bridge in the world, I informed Paul. I would sure like to see it.

They also enjoy a warm sunny climate out there, we told each other. Everyone, it seemed, from established American Jews to recently arrived refugees, wanted to move there. Neither Paul nor I, though, had anything to lose. So, without any hesitation, we went in, walked up to the counter, and bought two one-way tickets on a bus leaving the next day. It wasn't that different than my decision to cross the Atlantic. In Europe, America was everybody's first choice, and in America the best place appeared to be California.[4]

Yosel Epelbaum, Podlaska, Poland

After traveling four days of quietly observing all the different landscapes, road signs and Americana, Yosel marveled at his new home. Once arrived in California, he changed his name to Joseph Pell and began his climb skyward. His beginnings were in an ice cream store called Shirley's, which he eventually bought. The ice cream business became extremely successful, and he was able to build a four-apartment building where he lived in one unit and rented out the other three. It was this purchase that launched Joseph's career in the business that would result in him rising to become one of northern California's most successful real estate developers.

From a desperately dangerous life in Europe to an American success, his story is one of many marked by both personal endeavor and the consistent determination to find opportunities and seize them wherever possible.

Yassin Terou, now of Knoxville, Tennessee, came as a refugee from Syria, and currently operates two successful restaurants, *Yassin's Falafel House*. He has faced numerous barriers to American success along the way, yet his family values, work ethic, persistence, and continued growth as a businessman paved the way for his new life in America. His is a story of what can happen when one sets both his or her mind and actions on day-to-day work in order to reach a better place in life. For Yassin, his path was not always clear, but he was confident he and his family would ultimately triumph over the various setbacks that invariably take place; it was only a matter of time. His personal interview along with a few excerpted passages from a Knoxville News Sentinel editorial titled, *Welcoming Refugees Like Me is What Makes America Great*, provided the material for this story.[5]

> *I grew up in the capital of Damascus. My four siblings and I enjoyed a quiet, middle-class upbringing, and we were heartbroken when violence and war broke out in our beloved country. In 2010 I was working in public relations for a Kia dealership, but because I had been critical of the government, the secret police questioned me and held me in captivity. When I was finally released, I knew it was no longer safe for me to remain in Syria. I ultimately applied for asylum in America and started my new life as a refugee. As hard as it's been at times, I believe it was the right decision.*

> *When I arrived, I rented a studio for $300 a month. I didn't speak English and struggled to find a job. I was determined to be self-sufficient, so I asked at a local mosque if I could sell sandwiches outside after services. I was amazed at the reception from the people, and my sandwiches sold.*

> *Eventually I was able to rent a small space where I could make and sell my sandwiches. The little sandwich business kept growing in popularity and we were able to eventually grow this into a real business. In 2014, I opened*

Yassin's Falafel House with two plastic tables, a credit card machine, and a gallon of water. We didn't even have a kitchen at first. But the little business has grown ever since. Along the way I met my wife, a Palestinian immigrant. We're proud to be a part of this country and build a future for our children here.

Two years ago, when my restaurant was vandalized with a white supremacist slogan, I decided not to press charges. Instead, I told my customers and friends that whoever was responsible was welcome to come in for a meal and ask me any questions he or she might have about my experience as a Syrian refugee.

Back home in Syria, I was raised to be understanding of others, and it's how I'm raising my children here in America. Because of the current travel ban, no Syrian refugees are allowed to enter the country right now. This saddens me because I know how much refugees can benefit America. Here in Knoxville, I now own two falafel restaurants, serve roughly 4,000 people a week, and employ nearly 30 people. Some of my employees are refugees like myself, but I also hire U.S.-born Tennesseans, including ex-cons, recovering drug addicts, and women who have survived domestic violence. We're planning to open two more stores within the next year and increase our employee base to fifty or more.

All of this was possible because the United States welcomed me and my family when we were most in need. I hope all of this demonstrates that there is no reason to fear newcomers like myself. In truth, I know the person who vandalized my sign is part of a tiny minority. My

*customers are kind and welcoming. They are the America
I know. They believe in my motto: "When you break bread,
you break hate."*

Yassin Terou, Syria

Two important messages are embodied in Yassin's story.
The first involves the untapped resource of refugees who
might arrive with a desire to make themselves and America
better. The second is the power of love and a welcoming spirit
to build better communities. As Yassin pointed out, there was
a ban on refugees from mostly Muslim countries, and at the
time it virtually closed the door to those who wished to gain
asylum. That ban is currently suspended. Yassin's more central
point was the idea that refugees often bring great benefit to
America. This is certainly true in a great many cases, and it
underscores an area on which this country should work for
improvement. We must continue to seek ways to assist those
who present no risk to come and hopefully rebuild their lives.
This decision-making process will not be easy, but it is worthy
of our effort to find and open such a door. It is, after all, part
of our heritage and founding DNA.

Yassin spoke at length of the various steps required to gain
his classification as a refugee. He described numerous sessions
of lengthy questions, reviews of personal documents, and constant delays. By the end, Yassin's perseverance and determination was rewarded. As is often noted, however, that was only
the beginning of his family's much longer journey in the
United States. Yassin is now a respected member of the
business community and has received national recognition by
Reader's Digest for his welcoming, friendly business atmosphere. His story is one that has earned the respect of everyone

who knows him. Yassin is hopeful that one day others of his family can join him, and he can help them pursue their own dreams in America.

Not every immigrant has arrived from a country where the culture and language were entirely different. Kathryn Court is a well-educated English woman who began her career in London. Coming from university, she initially took a position in a London investment bank where she was the only woman on a staff of 52. As Kathryn put it, *"It was unbearable and I hated it; not the work, but the environment."* She began looking for other work when she came across an ad for a position in the publishing business where "experience" was not needed. As a member of a panel discussion entitled, "Powerful Women in America," she described her subsequent journey and transition to America.

> *Then I saw an ad in the paper that said editorial assistant needed, no experience essential. I thought, well, I could do that. When I sat for the interview, I was asked, "You don't have any experience, do you?" I said, no, but anyway, at the level of salary we were talking, it was I think 400 pounds a year or something, I thought, well, what do they want? So, we went to this Italian restaurant, and I ordered the pasta and realized the interviewer was watching very carefully if I could properly eat this, and then she explained to me that the reason I couldn't have any experience was actually that she was going to get half of my magnificent salary should I get the job from something called the Publishers Training Board. So, in fact, I was only going to cost her a couple of hundred pounds a year. Oh, and by the way, did I have a private income? I thought*

this was really a very good beginning place for getting into the publishing world because it somewhat set the tone.

After that, I have to say I was really rather lucky. I spent a few years in publishing there in England, but then I moved to New York and ultimately found a job at Penguin Books. I had the initial experience of working for a very nice man in one of their departments in a very junior capacity. Within quite a short space of time, everybody up the ladder from me had left because either they wanted to earn much more money, or went to law school, or did smart things like that. Finally, the chair left the department, and somebody I knew very well said to me, well, you know you have to apply in order to be the editor-in-chief. I said, well, I don't think so. I'm here only a very short time and well, I don't think so. But then I thought, well, I suppose this is the American way. Be aggressive, don't be this little polite English flower. Go in there and tell them you want this job, so that's what I did. And, of course, I didn't hear anything for a bit, but I ran the content for six or seven months and was basically the head of the company. There was no more money or anything while the company interviewed everybody and their dog. Probably nobody wanted the job because it didn't pay enough, and so I got it. I was terrified, absolutely petrified. I don't know if I could ever come to realize I actually could do it, but it would be fun, so I went ahead. We would have to work as a team, and we gradually would build that team; it was going to be really exciting.

I suppose the first thing I learned is that I had to find the very best people to be my colleagues. I had to hire people, if possible, who are brighter than me, more experienced than me, and who had a good sense of humor. I had great luck. I had some fabulous people, and we had a bloody good time. We published some really fabulous books, and some of them even sold. It seemed to me it was a great way of making a living. It's sort of been chaotic over these twenty years; it's had a lot of challenges.

There are a few things that strike me as being very important to anybody, probably in any business, but especially maybe in ours. First, CLARITY. The ability to speak very clearly about what you want to do and why you want to do it. Second, COURAGE. Being able to go forward with things you really want to do, even though others are very skeptical. You know, trust your own instincts. Third, be very, very DETERMINED. When I first came to America. I went to interview with about sixty people before I got Penguin. I had all these little notes in a tiny little notebook and over the years almost every one of those people who saw me kindly then became colleagues.[6]

Kathryn Court, London, England

As Kathryn found, making a change to America opened doors for her that might not have opened in her home of London, England. The important lesson of her story, however, is that one has to knock on those doors, and one has to have the courage to walk through them if they open. Clearly, she had some concerns that perhaps the job of editor-in-chief might be too large a step for someone so young in the industry, yet she took a chance on herself and pressed on. She did not allow her self-doubts to limit her future. Whether immigrant or native-born, it is essential one be willing to take a risk, especially when that risk is on yourself!

Many immigrants, particularly some of our current day Americans, have come here as students. Perhaps when they arrived, they had no real intention of making America their permanent home, but then later decided to stay. Others hoped their studies and degree would lead to greater things in this so-called land of opportunity. Most, however, came unaware of the difficulties that would confront them once they graduated and attempted to make the transition from international student to permanent American status. One such student was Bob Mwiti from Kenya, Africa.

Bob is currently the CEO of his own IT consulting company in Tampa, Florida. He works with other immigrants and assists them in making the transition from their home country to somewhere here in the United States. He uses the many lessons learned through his experience to guide others through their own process of finding employment and making an application for permanent residency. His road was not smooth, nor was it the one he had envisioned it might be.

I grew up in a very humble family back in the village on the slopes of Mount Kenya at a place called Meru. I came to the USA in 2009 as a student. I grew up in a typical African village and lived with my grandparents. For my education, I attended the local primary school, and then from there went on to the high school which was not far away. I had hoped to go to a much better high school after my primary school examinations but wasn't able to go to that school. I was forced to attend a school that was closer to home and much less expensive.

Like most of the children from Meru, that was how we grew up. In those early days, I never really thought of coming to the U.S. My dream as a boy was to go to the big city, Nairobi. When I was growing up, I had heard so many stories of that city and the Europeans who lived there. In Kenya, you usually have a chance to choose the school that you want to go to, but where you actually go is determined by your exam scores. For me, Nairobi was the goal. Coming to the United States was something that came much later in life and well after I graduated from high school.

My father lived in London, and he had told me about the opportunities that are out there in other countries, countries outside Kenya. It wasn't until my father had described the kinds of opportunities that existed in all these other countries that I began thinking about leaving Kenya and going to some other country. My first idea was to go to the UK, not the USA. My father had left our family when I was quite young to live in England. Although we did not have a close relationship when I was growing up, we were able to somewhat reconnect in my older years. He had told me many good things about life in the UK, and I thought them to be really attractive. Unfortunately, my United Kingdom visa application was denied four times and I had no chance at all to go there. Apparently, because my father lived in England, I was deemed to have family ties in England rather than Africa. The UK government wanted to know that when you finish your studies you will go back to Africa, so on that basis my application wasn't granted. After being denied the fourth time, I decided to try to come to America.

I got a student visa because I was able to gain acceptance to Indiana University of Pennsylvania. I had been looking on the internet for schools online and that was one of those schools that accepted foreign students on visas. I now had my visa, an educational opportunity, residence here in America, and my life in front of me. However, I have to stop here because this is what a lot of people don't know. Those people from my background in Africa, we tend to think that it is "successful" when they attain their status as just being a student. But for me, I first got my undergraduate degree in Africa, and then came here for more school. I didn't just come to the United States, and that was my only goal. I was looking for bigger things. At the time, though, I had only a general idea of my future, but I had no actual plan of what I was going to do once I graduated with my advanced degree. Even worse, I had no idea what my next steps would be after graduation. All I knew was that I first needed a job as that was essential if you wanted to stay in America. For me, it was not just OK to just be in the U.S. So here I was, on my own with no job and no plan. It did not turn out to be smooth sailing. There were a lot of challenges.

When you come here as an international student and you graduate from college on your student visa, you can apply for something called an optional practical training. If you have a STEM degree (Science, Technology, Engineering, and Mathematics), you can usually get good employment and do well right away. But still, I had one problem in that

I actually had to find a job that will accept and hire you. I did not have a STEM background. Something else many do not understand is that when you look for work in the U. S., the job opportunity absolutely has to be tied to what you had studied in college and your chosen field. For example, I came here as a master's degree student with a bachelor's degree in Accounting and Finance. I had to find work in that area only. My work authorization was only for the one year, and I needed to find something as soon as possible.

The employment requirement is a big challenge for a lot of African immigrants who come here as students. They don't realize that companies, when they're hiring international students, are very picky and cautious. They are not sure how it will work out, and there are a number of additional things required of African immigrants at the time they are hired. Hiring is expensive, so many companies ignore even brilliant students because they only have that one year before they might have to leave.

Most companies are understandably looking for someone long-term, which places international graduates at a big disadvantage. I didn't know about any of those things when I came. I had to learn all these things the hard way. I went for interview after interview, but I didn't pass any of them! I'm thinking, "I'm smart, I'm ambitious and I know I will be a good worker. What am I doing wrong?" I realized at this point, I have to do something differently; this can't be allowed to go on.

Luckily, I have always been very motivated and observant, so I didn't just sit there. I began to pay attention and look at others who were getting jobs to see what they were doing. In particular, I took notice of the international students, no matter what their native country. I saw how Asian students were doing noticeably better than people from my background, especially the Indian students. They were really good at finding employment fairly fast. There were jobs out there, but I had a business degree in accounting and there were not as many job openings in that field. I thought perhaps I could transition into a field where there was a shortage of applicants. I conducted my own research to which skills were in demand and where there might be a shortage of applicants. Where were the companies who were outsourcing work or positions and what skill sets would fill those needs? I found the tech industry was one of the most understaffed. I thought to myself, this could be a way out for me; I might actually get a job in the IT industry, but I would have to retrain for that industry.

I began my renewed path by training for the specific tech skills where I saw an immediate need. I went back and trained to become an Oracle consultant. I could go out and help a client start using Oracle to run his daily business. There are many corporations that rely on financial systems supported by an Oracle system. I saw how they needed people to help them operate that program effectively and there just weren't enough individuals to fill that need. I spent the next five months training to be that *person, and that was really where my consulting business began.*

As I continued to work in that field, I gradually gained stronger skills and sharpened my analytic ability to where I became a senior consultant in Oracle Financial Systems. In time I branched out and started my own company, Appstec America. The company mission was to create an Oracle E-Business Suite training platform that specifically focused on helping "brilliant Kenyans" study here in the United States. We assist good students in their visa application process, and once they are here to then train them in the Oracle IT business. I've been blessed to have learned and achieved so much in my consulting career. My life has measurably changed. I've now made it my mission to give back and serve others beyond myself. I want my story to inspire others and help them come to the United States to make their dreams come true just like I did.

Robert Mwiti, Kenya

In some cases, immigrants who have arrived in America had someone else to pave the way. It may have been an existing family member, a spouse, or just a sponsor who already arranged for the necessities. In those cases, the move to their new country was likely to have been less complicated. Kim Oksun-Comazzi came to be with her husband and his family. There was already a solid living situation with people who loved her and were anxious to make her new American home as pleasant as possible. Yet, even then, the adjustment to America and establishing a new life took time. Kim offered these observations about her experiences and journey in America.

For the first two years that I was here, I just stayed at home. I did the cleaning, I made meals, and I did things for my husband like his shoes and laundry. But other people were telling me things like, "You didn't come all the way to America to be a maid. Why don't you go out and do something?" Of course, I didn't really know exactly what they were telling me. Isn't this what you are supposed to do when you are married? And what would I do, this "go out and do something?" So, I just went and began looking for some kind of work I could do. My first job was at a factory making brassieres. I stayed there a while, but I knew I could do better than that, so I got another job, this time at a cigarette plant. I was stamping cigarettes, packing orders, making certain the orders got out to wherever they were going, and whatever else they needed at the time. It was all right, but I wasn't satisfied there either. Where could I go with that experience? Was there something above what I was doing? Finally, I found work with Hewlett-Packard. This was really good. It was here where I started interacting with other people, talking with the other girls. It was funny what happened. One day we were talking about what we were making our husbands for dinner, and a number of them said, "Oh, I don't bother cooking, I just make him a TV dinner or something." I thought that was good and how easily it was done. When I got home, I told my husband we needed to go out shopping so I could get him some TV dinners. You can imagine how that idea was received. But it was through all these conversations and making friendships with these *women that I began to understand and become part of American culture. I was having a good time.*

Eventually, Hewlett sent me to college for two years and I became a computer technician. The management people were always telling me how much they appreciated how hard I worked, and how whatever they asked I would do without complaint. In fact, because they liked the way I worked, I was able to get jobs in the company for a lot of the Korean girls I would meet on the outside. I would talk to them and teach them things on how to work and fit into the everyday life at the company. Over time, however, men and women with four-year college degrees began to come in and establish themselves in the same technical field with me. I realized I was not going to get a management position or move up unless I went back to college. I would have to do something else if I wanted something more.

Over this time, most of my family from Korea had also immigrated to America and a few of them had started their own businesses in California. They were doing well, and I began to think I wanted to start a business of my own. My husband, though, was a kind of conservative American man. As he told me many times, he was not a "risk taker." He liked his weekly paychecks that he could plan on and was not especially encouraging of my idea to start my own business. What business experience did I have? How would I be able to finance everything? What business did I even want to get into? What happens if it didn't work? I suppose these were all good questions and concerns, but I wanted to start my own business; that was all I knew. I would figure something out if I could just get the chance. I cried and cried, and tried to convince him, but there was always resistance. Finally, with just a small amount of approval, I simply went out and began looking at businesses for sale. I finally found a local doughnut shop that was available, and I convinced my husband to come and try with me. We opened the doors and over time it did well. We eventually sold that business and opened a restaurant business in a nearby town. We operated the restaurant until we sold it and retired to Florida, where we now have a beautiful home and wonderful friends.

I am blessed to have had all these chances and live here. None of this would have happened for me had I not met my husband and come here. In fact, none if it would have happened for all my sisters and family, either. Yes, truly blessed, that's what we are.

Kim Oksun-Comazzi, Korea

Sly Dumitru of Romania originally came to the United States with his mother in 2001. His journey has a followed a path similar to many others who have come to call America their home. Sly did not arrive with a complete plan or set of expectations as to how he would establish himself once he got here. He simply came to help reunite his family and give America a try. He wondered if everything was going to live up to what he had heard. Was it in fact a place where there were better opportunities, better lifestyles, and greater freedoms? He even wondered if America was even the place where he would ultimately stay. Once arrived, he bounced through a variety of jobs and locations. He had to confront and overcome a number of challenges regarding what he described as "learning the American ways." His story is his alone, but there are elements that typify the struggles of so many others. They are worth the time to examine.

> *When we first got here, we were in Florida. For me that was a complete change from Bucharest. Just the weather and topography themselves were a complete adjustment. It was flat, flat, flat. The weather was so hot. There seemed to be everything going on around me. It was dizzying. My idea when leaving Romania was when I got to America I might just pick up where I left off in college. Since I had been going to college in Romania for the past two years, it seemed a logical place to begin. Unfortunately, I had no clue how to find a college, what I needed to get in, or how I was going to pay for it. In Romania, the college I was attending was basically free and was no problem getting in, but that was certainly not the case here. I hadn't thought about that.*
>
> *At first, I just had to live with my parents while I tried to sort things out. There were also a couple of other Romanians where we lived, and they were in the construction industry as tile installers. I got my first job with them and became a tile installer for nearly ten months. I later got a job at a swimming pool company, but that was another job I totally disliked. To hopefully free myself from these entry jobs, I even took some courses in computers. During those first years I had so many different jobs to just make a living. None of them were anything I wanted to do as a career. I was becoming less and less happy.*
>
> *I had also come to miss the change of seasons, the mountains, and the cool climate of my home in Romania.*

A friend had told me about Colorado and how beautiful it was, so I just up and left Florida and moved to Colorado. Here, too, I found myself in need of a job and found work with a debt relief company. As with Florida, the work was neither fulfilling nor enjoyable. I was faced with another decision about my future. This was leading nowhere, and here is where I made a choice that threw my life in an entirely different direction. I joined the Army! I had for some time held military service in the back of my mind and thought perhaps I might one day join. Now seemed to be that time. I spoke with the recruiters and told them if they could get me into a position where I could drive a Humvee and learn to operate a variety of weapons I would sign. My next four years were sealed. I was deployed to both Kuwait and Iraq where I drove a variety of vehicles and used almost every weapon we had. I got what I had asked for, and I was involved with the rest of my unit where we all had to work together. It was a good experience for me. Between active duty and the reserves, I spent about six and a half years in the service.

When I completed my last tour and received my discharge, I found I had all the GI Bill benefits. The military changed my world. Now I was motivated, and the Army benefits would help pay for my college. I went to full-time college at Colorado Technical University where I got my BA and MA degrees in computer science. I also met my wife-to-be while I was later teaching at Colorado State. I became a teaching assistant at the college for a while, then later left college teaching for a full-time job doing Android phone development. I began my work for Seagate and moved to Knoxville, Tennessee in 2020. I still live there today and

*work for the Oak Ridge National Laboratory. I never
could have done all this had I stayed in Romania. Never.*

Sly Silviu-Cristian Dumitru, Bucharest, Romania

In looking at Sly's path, it is easy to see where things began to change. Having already lived in two different states and been employed in numerous occupations, he chose to join the Army. Subsequent to all his combat experiences and receipt of the GI Bill, he was able to go on to college, obtain his advanced degrees, find a wife, and take advantage of the excellent career opportunities he found along the way. His life took on an entirely different trajectory almost overnight. Everyone's life is full of choices. Some of them are life-altering. At the end of the day, what we have and all we will become is the sum of those choices and what we have made of them. For Sly, he has moved himself from a relatively unaware immigrant in Florida to a successful family man living a worthwhile and fulfilling life as an American.

As this chapter began, I mentioned how our individual stories are more durable to the test of time than such things as our youth and health. But even our stories can be eroded by time unless we have chronicled them in some lasting way. For most of us, our personal history will rarely extend much beyond two generations...our children and perhaps grand-children. Immigrants with so many wonderful experiences and narratives to share may lose their marvelous accounts of days gone by as well. Loss of these living histories is far too often a family tragedy. How many times has it been exclaimed, "Oh, how I wish (insert favorite name) would have written down that story?" Countless. There is perhaps no better reason than this for us to have spent a few moments sharing and enjoying just a few of these rich life-time experiences from our fellow American travelers.

CHAPTER 4

Realities in America

> *The use of traveling is to regulate imagination by reality, and instead of thinking how things may be, to see them as they are.*
>
> —SAMUEL JOHNSON

America is not a perfect country. That may seem a strange statement to make for a book entitled *America the Beautiful*. However, in reality, there is no such place as Utopia, no promised land. America, like all countries, has its blemishes, has not always lived up to its founding principles, and had to overcome errors of both omission and commission. She is working on many of those problems still today. For many of its immigrants, America has been considerably different than what they perhaps envisioned; it has been more challenging than they realized. There were elements of America they may have found less than attractive, not what they anticipated. In other cases, America came to be even more than they had hoped. Either way, America has without question been the one land to which millions of immigrants have come to pursue their dreams, make homes for their families, and seek prosperity. It is now, and has been throughout its history, the most free, most exciting, and most vibrant country in the world. It is that place upon which dreams can be built. It is that place to which our nation's immigrants have pinned their hopes for a better future. It speaks of its promise across every land to the peoples of the world.

> Even though America is a young country, we have contributed so very much to humanity and society. Think about what has been accomplished; our innovation has brought us cars, airplanes, medical equipment, advanced communication, computers, and so much more. In every way you look at it, America has been the foundation of our advanced society. Our people live the best lives imaginable and what is the reason? It is our founding fathers and the design for this America they gave us. People came to this land with very little, almost nothing. All they had was their faith and their work ethic. That was the entire reason this country succeeded! In my experience, almost every person who migrated to the United States has come with the same drive and honest hope to succeed.
>
> Shegitu Kebede, Ethiopia

Of all human qualities, the ability to formulate a vision of the future is perhaps one of the most unique. We can all imagine the places we might go, the experiences we might have, and the kind of life we might enjoy in our coming days. For each immigrant who has longed to come to America, there has first been that concept of how life might be in this new land. Such images are born from a variety of sources, and each one is exclusive to that person. It is not surprising that the realities of America were often different from those initial views. In times gone by, much of America's image arose from second and third-hand narratives told by other people, relatives, or acquaintances who had returned from living in the United States. Their stories were often filled with over-embellished accounts of American lifestyle, employment successes, and general prosperity. The relative wealth of the average American seemed easily within reach, and there was an almost insatiable thirst to hear such fascinating tales. Few questioned their authenticity. Marcus Ravage, in trying to convince his father to allow him to leave Vaslui, Romania and seek his fortune in America, described his view of America as follows:

> Had they forgotten the wonderful man from New York who had recently visited us? Had they forgotten his jewels, his clothes, his trunks, his fine impressive appearance, his cultured manners, his official position? That was what America was making out of her men. For our visitor, by his own confession, was not the only one who had been so marvelously transformed in that great country. Everybody who went there became a millionaire overnight, and a doctor or a teacher into the bargain. There, in America, was my future as well as theirs. For it would take me only a few weeks to make enough money to send for the whole family.[1]

> Marcus Ravage, 1909

Such was hardly an accurate depiction of turn-of-the-century New York, but that was the picture painted by many of those countrymen who had returned home to speak of their exploits. It is only natural so many of these returnees would magnify both their own success and the grandeur of their new home; and, as one can see, such accounts left lasting impressions on their audiences. Marcus, as we will see later, was in for a severe disappointment.

In more contemporary times, television, movies, print materials and other visuals have provided a broader concept of American life, but even that has not always been a true reflection of what someone's life might be like were they to come live here. Often, the prospective immigrant sees on display a nation where almost everyone seems to drive a modern car, enjoy a well-paid job, and live in a pleasant house or apartment. Such images speak to what might be if only he or she could make their way to this land of plenty.

> Before I came here, I had some good idea of what life was like. I watched a lot of American TV programs where I would see pretty much what life could be, or at least what I thought it would be like, anyway. I remember I would see people driving their convertible cars down the coastal highway in California, and I would imagine myself doing that; the freedom and bright ocean air were exciting! I wanted to do that. And you know what? After I was here for a little while, I did do that. It was so wonderful.
>
> Maria Flores, Peru

No one abandons his or her existing homeland without a vision, without a dream. Along with such dreams, however, almost always comes some degree of apprehension, some doubt. If there is any lesson in life more soundly learned, it is nothing is guaranteed. Rarely does everything turn out exactly as planned. Immigrants have universally found this to be the case upon their arrival to America. The experiences and initial observations of a newly arrived immigrant can often be quite disparate from his or her original expectation. It is important to understand how they coped with these disparities if one is to understand their stories. Such will give greater light to America's character when seen by those who came with understandably high hopes and aspirations, but ultimately had to deal with reality. These observations also serve to inform potential future immigrants as to the unexpected conditions they might face, circumstances they might expect.

Each individual experience can be greatly influenced by any number of personal factors. For example, those who arrived with no or limited mastery of English would have had different barriers to face than those fluent in the language. Those with a more narrow education might have found fewer employment opportunities. Those from impoverished circumstances would likely have found things more difficult than those with more affluent means. Yet, there are literally hundreds of thousands who have come to America with all these limitations who are now living full, happy lives. Their initial observations of America's realities may have been different, but their ultimate successes are in many ways refreshingly similar.

> I remember a mixed bag of emotions of those early years: excitement, curiosity, enjoyment, homesickness, confusion, disorientation. The first couple of years, I felt like a tourist, unable to engage fully with the culture here.
>
> I'd switch on the TV, see Oprah on but be unable to relate to the things she talked about. I'd scan the newspaper and it'd just be a sea of words, utterly foreign to me. I chuckle

now at how delicate my sensibilities were then, for I'd be constantly shocked by the prurience and profanity on TV.

Assimilation happened to me, gradually, inexorably, but what also helped were the many Americans along the way who were warm, generous, helpful, and accepting of all the ways I was different from them.

For several of those early years, there was financial struggle, and a cycle of being broke and borrowing each month-end. I spent hours on the public bus each day going to work in Orlando and then in Dallas as we couldn't afford a second car.

I'm grateful for those hardships: they keep me from being self-satisfied now, from taking anything for granted, and have me seeing anyone less fortunate and thinking, "There but for the grace of God go I."

The best part of immigration and assimilation is that you feel like you're at a giant buffet where you get to pick, choose, and retain the best from both worlds. That's the hidden gift of all these years of change and adopting and adapting.

My American story is a personal one, yet it mirrors that of millions of foreign-born Americans: of one who goes from an "other" to being an American but who also still retains aspects of the other.[2]

Saritha Prabhu, India 2019

Yes, it was, "by the grace of God," Saritha is where she is today as noted by the USA Today columnist who related her story. But it has also been due to her perseverance, faith, and constant striving to make herself a better person. Immigrant or native-born, there is no substitute for continuous hard work in yielding personal success. It has always been and must still continue as "the American way."

Even some who came from more elevated positions in their native country may have found the adjustment to their position in America a challenge. As related by his son, consider the case of Selwar Hanna, an immigrant from Baghdad, Iraq who had held a high government position.

> I remember how my dad had related how his brother had been telling him that the United States was like a total land of opportunity. "There you could do whatever you want to try and make a life for your family," he told my father. My dad thought that is amazing; perhaps it is almost unbelievable. He would ask my uncle: can you do this? Can you do that? And my uncle would say, "Yes, you can do any of those things." We had never experienced anything like that in Iraq. My father's main objective was always to keep his family safe and give his children a future where they could be whatever they wanted to be. But could everything my uncle had said really be true? When we finally got here and realized my uncle was right, we were somewhat taken aback. In many ways, the family almost couldn't quite believe how lucky we were to be here and have the opportunity to live this, this American dream.
>
> Of course, it wasn't quite as easy an adjustment for my father. At home in Iraq, my father was a very highly respected official. His job as one of the Bishop's top bodyguards had taken him all over the country where he had met many important men and been given numerous

special privileges. The post of a top bodyguard for the Bishop would be similar to a secret service agent for the President in this country. Once we came to America, however, my father had to take a position in a regular nine-to-five job where there was no special protection or status attached. He was just working to take care of pallets and to drive a forklift. It was a big change for him, and I know he probably missed some of that high respect and position he used to have, but he never really showed or spoke about it.

So yes, we had lots of opportunities, but for him, it was a much less important position than he was used to. I have to say as well, this change of lifestyle didn't really surprise my father. He always would say, he expected things would be different. So yes, although that difference in his influence and position has not always been easy, he and all our family still feel entirely blessed to be in this country where everyone is safe.

Selvar Hanna, Baghdad, Iraq

The central goals for the Hanna family in America included safety and the opportunity to live their lives free of an intrusive (and sometimes dangerous) government. Life sometimes presents choices where one thing must be given up in order to attain a larger objective. In this case, it was position and prestige for a better life for their children. Yes, the realities of this new life in America required significant adjustment. It takes time, effort, and sacrifice to incorporate an entirely new culture, but these expenses must be balanced against someone's reason for coming in the first place. Like the Hanna family, immigrants have almost universally agreed that opportunity and the freedom to pursue their own path was a major motivation in their decision. For Selvar, who came with his parents, he will soon be going on to university and begin building his own future...just as his father had intended all those years ago.

For Ilya Somin, who came to America with his family at age five, he can only talk to what his father might have found different. As the family had come from what was the former Soviet Union and lived under communism, the general living conditions here stood in stark contrast to those in Russia. Not only did America have different social customs, but the restrictions, laws, and general guidelines governing everyday life were completely new. Things like employment practices and achieving personal advancement were greatly changed. Ilya speaks about this in the following way.

> I can't fully talk about what my father may have thought about this, although he wrote his own memoir and probably made a more complete description there. But, as I think about it, one issue might be that maybe he, as well as a lot of other immigrants from socialist nations, had underestimated the extent to which you have such a wide range of choices available to make in this country. Under a socialist or communist system, it is much more constricted than in a freer society. Here is much less limited with regard to where you want to work or what kind of product to buy, or even if some products are available to purchase. That aspect is actually quite good. Other than that, the country itself obviously takes some getting used to; American culture is very different from Russian in various respects. Some of them you could perhaps foresee ahead of time, others were a bit more difficult with which to adjust.

You would need to look at his memoir to really understand his feelings on this. One of the distinct differences I can say is that in Russian society there is more corrupted kind of government economic system. Things work very much on connections and contacts in that world. There's a kind of black-market activity and informality that exists. That doesn't mean that connections are unimportant in the U.S.; even here, they obviously are. That is the case in almost any society, but people take rules more seriously. Here there is perhaps less premium put on who you know and doing everything through connections or through friends and family members. In Russia, however, they may well conduct a lot of that same activity under table or at least out of view. Certainly, we have that too, but not to the same extent as in the Soviet Union or even the Russia of today. As I said, it takes adjustment.

Ilya Somin, Leningrad, Russia

Yes, America has many differences immigrants must negotiate. But for those coming from totalitarian regimes, the level of freedom and ability to set your own course has often been noted as worth the effort. Opportunities to choose whatever kind of work you want to do, shop wherever you like, buy anything you see on the shelf, and move forward without needing connections or approvals from government authorities were valued perhaps above all else. Freedom of choice is so easily undervalued when you are born into a free system and never experience the realities of other more authoritarian societies. It is clearly evident today how many Americans unwittingly take for granted so much of what this country provides. Such is less likely the case when someone has lived under a system where the government determines almost every aspect of life.

Beyond politics, there are other contrasts of life that can make the adjustment to a new country challenging. For example, someone may have grown up in a rural setting of their country and be unaccustomed to life in a larger, more complex world outside. For Kim Oksun-Comazzi, she had lived in Suwon, a small town outside Seoul, Korea and knew only what she had heard from others about the United States. Certainly, she had seen pictures of various big cities, studied some of America's history in school, and been vaguely familiar with its general nature. And, too, Kim had been to Seoul and experienced at least some of what life might be like in a bigger city. She had also worked on an American Air Force base and met many service men and women who had told her stories of America. These were experiences of a sort. However, seeing pictures and hearing about another country rarely provides sufficient perspective to fully grasp its realities. For Kim, it was an awe-inspiring event to simply fly into New York. Everything looked so remarkable. Yet, the small town to which she would come to live with her new husband was not especially different from the one in which she grew up in Korea. It was a dissimilar house, a different topography, and the people were in some ways a bit different than those in her Korean hometown. And yet, there were similarities as well. Families lived together, shopped together, had comparable demeanors, and the rural atmosphere seemed recognizable. She quickly settled in and felt relatively comfortable in this new environment. Amidst this process of readjusting to her new life, Kim began to take notice of her surroundings. Even the different sounds of nature near her home, though perhaps small things, provided unexpected enjoyment. There were larger things to be confronted in this new America as well. Shortly after arrival, her husband took her on an excursion to New York City where she was introduced to an almost entirely new world. Her recollection of these two experiences tells of her emotions and reactions coming face to face with these events.

> Well, I'm just in this country a few weeks, and it may seem funny, but something I noticed right away when I got to our house was the birds. You could hear them and see them all the time. And in the morning if I went out, they would be there singing. I remember listening and thinking how happy they made me. It was somewhat different than home, but I really liked it so much.
>
> Only a week or so later, I had something else I couldn't have imagined happen for me. My husband took me to New York. Just the ride from our house in New Jersey to New York was remarkable. We came through mountains, passed little cities and towns everywhere, and the highways were full of cars I had never seen. When I came into New York, it was teeming with people, the streets were lined with hundreds of businesses and restaurants, giant buildings everywhere I looked, and the entire city seemed alive with activity and life. It was beyond amazing. I'm looking, and almost everywhere I look there is something else that is wonderful. You know, I can only say at the time, "WOW!" I am overwhelmed at everything I am seeing. Then we go to the Empire State Building, and we go up this elevator all the way to the top! I am walking around looking out everywhere. It was incredible. Again, all I am saying is, WOW! You know, I didn't know what to expect or if I ever could even have imagined anything like this.

But what I saw...it was just awe-inspiring. I think that is the right word. Maybe it was overwhelming, too.

While we were there, we were meeting people and talking. It was so exciting for me and so much fun. Everyone seemed so nice and friendly. We even met a nice couple from France who spoke English and took our picture with all those great views. They said, "You two make such a beautiful couple." It was just so nice of them. I don't know how to explain it, but I never expected a day like this. I could not quite fit everything I was feeling about that day here in America into words. It was wonderful.

These are just two special memories that live on for Kim even today. At times, the observations made by our new immigrants are not only the big things one might expect. Sometimes they are things we Americans might almost take for granted, like birds you are not used to hearing. The impact and value of such emotions should not be dismissed or undervalued. For Kim and her first days, America was beginning to come to life. She was finally seeing and experiencing this new country, the one about which she had previously only read and heard. As she continued life with her husband and newly adopted family, Kim came to realize other more important features of this country; it seemed many of those things were even better than she had originally hoped.

You know, there are things I found that make this place so special, things that perhaps I didn't really recognize before I came. When I came, I right away was able to find a nice job. It wasn't the job I always wanted or the job I kept a long time, but it was easy for me to find work for myself. But then I was able to keep getting better positions. I had the opportunity to do whatever I actually wanted. It was so...so open with opportunities. I was even able to later just go buy a business. Who could have believed there was a place like this? We have such freedom. We can say what we like, we have wonderful medical care, we have freedom to go to church. America, yes, as I said, it is such a special place, and we are so blessed!

But you asked me too if there is something I don't like, and yes, there is. Something I now find ugly is all the burning of cities, and looting, and burning our flag. My heart is aching. If these people only knew how much they were hurting themselves. All immigrants like me are trying to build this country, not destroy it. You know, I am feeling like a "chosen person" to live here, here in this great country. We can't lose it. There is no place else to go like this. After I had been here for five years and obtained my citizenship, I was able to have all six of my sisters and mother come to live in America, too. My family was back together again! I could give them a chance at the opportunities that I was having. And they took advantage of America's opportunities because all six went on to being successful throughout many states and in lots of ways. They were business owners in agriculture, fast food restaurants, and motor repair facilities. Two of my other sisters worked in great positions for large companies and in the healthcare industry, while another earned her master's degree and became a teacher. Even my sixty-year-old mother got a driver's license and owned her own home. I love my home of Korea, but I know these things would never have happened for us back in my country. But people are trying to burn it down? And our flag? That is not attractive, and it hurts...deeply.

Kim Oksun-Comazzi, Korea

What Kim speaks of in these few lines has been echoed many times throughout these interviews. Almost every immigrant has identified their ability to chase down opportunities and seize them as the gift that most led to where they are today. But they wonder what it is about those rioting and burning the flag that makes some so hateful of their own country, so unable to see what they have in a place so full of possibilities. For many of those immigrants, they came with nothing, didn't speak the language, and had limited educations, yet they found success. It wasn't fast. It wasn't without hardship. They may have worked at numerous jobs along the way but somehow kept moving up with each step. Why not everyone? They repeatedly asked, why is it that others don't see how to take advantage of all the things this country offers? Why do they see so little hope? For a great many, answers to those questions seem extraordinarily limited.

Greg Lhamon, a world-renowned storyteller, marketer, mentor, and speaker told a story about a conversation with his daughter that directly reflects on that special quality of America called "hope."[3]

I used to grumble a lot about politics. But one of my daughters put an end to that. I was railing one day about some issue or another when she interrupted me.

"Dad...I know we've got problems in this country. And I know they need to be addressed. But I want to have hope about my future. When you complain about this or that, it

sucks the life out of me. Please stop. Help me to see what's possible instead." She was right. My complaining was robbing her of hope. And I had no right to do that to her. Or anyone else, for that matter.

Do we have problems in America? Are there still evils that must be corrected? Of course. And each of us should get busy fixing them. But in the process, I would rather help people see a vision of what could be and then get my hands dirty trying to achieve it than complain and denigrate and drag others down in the process.

After all, so much is possible here. How many countries are there where a person can arrive with a few personal belongings and build a wildly successful life with just a four-inch book of recipes and a dream?[4]

Greg Lhamon

Former Secretary of Education Bill Bennet once outlined a small quiz a country could administer to determine its attractiveness to the outside world. He called it, "The Gates Test." He wrote, *"Someone can judge a country by which direction people run when the country erects gates: Do they flee in, or do they risk life and limb to get out?"* By that measure, the United States is a country to be envied; it is a country with great hope![5]

Still, America is not, and has never been, a perfect place. Not every immigrant has arrived and found this to be the place they had imagined. There have been times when the realities of America *have not* been so positive. There have been times past when our country was seen as the ultimate safe haven, but on arrival, it was found to be far less welcoming than originally thought. For an immigrant at the turn of the twentieth century, this contrast between the homeland and a place called America was quite stark. Often, this led to a harsh, unwelcoming reality in making that transition between one's former culture and this entirely new culture with all its unfamiliar people and social barriers.

You may recall our Marcus Ravage, from Vaslui, Romania, who had arrived in America with an image of success on every corner, employment opportunities by the hundreds, and a place where nearly everyone enjoyed extraordinary wealth. He had been convinced everything would fall into place if he could only reach New York's shores. He had been sadly misled and greatly mistaken. His introduction to turn-of-the-century New York and its unfathomable lifestyle was a shock of immense proportion.

Shortly after his arrival, he wrote home that he hated it in America; it was a *"totally foreign place of strange customs and behaviors!"* When some well-meaning person unwittingly asked, "How do you like America?" his response was completely unexpected, dispirited, and negative. Marcus's first impressions had been completely unlike anything he had ever experienced or valued. He saw almost nothing but decline and decay.

> *No, my first impression of America was right, and no mistake. With every day that passed I became more and more overwhelmed at the degeneration of my fellow countrymen in this new home of theirs. Even their names had become emasculated and devoid of either character or meaning. Mordecai—a name full of romantic association—had been changed to the insipid monosyllable Max. Rebecca—mother of the race—was, in America, Becky. With womenfolk, matters were even worse. It did not seem to matter at all what one had been called at*

home. The first step toward Americanization was to fall into one or the other of the two great tribes of Rosies and Annies.

Cut adrift suddenly from their ancient moorings, they were floundering in a sort of moral void. Good manners and good conduct, reverence and religion, had all gone by the board, and the reason was that these things were not American. A grossness of behavior, a loudness of speech, a certain repellent "American" smartness in intercourse, were thought necessary if one did not want to be taken for a greenhorn [a recent, non-Americanized immigrant] or a bore. The ancient racial respect for elders had completely disappeared. Everybody alike was addressed as "thou" and "say"; and the worst of it was that when one contemplated American old age, one was compelled to admit that there was a good deal of justification for slighting it. It had forfeited its claim to deference because it had thrown away its dignity. Tottering grandfathers, with one foot in the grave, had snipped off their white beards and laid aside their skullcaps and their snuffboxes and paraded around the streets of a Saturday afternoon with cigarettes in their mouths, when they should have been lamenting the loss of the Holy City in the study-room adjoining the synagogue.

Mere slips of boys and girls went around together and called it love after the American fashion. The dancehalls were thronged with them. The parks saw them on the benches in pairs until all hours of the morning, and they ran things in their parents' homes to suit themselves.

Well, after what I have given you of my impressions, you may readily guess that I did not like America; that, indeed, I very emphatically hated America. Yes, I hated America very earnestly on my first acquaintance with her. And yet I must confess, here and now, that for a whole year every letter that came from my parents in Vaslui was an offer to return home, and that I steadily refused to accept it. Those letters, by the by, added their very considerable share to the tragic burden of my readjustment, for my parents suggested that, if I liked America well enough to remain there, they would endeavor to raise the money and join me. And to this I was constrained to reply, "Vaslui is not for me, and America is not for you, dear parents of mine." These words were obviously a confession that our separation must remain indefinite. I did not want my parents to come to America, because I could not endure the thought of father as a match-peddler on Orchard Street; and since he was neither a shoemaker nor a woman's tailor nor a master of any other profitable professions in America, and since I was as yet far from equal to the task of supporting the family, there was nothing for us to do but rest apart. Somehow, even in those dark days of greenhornhood, another occasional ray would penetrate through the gloom and reveal another America than that of the slums.

Yet, in the midst of this slum and all the difficulties finding a position or convincing prospective employers to even give a greenhorn a chance, there were others who still *provided some ray of hope; somehow, I knew I too could be successful if I just learned "the American way."*

Here, for instance, was Louis Carniol, whom everybody at home had considered a ne'er do well—a "schlim-mezalnik." Did I notice how nicely he was dressed: Did I know that he had money in the bank? Yes, I need not look incredulous, for only the week before he had sent home fifty francs. And there was Rose Marculescu, a mere girl, and in three months she had nearly paid for the steamer ticket her brother had sent her. Of course, the lucky ones and the clever ones got jobs. But what could a body do? In the land of Columbus, one did what one could, and there was no disgrace in doing anything. A shoemaker was just as good in America as a doctor, as long as he worked and made money, and paid for everything.[6]

Marcus Ravage, Romania

To be certain, things were not easy to reconcile, and America was a place so vastly different than his Jewish community in Romania that adjustment to this new country seemed near impossible. Understanding and finding "the American way" took both time and study. Marcus did manage to adjust as he moved ahead in his life, but there remained elements of the American lifestyle he always found dis-respectful and distasteful. In many ways, immigrants of today might suffer similar culture shock.

When people make the momentous decision to immigrate, that decision removes them from their traditional accustomed worlds and transplants them in a strange new world, strangers among strangers with strange customs. Such was the case for Marcus, and it took him many years to reconcile his former life in Vaslui to the America of his imagination and then to the America that actually was.

Marcus arrived as an adult who had to make his own way. Others, however, came as young adults, brought by their parents, and their experiences were far less stressful. As a result, they were able to look at America through a different lens and more fully appreciate its history and culture. Raised in a well-to-do family of shopkeepers in what is now Belarus, Mary Antin's introduction to America was entirely different. Her early life had been relatively comfortable, and she had received a good education. She was an unusually bright young girl and a voracious reader, which made her transition to America at the turn of the century much easier. She quickly learned to read and write English, and avidly read books about America, its founding, and the patriots who had done so much to establish this country, her new homeland. In her highly successful memoir, *The Promised Land*, she explains her elation when she came to realize she was a part of America; *she was a citizen* of a country with what she describes as a deep and wonderful history.[7]

> *What more could America give a child? Ahh, much more! As I read how the patriots planned the Revolution and the women gave their sons to die in battle, and the heroes led to victory, and the rejoicing people set up the Republic, it dawned on me gradually what was meant by "my country." The people all desiring noble things, and striving for them together, defying their oppressors, giving their lives for each other—all this it was that made "my country." It was not a thing that I understood; I could not go home and tell Freda about it as I told her other things that I learned at school. But I knew one could say "my*

country" and feel it, as one felt "God" or "myself." For the Country was for all citizens, and I was a Citizen! And when we stood up to sing "America," I shouted the words with all my might. I was in very earnest proclaiming to the world my love for my new-found country.[8]

"I love thy rocks and rills,
Thy woods and templed hills."

Mary Antin, Belarus, Russia

Mary Antin was, of course, a young girl at the time she describes this experience, and as such might display a certain youthful enthusiasm that might not be attendant to the masses of today. Nonetheless, her observation of how important it was that she was "a citizen" and a part of these United States, *continues to be* an important element of the immigrant experience even today. When our newest citizens are initially sworn in, there is an unmistakable pride in their voices as they make their initial recitation of the Pledge of Allegiance and sing the *Star-Spangled Banner*. Without question, it is a magical moment. They too will now become part of America's history.

Kirsten Epley came as a child with her parents from Norway, and the America they found was markedly different than their homeland. Her mother in particular did not like America when she initially arrived. At first, things were not easy. Her father got a job in a factory and her mother cleaned houses with another immigrant Italian woman. There was separation anxiety, a new language to learn, a new culture to which they had to adjust, and at times it seemed too much. After five years, her mother decided to return to Norway with the children. Kirsten describes what happened.

Well, at the time we didn't have a lot of money, or clothes, or shoes. We had our Sunday stuff, of course, but we didn't really have any what you might call luxuries. But then, nobody had any money where I lived, so we were fine. We weren't afraid of work, and we all worked together. But as I said, my mother did not like America when we first came here. She was unhappy here and missed Norway. My father said, "Well, we will stay five years, and if you don't like it, you can go back." So, after five years, my mother actually did return back to Norway, and she took me and my brother with her. Once she got back to Norway and she saw how things were, she had a change of heart and came back to the States. Just as things had changed in the United States over those five years, so too had they changed in Norway. In Norway, she didn't have a car. She had to walk everywhere. To go to the store, or visit, or go anywhere at all, she had to walk. Also, there weren't the conveniences of life that had been available to her when she was living in Chicago. In Chicago, she had a car, she could get wherever she wanted to go, stores had whatever she needed, and there was a variety of things she could do here that she found unavailable back home. Everything just seemed more at hand. It was hard for my mother emotionally. It was so difficult for her to leave her own mother, our little family that remained in Norway. It was hard on my grandmother, too. I think a lot of my mother's unhappiness came from guilt, you know, leaving her mother behind. Ultimately, my mother returned here with us to the U.S. and our father. People don't always understand that it isn't just the differences of how we may have thought things would work in this country; it is the *reality of leaving behind pieces of your family and people you love...pieces of yourself.*

Kirsten Langoy-Epley, Stavanger Norway

For those who arrived from countries more similar to the United States, the culture shock was not so great. Coming from somewhere such as England, where the language and social customs are more similar, the transition to American life could be nearly seamless. The new realities are less stark. The absence of cultural barriers allows for a more immediate assimilation and ability to focus on larger goals with a faster start.

Such was the case for Kathryn Court, who came from a small town near London, England. Although she was well educated, she found herself struggling to find the right employment in the London publishing business. She noted there was a certain snobbishness within the industry, and one needed a degree from "the right university" to be seriously considered. Being a woman did not help matters, either. Kathryn soon found you also needed a letter of reference from "one of the better companies" to gain entry to positions of any significance. She decided that, if she were to make a success of herself, it would be better to make her way somewhere other than the London publishing houses. Although she had only been here once, she thought she knew a little about America and it might offer better opportunities.

After moving to America to live with her boyfriend, she found things considerably different.

Before I came to live in New York, I had been to America once before. I came on a three-week holiday when my boyfriend at the time was finishing medical training courses in Arizona. I found America quite surprising because I grew up without a TV. My English friends always had a "romantic" view of America. They'd tell me about movies they'd seen and all the wonderful things that were involved. Because I was very unfamiliar with all these images my friends had romanticized, it was very fresh to come here.

I remember thinking that New York was stunningly beautiful. And the west, to me, was quite extraordinary...the Arizona desert, southern California, and Yellowstone Park in Wyoming were spectacular, but I never thought I would live here.

Kathryn Court, London, England

As noted earlier, Kathryn's American adventure became quite the success story. She ultimately became editor-in-chief at Penguin Books, worked with numerous luminaries of the publishing industry, and published books from some of the finest authors. But none of this came easily, even for someone as brilliant and gifted as Ms. Court. Before she even found her first job in the American publishing industry, she had gone on more than fifty interviews. In the end, however, her tenacity and strong personality won out. It was only then that she could display her talent and ambition.

Many of our immigrants in recent decades have come to America as students. They have been intelligent, well-informed men and women with a solid grounding in reality. Many have not looked at America as a Utopia, but rather cultivated more realistic expectations. But, even here, there can be a difference between the image of America and its reality. A graduate student from Africa describes his experience when asked about such disparities.

> *Yes, well, I had in my mind many ideas like everybody else out there. Before you get here, you think, "OK, American people have good lives, lots of good things like houses, good jobs, cars, and so on; perhaps this is a good place where you can come, and would like to have a little money, and live nice." But when I got here, I found things to be different. Yes, here in the U.S. there are opportunities and ways you can go, but you have to go grab those opportunities. You have to find the way to go for yourself. You can't just come, and things will happen. Yes, you can spend money, have jobs, and stuff like that; but even more important, you soon realize that you have to start from somewhere. When you get here, you don't really have anything, just maybe an idea. Then you have to find some way to make that idea happen, and no one is there to just give you the way to do that. That's what people don't realize; you actually have to start from the bottom, and then work and find ways to go up. But no one tells you how or shows you the way. You have to find it for yourself. That can be hard for someone who recently arrived with basically nothing.*
>
> *Bob Mwiti, Kenya, Africa*

Sly Dumitru of Romania, in his words, confronted any number of "setbacks" in his attempt to establish himself, many of which had to do with his adjusting the expectations he had for life in America. When asked if he found any differences between what he might have envisioned life would be like in

America as opposed to what he experienced, he simply laughed. There was a reason for his laughter.

> Perhaps the one shock I had was I fully expected America to be even more free than it is. In some respects, it seemed I was more free in Romania than I was here. As I was going about things day to day, I realized there were a great many rules or laws I hadn't recognized would be the case in America. For example, if you want to travel on mass transit, you have to pay. Travel from one place to another generally required a car or, if there was a bus or train, there was a cost; it was not a small cost, either. In Bucharest I could go from place to place on trams or bus very inexpensively. Most importantly, where I had lived, the mass transit system could take you to almost any place you wanted to go. This was not the case in Florida. There were many places with no mass transit available. Also, perhaps I just wanted to go for a hike as I liked to do in Romania. That, too, was different here. In Florida I had to realize that lots of places were either private property or part of some preserve or restricted area where hiking was not allowed. You can't just trespass on private property. As far as transportation was concerned, perhaps my biggest challenge was getting to and from work without a car. When I first started working, I always had to rely on someone else to drive me.
>
> Oh, wow, Florida was so very different from Romania. I expected there would be differences, but I had no idea how big those differences would be. The speed of things, cars everywhere, buildings, stores, and the various aspects of life all came at me at once. Something else I didn't realize;

I had no idea how money worked. How do I open a bank account? I didn't even have one in Romania, but you can't do without one here. What is credit? Credit score? Another mystery. But if you wanted to buy a car, you had better know about all these things. And what about colleges? How do they work? How do I get in or even apply? These things were simple in Romania...and pretty much free or very low cost. Here, I found money and finances to be a much larger issue than I had ever imagined. As a result, I got myself into credit problems, I was swindled by a college credit scam, and ultimately found myself in bankruptcy. All of these things were different than I imagined if I even imagined such things at all. No, America was in many respects much different than I might have thought.

Sly Silviu-Cristian Dumitru, Bucharest, Romania

As Americans, we take so many things for granted. We don't realize how just simple aspects of American life can be complete obscurities to someone from another country. Discovering the mechanics of everyday life was something Sly did not confront until after he arrived. His observations on freedom were also unique to him. Most often, the concept was viewed through the perspective of freedom from government intrusions or freedom to pursue economic opportunities. But Sly's confrontation with unfamiliar laws and regulations was yet another aspect of daily life he had to negotiate.

The Americanization process gradually blends all the realities of "here" with all the histories, understandings, and experiences of the "there" that a new immigrant brings. It is that battle between different realities that must be somehow reconciled before one can really call America theirs.

Reality, like beauty, is in the eyes of the beholder. For each of the travelers making America home, each sees different aspects of the national landscape, different vistas outlining their paths forward. As noted by just the few experiences related here, each reality contained its own unique observations; there were differences in each view. But among those differences, there were also connections, characteristics of the nation's essence they shared. One of those characteristics was the collective idea that wherever they were today, there was something more waiting in the future. In America, people don't need to be defined by their current situation, or even what other people might see in them. America's reality depends upon each individual's willingness to grasp life and wrestle out of it every ounce of goodness it can. In America, that can happen. That is America's promise. Listen to how another important American fashioned that same idea.

> We may have different backgrounds, but we believe in the same dream that says this is a country where anything is possible. No matter who you are. No matter where you came from.

> Barack Obama, 44th President of the United States

So what, then, is the reality of America? Her reality is for you to decide. It is for you to see and experience. It is contained in that dream you created for your future and what you see along the path toward its fulfillment. America is waiting for your story to help shape her reality.

CHAPTER 5

Confronting Obstacles in America

> *As each new wave of immigrants has reached America, it has been faced with problems... Somehow, the difficult adjustments are made, and people get down to the tasks of earning a living, raising a family, living with their neighbors, and in the process, building a nation.*
>
> —JOHN F. KENNEDY

Virtually no personal success or attainment of worthy goals has been realized without overcoming a wide variety of challenges along the way. Nonetheless, immigrants from across the globe continue to come in hopes of seizing the opportunities they have heard of; they are intent on making America their own. They are buoyed by the fact that hundreds of thousands have already arrived and achieved similar hopes and dreams. Few of those earlier arrivals, however, have done so without first successfully confronting the numerous obstacles and setbacks in their path. For the immigrant, overcoming hardships at times consumed their entire existence. It required every ounce of their energy and courage to push forward. Success has always seemed to reward the persistent, and America's immigrant class has embodied that quality in great measure. There is much to be learned in examining some of their experiences.

Identifying and understanding how successful immigrants negotiated the barriers to their future success will provide insight unavailable anywhere else. It is often said that "experience is the best teacher." If that is true, then the stories of our immigrants can help guide both the recently arrived and others who may make America their future home.

The Barrier: Gaining Initial Entry to America

Perhaps the first and most troublesome hurdle for any immigrant is the attainment of his or her initial visa for entry to the country. Some argue the process is more difficult today than at times in the past, although that may be changing to become less challenging. Still, there are numerous accounts of those who applied for a visa multiple times and were refused. But there are also millions of others who found success. It is important to focus on this latter group. What process offers the prospective immigrant the highest likelihood of success?

To understand how this challenge was successfully met by others, it is essential one understand America's visa process. Although some of our stories involve those who came as refugees or were granted political asylum, most had to negotiate the visa application task at some point.

For immigrants already here, their visa process greatly depended upon when they applied and their personal circumstances at the time of that application. Prior to 9/11, the process was much simpler, and considerably more visas were approved. Post 9/11, with the rise in terrorist threats, the screening process for entry visas grew by an exponential factor. Today, there are countries from which it is difficult to obtain a visa other than as a refugee or political asylum status. Current immigrants will find the visa process more difficult than those who applied prior to the year 2000. There are a number of visa categories, but no matter which one applies, the process is not likely to be easily negotiated, and you may need assistance to be successful.

In years prior to 1965, immigration had been highly controlled. There was a quota system, immigrants needed a sponsor, and preferably had a waiting job to show they would not "be a burden on the American taxpayer." Strict health examinations were also administered, and those with specific health issues were either denied entry or placed in quarantine. Prior to 1965, each country had a quota with only a set number of visas granted per year.

Kirsten Epley's family came from Norway in the 1950s and she describes what was required of her father before they could obtain their visas to the United States:

> After World War II in Norway, employment was a little hard to find, and my father took a job in a gardening center. His brother and other family members had already come to the United States, and they would frequently talk about the kinds of opportunities that were here. My father's brother was originally going to sponsor my father

to come to North Dakota; however, he passed away before that could happen. My dad then had to get my mother's cousin to sponsor us out to Chicago. But even with a sponsor, visas were not always easy to obtain. The United States only allowed so many from every country to come and there was quite a crowd waiting, so I don't know how long my father waited before we finally got the visa application approved. Understand that, at that time, it wasn't enough just to have a sponsor. You also had to show you had somewhere to live and a job waiting when you arrived. Fortunately for us, my mother's cousin arranged all that and we finally made it to this country.

Kirsten Langoy-Epley, Stavanger, Norway

Times have changed since Kirsten's family went through the visa process. The requirement for sponsors, established living quarters, and prearranged employment has been abandoned. These changes were made when the U.S. Congress passed Ted Kennedy's Immigration and Naturalization Act of 1965. In addition to eliminating most of the previous requirements, it also put an end to long-standing, national-origin quotas that had favored those from northern and western Europe. With the diminished entrance requirements, the number of immigrants quadrupled in a relatively short period of time.

Although today, the visa application process is less constricted by quota numbers and burdensome requirements, it continues to be a significant hurdle. Prospective immigrants should understand the different kinds of visas and to whom each applies.

There are basically ten different kinds of visas for which one might apply. These are separated into two distinct groups: there are "nonimmigrant visas" and "immigrant visas." It is important to take care in identifying which visa is applicable to your situation. Many have been rejected simply because the wrong application form was submitted (US Visa Guide, 2020).[1]

1. **Non-immigrant visas** are for those who **will not be staying permanently** in the United States. Non-immigrant visas are for most businesspeople, tourists, or students. When applying for the non-immigrant visa you must prove to the consular officer at the embassy that you will return to your home country after your temporary residence in the United States concludes. Those who come for business purposes can obtain one of the two B-type visas. **The B-visa requires** proof of legitimate business affiliations and the bona fide reasons one would need to be in the country; these might include such things as attendance at a conference, fulfilling a unique job function, or business travel for necessary purposes. Non-immigrant visas are perhaps the easiest to obtain.

2. **Immigrant visas** simply mean you plan to stay permanently in the United States. For obvious reasons, these are considerably more difficult to obtain. Although not all visa categories are included in this group, the most common are listed below:

   • **Work Visa:** Those who wish to live and work in the USA, even on a temporary basis, need a particular type of visa based on their specific job description.

Check at the U.S. Consulate and determine which best applies in your case. Know, too, there is USCIS Form I-129 that must get approved *before* you can apply for a U.S. Work Visa. After the I-129 is completed and reviewed, the employer will receive a Form I-797 that will serve as the petition approval notification. These two forms must be completed *before* you go for an interview, and you can find out more on them from the Consulate Office.

- **Student Visas**: To apply for a U.S. Student Visa, you must *first have been accepted by* an accredited school or program of studies. Your acceptance letter will serve to meet this requirement and will be attached to your completed I-120 form. Once these have been submitted, students must apply for their visas within 120 days. Be aware that there are two types of student visas. The first is an F-1 Student Visa for students who will attend full time at an approved school or ESL program. F-1 visas require school attendance for a minimum eighteen hours per week. The other is an M-1 Student Visa for those coming for non-academic or vocational training. Separate requirements vary.

- **Religious Worker Visa:** These are for those who wish to work in religious fields on a temporary basis. The application will have to include a written recommendation from a duly certified and recognized individual licensed to conduct religious activities.

- **Domestic Employee Visa:** Someone working as a non-government domestic servant and wishes to travel with their employer can apply for a B-1 Visa.

These visas are specifically for housemaids, valets, cooks, butlers, chauffeurs, nannies, or paid companions.

3. Other categories: Immediate family members, minor children, and fiancée or spouse of a green card holder can also get special visas. Anyone wishing to come in that status must visit the U.S. Consulate in their country of origin regarding the necessary documentation and process.

The Lesson: There are many kinds of visa applications, but each has its own specific requirements. You must match your background, goals, and abilities such that it maximizes your chances of successfully negotiating the process. The advice of many successful immigrants is to obtain professional assistance in this matter if you can afford it. It is unwise to simply present yourself at the American Consulate's office to begin the process. Applicants are too often denied a visa because they either applied for the wrong type or improperly completed the forms. Keep in mind that whatever is on your application may require proof.

Completing the necessary documents and negotiating the process is at times an arduous task. Bob Mwiti of Kenya now operates a consulting company that aids foreign students with their visa process, and he offers this advice.

Documents! It's a big deal. In this country we have about twelve million undocumented immigrants, so for immigrants who wish to stay, getting a green card is really the best thing, but it is not easy to obtain. Having a green card basically means you can work and live here permanently. If you come to America and don't intend to go back to your country, getting that green card is almost essential. Realize that if you don't have steady work where an employer is willing to sponsor you, there's no simple path to get that green card. Of course, one of the other ways to obtain your card is to perhaps fall in love with an American citizen and get married. It happens.

If you are an international student graduating from college, then you need to get the required work authorization, which is only good for one year. To stay longer, the employer has to be willing to sponsor you long term. That was one of the challenges that I personally faced. Of course, I wanted a good, well-paying job, but I also had to worry about making certain my visas and other documents were up to date. Even if a company gave me a job, it also had to be willing to sponsor me. I was able to get the job, but then I had just three years before I had to let the company know I wanted to stay longer. At that point, the company can start the process to have you extended for an additional three years. Once I completed those three years, I was able apply for permanent residency and get that all-important green card.

Even with all I knew of the required procedures, that process still did not go smoothly. When I got the job with my first company, they had promised to help me get my permanent residency. Unfortunately, after I worked with them for a time, they changed their mind and told me they were not going to do that for me. That put me back to square one, and I had to start the search to find another company all over again. This time I had to make double sure it would be a company willing to sponsor me. I was not interested in just staying for three years; I wanted that green card.

A big hurdle in finding such employment are the government regulations companies must follow. The employer has to prove you have skill sets that other Americans don't have, or at least too few Americans, to meet their needs. There has to be a shortage in that part of the labor force, so if you don't have somewhat unique skills, a company is not in a position to fight for you. They need to follow the immigration law to the letter. Luckily for me, I am a very proactive person. I knew the laws, and I knew which skill areas offered the best opportunities. As a result, I found a company with a Green Card processing staff, and in a few years, I finally got my Green Card.

What so many students who come here fail to understand is that if you are studying in an area where there are too many Americans with that same skill set, you are going to find it extremely hard to find a company able to sponsor you. Even if the company likes you and would otherwise be willing to keep you, that company will not be able to meet the requirements of the law if there are lots of Americans to do the same work. It's important you really do your homework and prepare for jobs with more specialized skills. Realize you are not here just to get a degree; you want to make a home here and you need to choose carefully how you train for work.

Bob Mwiti, Kenya, Africa

The Lesson: Take Mwiti's last statement first. If you are coming to America as a student and want to make your stay permanent, plan for that! It is critically important what field of study you choose. You must decide in advance if you are here to simply get an education or are you here to start a life? Is whatever you are studying likely to qualify you for a specialty field or provide expertise that is hard to find? Will you have taken sufficient ESL and literacy courses to afford you a solid ability to communicate in English? Have you investigated companies or prospective employers where you might work after graduation? Unless you have preplanned your qualifications and undertaken the necessary steps to make yourself a special talent, you can easily find you are unable to secure the kind of position that will lead to a sponsoring employer.

Maria Flores-Guerra of Peru initially came on a tourist visa, translated that into a Green Card, and ultimately obtained her citizenship. Her experience outlines a different path toward permanent residence in the United States.

> For me to come to America was a bit of a process. I first had to make an appointment at the American Embassy in Lima in 1997; that was more than twenty years ago. At the time, I was working and studying at the Institute. When I had my interview, I had to answer a lot of questions and fill out question sheets at the Embassy. They wanted to know things like what you do for living, was I currently full time in the University, what was I doing to earn money, and did I have family or children I intended to bring? Then I had to give them a complete outline of what I planned to do once I was in the United States. I said, "Oh, I am in the Institute to study computer science." That was not good enough; they wanted to see a current university ID to prove what I said. I had to tell them I was working as something like a secretary so they knew I

would have some money. As to what I planned to do, I said, "Oh, I just want to travel and see the country and the coast." I was interested in seeing the different cities and general life in America. I didn't tell him I had any long-term plans or wanted to work in the U.S. at that point. That initial interview appointment had only gone about thirty minutes before the man got up and said, "OK. Congratulations," and closed the folder. "I hope you can have a good trip." I got my tourist B-2 Visa. Of course, that was just a travel and tourist visa, so it was only stamped for six months.

My mother, who was already in America, had sent me all the money, plane tickets, and other things I might need to make the journey, so that part was happily taken care of. When I flew into the U.S., I landed in Los Angeles at LAX with my tourist visa in hand. I was relieved to just go right through customs.

But, of course, I am not intending to stay just six months as a tourist; I wanted to stay longer. So, after my six months were up, I had to go apply again and be approved to stay an additional six months. Years ago, back in 1998, this was a fairly simple thing to do, but after 9/11 happened, everything became nearly impossible. In 1998, I was approved for the additional six months because there were no complaints against me. I just had to pay the fee.

In the meantime, my mother had begun work as a companion for a woman in an assisted living community. The agent asked if I wanted the forms for my mother to stay as well. Once everything was completed, I was *elevated to a different status where I was later able to apply for a one-year work permit. That application was also approved, so that let me stay in America for another year. During that additional year, I started the process to get my Green Card.*

I finally got my Green Card, and after five years I applied for citizenship. The citizenship process was much longer and a lot more difficult than most people realize. I had to study American History because they give you a pretty hard test. There were a hundred questions you had to get right. Also, I had to speak, read, write English. They gave me a book and had me read a page or so to them. Then I had to write something they dictated to me to show I knew how to communicate in writing. It took a lot of study and time, but I finally got my citizenship. So, from tourist visa to American citizen, here I am today.

Maria Flores-Guerra, Peru

| *The Lesson:*

It is not where you begin, but where you end that is important. A person might have as his or her goal permanent residence in America. Individuals want to come, perhaps later bring their family, start a business, or obtain a good job; they want to begin their life anew. As was the case for Maria, that process can begin with a small action. It can start with the simple task of completing an initial visa application. As we have seen in Maria's story, there are other ways forward once you are here. From there, it will simply be a continued series of small steps one after the other that move you toward that better future. Things do not happen all at once. Be patient and commit yourself to consistent efforts. The human spirit is always heightened when small victories lead from one desired outcome to the next. Commit to the idea that success and fulfillment of your goals is the only acceptable outcome, no matter how long it takes or what sacrifices must be made. Most of all, be patient with yourself and with the process. Persistence to your goal is essential, and time is on your side.

The Barrier: Other Discrimination in Various Forms

America's immigrants have frequently been confronted by negative preconceptions and rejections based on their appearance, accent, color, or some other facet of their person. In some cases, the experience has simply been a result of plain racism. This can be especially true if they are from a part of the world where color and language differences exist. Stories of racial discrimination have frequently been attributed to incidents in the South. However, the assumption of "obvious racism" can sometimes be too easily reached when events are quickly and superficially viewed. Within today's hypersensitive society (both North *and* South), some immigrant experiences require deeper consideration and wider context.

The *New York Times* once interviewed a woman who had immigrated to America with her parents from the Punjab region of India at age four. The reporter was particularly interested in a story from her youth that had taken place near her family residence in rural Bamberg, South Carolina. The story below is recounted exactly from the writings of this young woman, and it is demonstrative of how one family viewed their experience:

(As excerpted from the book, Can't Is Not an Option; My American Story (2012)2

The reporter had heard a story about Simmi and me as four- and eight-year-old contestants in the Wee Miss Bamberg pageant. It quickly became one of the stories the media most like to repeat about me. For too many of them, it confirmed their preconceived notions of life in the South, particularly in the small town, rural South of Bamberg, South Carolina.

To this day I'm not sure why my mom decided it was a good idea to enter Simmi and me in the pageant. We weren't a family that put a lot of stock in those kinds of things. But I remember I wore a ruffly white dress. My talent, such as it was, was singing, and my song was, "This Land is Your Land." I remember my brother Mitti playing in the band below the stage as I sang my song. He watched me and started laughing when I forgot the words.

After all the little girls had performed, they lined us all up on the stage. The little white girls were on one side, the little black girls were on the other, and Simmi and I were in the middle. The pageant traditionally had two winners, a black queen and white queen. But, before they revealed who the winners were, the organizers of the pageant said they had an announcement to make. They called Simmi and me out of line and said, "We don't have a place for you." Then they thanked us and handed us gifts. I got a beach ball. I didn't understand. I thought they were giving me a present because everyone liked my song. I remember thinking that when I got home, I was going to rub it in my brother's face for laughing at me.

The beach ball was a disqualification gift. What Simmi understood—and every adult in that auditorium understood but I didn't — was that my sister and I didn't fit into either of the categories, (black or white) by which the pageant judged the winners. Not wanting either race to get upset, the judges disqualified us. I remember being happy that I was able to sing my song. Besides, I loved my beach ball. My parents praised us when we got home and said how great we were. But other than that, we never talked about the incident again.

Many people have found this story shocking, and I suppose to someone who hasn't seen it in context it is. But I do see it in context, and I see it differently. My family and I have some disheartening stories, but every family does. What matters isn't the stories themselves; it's how the stories end.

The year after Simmi and I were disqualified from the pageant, the lady next door, who had originally recommended that my mom enter us in the contest, said she thought we should compete again. I don't know if she hadn't heard about what had happened to us or what. But my mother told her in no uncertain terms that as long as the pageant was segregating the little girls who competed *in it, her girls would never have another thing to do with it.*

Yes, I was disqualified from the pageant, but the same town that disqualified me was the one that accepted me into a Girl Scout troop, helped my dad get a job in the community college, and helped my mom get a job as a sixth-grade social studies teacher. Over time that town, Bamberg, adopted us as its own. It was a place where I saw firsthand neighbors helping neighbors, I saw the power in the goodness of people doing for one another in good times and bad. Bamberg was a town of faith, values, and patriotism, a town that supported and comforted us when my brother was deployed and fought in the Persian Gulf War.

That was the story I wanted to tell the press: The wonderfully, uniquely American story of a small southern town that accepted an Indian family despite our cultural differences. Was it a perfect place? No place is. But the town of Bamberg showed us that it too could change, and that says more about South Carolina and about America than an awkward day at a kid's pageant.

> Nikki Haley, Punjab, India
> Governor of South Carolina
> Ambassador to the United Nations

| *The Lesson:*

The essence of this short narrative is one of great importance when looking at the true spirit of America. All of us are likely to meet people and have experiences that are unkind or unfair. In every society, there are those who are bigoted, ill-spoken, or ignorant, and encountering them seems an unfortunate part of almost every life. Immigrants are perhaps even more subject to this kind of treatment, particularly those with a racial component. The important lesson, whether immigrant or native-born, is to never let momentary unkindness deter you from your path and to look at these things in their wider context. Do not allow temporary discomfort or anger dissuade you from pursuing your future and your goals. Single incidents such as Ambassador Haley describes are neither reflective of the character of America nor its society as a whole. America is bigger than that. You are bigger than that. Nikki Haley, through her own immigrant's eyes, saw the America of a caring community, not simply the unfortunate misjudgment of a few pageant directors. Ambassador Haley has gone on to become one of the most successful and influential women's leaders in the world partly because she saw this single incident, this single barrier, in its broader context. Should that not be a lesson on America for everyone?

The Barrier: Color and Cultural Adjustment

The barrier of color is not always rooted in simple racism. For example, when Shegitu Kebede arrived from Kenya as part of a UN Refugee Resettlement program, she was relocated to North Dakota. As she described it, it was "perhaps the whitest state in the country." Add the complete whiteout of snow, something else she had never experienced, and this ultra-white world was beyond anything she could fully comprehend. To suggest Shegitu felt out of place would infinitely understate the hurdle she had to climb. Not only did she not speak English, but now there were no people like her even in appearance. Fortunately, she had a support group within the church, and the people in her community were warm and welcoming. Even so, this initially seemed an almost impossible situation. She was understandably thrilled to be in the United States and out of physical danger, but how she could ever establish a life for herself in a world so unlike her remained a mystery. In a word, she was terrified.

Well, once you get the visa, you have no choice when or where to go unless you have a family member already in the United States who will sponsor you. In my case, I had no one in the United States, so the UN found a sponsoring church group in North Dakota. Coming from Kenya, North Dakota was a complete shock. I had no understanding of winter. As you know, there is no winter in Africa, especially the eastern part of Africa. I hadn't even experienced any kind of cold weather, so I had no ability to cope with it at all. On top of that, I didn't speak English, so when someone told me the winter will go away in a few months, I didn't understand. It was a very depressing moment for me. Africans depend on growing their own food in their back yard and that's what you live on. I was just thinking how will I make it out here without having any food? Who knew you could order food from a market? I was terrified and totally depressed at that moment. I had no idea what to expect in my future.

I had no real concept of what America was like when I was in the refugee camp. I really thought it would be like how I came from Ethiopia to Kenya. It would be OK. In the

West, the language may be different, but it would not be that much of a difference from what I just experienced. I thought, well yes, a different language but kind of nice weather, everybody friendly, that kind of thing. I was completely shocked! First, I came in the wintertime, and in the wintertime, you don't see people outside. I was thinking to myself, "Wow, what a big country with nobody in it. Where is everybody?" I was in an apartment building on the third floor. When I took the stairs from my third-floor apartment, I could see other people's apartment doors. By the door was a doormat that said, "Welcome." I thought, in Africa that means you are very welcome, come in. Let me go and knock on the door. But when you do that, people look at you. "What? Who are you? Why did you knock?" You don't realize that just because you live next door to people and they have out the "welcome mat," you don't just go up and invite yourself into their home. That was so strange to me. It was very enlightening, but also seemed so cold-hearted. Why do you have the "welcome" sign if you're not welcome?

You know, in the early to late-80s, there were basically no people of color in North Dakota. They didn't have any black people like me, so when I went out to the grocery store or to church, I really stood out! I was the only black person. That only added to my feeling of isolation. I was very lonely. However, there was one benefit I came to understand later. That isolation helped me to learn the English language much more quickly. To survive and assimilate to this strange new land, I had to be able to go in the marketplace and do the right thing. I had to try to become like everybody else. I had to buy food, go to work, and find daycare for my child. I needed the language of the town to be like them. That drove me to learn the language as quickly as I could.

I also had the sponsors from a couple of churches who came together in response to what I needed. They were some of the nicest people I ever met. They introduced me to another woman from South Africa who didn't see my accent and difficulty with English as a problem. She was so kind. She cooked dinner for me, welcomed me, and we had such a nice evening.

Of course, at that time, I didn't have a car and she didn't have a car either. Since we lived in different areas, we weren't able to get together that often. But I was able to get along. My sponsors took me out shopping, to the doctor's office, to the attorney's office to sign necessary legal papers so I could get Social Security, and to the ESL classes.

But acceptance and actually becoming American, finding a place for myself, a woman of color in this strange world, took longer. I have my own way of living life. I'm a Bible believer, a Christian. I believe in the God of Abraham, Isaac, and Jacob. For me, it wasn't so much a requirement that people be friendly to me. I just went by the Bible teaching to do unto others what we will want them to give back. That's the cycle God had created for us. I reached out to people and became very friendly to them. I wanted to let them know that I am just like them. I have done these things all of my life. By reaching out as a friend, I think people then accepted me.

When I first moved to where I am now in Minnesota, I picked a small town where there would not be a lot of *traffic. My friends were thinking, how are you going to survive in that rural area? The first thing I did was to go around my neighborhood and meet as many of my neighbors as possible; I took a sidewalk tour. I invited people from one block at a time to come to my house for coffee. I set up my very best china and a beautiful table. From outside and not really knowing me, they may have already had a certain mindset about me, but when they came into my house and looked at how I set my table and how welcoming I was, then they found we had something in common. One lady said she collected things similar to me, so we connected together right there. Another lady was a gardener and gave me pointers about the new soil and the best things to grow in that area. That's how I made friends. I reached out to my neighbors. I don't really just expect people will walk up and be my friend. I reach out to them and try to become part of the community. Like Doctor King said, you don't judge people by the color of their skin but by the content of their character. But when he was speaking, he was not just talking to white people to tell them not to judge by the color of someone's skin, but also to both parties. He was also saying you have to bring good values, an honorable character yourself so others will see it. I raise my children by that code, and I conduct*

my own life by that philosophy. That is great advice to
anybody, immigrant or not.

Shegitu Kebede, Ethiopia

The Lesson:

Where does one begin? There are so many lessons in this short autobiographical sketch that it is difficult to recount them all. Perhaps one of the most striking is the lesson Shegitu herself underscores regarding the way she broke the initial barrier of making friends; it was how she overcame potentially preconceived ideas others might have had regarding people of color. Rarely will personal connections and friendships "just happen." You need to extend yourself, be invitational, show others the similarities between you and them, open yourself to new ideas and new possibilities, and reach out to others who are in your immediate circle. The influence Dr. Martin Luther King had on Shegitu's life was profound and should not be under-appreciated, either. The point she makes regarding how important it is for each of us to base our opinions of one another on character, not color, is critically important. We must set a high standard for ourselves. We must try to see others as unique individuals, people like us who also have strengths, weaknesses, and their own pressing issues.

In those moments where we first meet, others may be less friendly than we had hoped. When Shegitu was faced with such receptions, it would have been easy to take those slights personally, perhaps even view them as racism. But she was patient and careful not to generalize such encounters. She kept looking for the good in the other person's character, linking values they might have with her own. By remaining friendly and continuing to treat others with care and kindness, barriers that might have existed were eliminated. Friends were made and social networks built. Adherence to her higher standards prevailed.

A second observation on Shegitu's experience reflects on her Christian faith. Not everyone is a Christian, or a Muslim, or a Jew, or perhaps any organized faith at all. Yet, as we previously observed, the lessons of treating others as you would want to be treated transcends religion. There is also an even deeper lesson in Shegitu's experience. By relying on that higher faith to guide her decisions, using her moral compass to light her way, and seeking a higher power when life became overwhelming, she found the added strength to meet her challenges. You are not alone. You do not have to shoulder all of life by yourself. It is comforting to have others who share that faith and provide their encouragement, kindness, and additional love. For Shegitu, her faith and the support of her church was indispensable. It seems a lesson from which we can all learn.

As Shegitu discovered, there are more people who want to help than get in your way. This theme was echoed in interview after interview. Said Fadloullah, the gentleman from Orlando who rose from "hamburger flipper" at Wendy's to a top sales manager in a major resort, said this:

> You know, Bob, I am here now over forty years, and in all that time I have never experienced racism or hate at all. It didn't happen even one time. Almost always, people tried to help me. They would explain how things were done, or try to help me learn my job, or they would show me how

something worked. No, about the only thing I had happen was people would say, "Said, you are not going to get that job, or no you can't talk to some boss, or that is not a job someone who doesn't speak English can do." But that was ok. I just go do it anyway. Yes, maybe there were people who looked down at me somewhere because of my accent or something, but then they just didn't say anything. I don't know. But I tell you what. If they had, I would have them to sit down and have a ten-minute conversation with me. At the end, they would have a new opinion, and I would have a new friend. No, this has been a fantastic country for me. It has given me more than I ever even dreamed could be my life. I even told my mother, "Mama, I'm sorry, but if anything ever happened that this country was in a fight with Morocco, I am with the United States. I am here. I'm an American."

Said Fadloullah, Morocco

Said's comments should not be taken to mean there is no racism, no bigotry. Unkindness and human malice are a part of every society. America is no exception. How we deal with these encounters, on the other hand, is perhaps the more important thing. Yassin Terou, who owns two Falafel House restaurants in Knoxville, was the victim of a racist attack. His approach was not what one might have expected.

Oh yes, there are people like that who don't like you because you are a Muslim, or foreigner, or whatever. So yes, there have been incidents of unkindness or mean comments from time to time. You know, every day cannot be sunny. There was the time someone set fire to my store and tried to burn it down. But afterward, there were so

196

many people who were angry about that and came to help me put everything back together and clean up what had been done. It was so inspiring for me to see how all these people came together! The police, they asked me if I wanted to sign complaints and press charges if they caught this guy. I said, "No. If you catch him, I want to meet him, and I will make him a sandwich and we will sit and talk over lunch. We will get to know one another better. Then there could be change. You know, you can't fix hate with more hate. That doesn't work.

Yassin Terou, Syria

Trong Nguyen from Vietnam unexpectedly experienced discrimination of a different sort when he took a position as a janitor in a large office building that had a largely Hispanic staff.

Just trying to begin a new life here, we had so many difficulties. When my wife and I began work as a janitor at the Water Tower Place, a coworker told me, "Trong, do you know that America is overpopulated? We have more than two-hundred million people! We don't need you. Go back where you belong." I was shocked to hear people trying to chase my wife and me out. I thought he was going to help me feed our children in America. A single income can never feed the family. Even though our youngest was just a baby, my wife also had to work. This job was everything for us.

One evening, a Mexican man said to me, "You come here and take our jobs. Go back wherever you came from." I was so upset I cried. They said so many hard things. One day, some of them said, "You come here to make money, and then go back home and live like kings!" That was too much. I couldn't hold it in anymore. I told them in a soft voice, "We are Vietnamese people. You don't have enough education to even know where our country is. Vietnam is a small country, but we did not come to America to look for jobs. We are political refugees. We can't go back home." I didn't call them bad names, but I added, "You are the ones who come here to make money and bring it back to your country. We spend our money right here." After that they didn't bother us very much.

I never got used to the fact that people could look down on me for just working. It is a very discomforting feeling. But I said to myself, "I've made it this far, and no way is anyone going to put me down. I'm as good as anybody else, and I've never asked for any favors."

Trong Nguyen, Vietnam

The Lesson: No single ethnicity owns the corner on racist feelings or actions. When people of other colors, other cultures, or other languages are encountered, it is entirely possible that misunderstandings and unkindness can surface. Such circumstances can make the adjustment to this new world of America all the more difficult. The word, however, is "difficult," not "impossible." As seen in all three previous examples, the temporary barrier of color or religion can be overcome through positive human relations or simply minimizing the event's importance by seeing larger contexts. Said, for example, put the idea of racism and bigotry so much to one side that he didn't even allow it to enter his life. His experience was defined by the way others helped him. He never allowed those who might have tried to limit his aspirations to interfere with his actions. In the process, he discovered how communication and empathy could win almost every battle.

Yassin Terou chose to fight hate with kindness. Human nature is such that when someone is kind and outgoing, it is difficult to not mirror those qualities. When someone does not react with anger and defensiveness, the other party's energy for bitterness loses intensity. What Yassin discovered from his experience was not hatred; it was kindness and love from an entire community that rose up to help him. That was the America he saw, not the narrow-minded actions of a sadly misguided individual.

In almost any setting, work or otherwise, one can encounter those who consider themselves better, the individuals who see someone else's presence as either unwelcome or a threat. In some cases, a person will be disliked simply on the basis he or she is not "one of them." Unkindness, insults, or even threats can be a part of comments from such people. Trong, however, came to exactly the right conclusion. He earned his station through his own merits. He is as good as anyone. He was not about to let someone who did not know him or the circumstances from which he came steal his dignity or position. He and his wife were focused on creating a life for themselves, and neither were about to let anyone stand in the way of providing for their children. You can always deflect hurtful remarks by weighing them against the larger goal of moving forward. In the end, the remark will be gone, but you will still be moving in a positive direction. Nothing can stop a determined spirit.

The Barrier: Finding and Securing Initial Employment

Regardless of what someone has heard concerning the abundance of employment opportunities in America, there is always a vetting process to navigate before a hiring can take place. As previously discussed, the realities of this can be frustratingly different than what was originally envisioned. This is not new. Our Romanian immigrant, Marcus Ravage, relates his experiences in 1909 which, although from some time ago, contain valuable lessons still pertinent today.

> Early in the morning I would go downstairs to buy a "World," and after breakfast I would get one of the children to translate the "want advertisements" for me. When I glanced at the length and the number of those columns, I saw that I would not be long in getting rich. There were hundreds of shops and factories and offices, it seemed, and they all wanted my help. They literally implored me to come. They promised me high wages, and regular pay, and fine working conditions. And then I would go and blunder around for hours trying to find where they were, stand in line with a hundred other applicants, approach timidly when my turn came, and be passed up with a significant glance at my appearance. Now and then, in a sweatshop, I would get a hearing; then the proposition was that if I wanted to work without pay for two weeks, and give $10 for my instruction, I would be taught to be a presser or an operator. I could not bridge

the gulf between the advertised appeals for help and this arrogant indifference of the employing superintendent.

There was only one way to succeed in America, my friends continually told me, and that was by constant, tireless, undiscriminating trying. If you failed in one place, or in ten places, or in a hundred places, you must not give up. Keep on trying and you are bound to be taken somewhere. The main thing was to say "yes" whenever you were asked whether you could do this or that. That was the way everyone got work. So, I followed the counsel of the wise, in so far as my limited spunk permitted, and knocked at every door in sight. But that ultimate inevitable success which I had been promised did not come.

At last, one morning a butcher in the upper eighties gave me the answer as to why I wasn't being hired with pungent frankness. When I saw, after our conversation, he was not about to hire me, I gathered all the pluck I could muster and demanded the reason. He looked me over from head to foot, and then, with a contemptuous glance at my shabby foreign shoes, he asked me whether I supposed he wanted a greenhorn in his store? Here, I thought, was a new light on America. In order to have an American job, one must have American clothes. One must "look American." But the only way to get American clothes was to find a job and earn the price. Altogether, a desperate situation. But, in the land of Columbus, one did what one could, and there was no disgrace in doing anything. A shoemaker was just as good in America as a doctor, as *long as he worked and made money and paid for everything.*[3]

Marcus Ravage, Romania 1909

The Lesson:

Marcus was finding this new American way of life almost incomprehensible. His appearance, accent, and lack of understanding had made him nearly unemployable for even the most menial of jobs. On the other hand, he was gaining valuable insights along the way that could be used in the future. The first of those insights regarded his appearance. That rule is as important today as it was then. If you intend to be taken seriously as a candidate, you must present a good appearance. You must look like you will fit the organization. Those first impressions are critical. It has often been noted that you cannot win a position in the first fifteen seconds of an interview, but you can often lose the position in those few seconds. An "American appearance" counts.

When someone comes from an entirely different culture that embodies standards and vastly different mores than those here, the task of becoming "American" enough to fit particular job requirements can be a difficult task. Yet, finding your first position can rely on making just that transition. There are some worthwhile steps in deciding what changes to make. Be observant of others. How do they look? How do they act? Be willing to make small alterations in yourself. Gradually grow your American identity. This should not be taken to mean you should abandon every vestige of your own background and heritage; it means incorporate the new with the old. A further message from Ravage is to be patient with yourself. When things seem insurmountable, continue forward anyway. You have already seen multiple examples of how that persistence has led to eventual success.

The third lesson to be learned was that finding suitable employment was a numbers game. You can never allow yourself to become discouraged because you didn't win a position, or even because you failed at a dozen positions. Try to learn from each experience, then put that knowledge to use the next time. Marcus realized he needed to change his appearance. That small recognition became a key to his future success. Moreover, he did not give up. He used that knowledge as he pressed forward with determination. There is no substitute for consistent effort and sufficient observation to continually adjust as you advance toward your goal.

The last lesson was about America itself. There is no such thing as a disgraceful way to earn a living in America. "If you are working hard, earning wages, and making your own way, you are a success!" In your community, you will be accepted and respected. You can always move up. You can always improve. Perhaps you can work more hours, or take second jobs, or go to school to learn a new skill. Know that, with persistence and continuous striving, there are no limits on what you might achieve or how high you might go.

The Barrier: Communication and the Americanization

Process: Communicating with others in America is a formidable endeavor if you come from a country where English is never spoken. Anyone will tell you: English is a difficult language to learn. Words with the same spelling have different meanings when used in different contexts. Then there is voice inflection, physical mannerisms, sarcasm, slang, idioms, and a thousand other small nuances that go into communicating in English. If you have traveled to a foreign country where no one spoke English, you have some understanding of what a new immigrant must face every day once they arrive in America. (And, knowing that, you might offer a little patience and understanding from time to time.) Things like employment, simple conversation, asking questions, all of these are made nearly impossible without at least a basic knowledge of English. Even though it is understood that tens of thousands of immigrants accomplished this task before you and went on to create wonderful lives, such recognition is of no consolation. The mountain remains unmoved, and it must be climbed.

There are avenues for newly arrived non-English speakers such ESL classes, computer programs, self-help books, tutors, and special immersion schools. However, no matter which path one chooses, the process takes time. The amount of time will differ from person to person. Some who have already had instruction in their home country will find the process a bit easier than those with no previous background. Young people seem to learn more rapidly than old. The more immersed will gain fluency more rapidly. Those who speak their native tongue at home and use English only when necessary, will likely find true fluency impossible to master. Whatever the circumstance, speaking English is the gatekeeper to much of America's opportunity. This being the case, what did others do to climb this mountain?

> *My parents, like most immigrants, faced many culture shocks. Such basic activities as buying a car, opening a bank account, and shopping in a supermarket were all new and unfamiliar.*
>
> *For my part, I had to attend summer camp and then school without speaking a word of English. Unlike my parents, I of course had not learned any English back in Leningrad. I wasn't even literate in my native Russian yet.*
>
> *There weren't any other Russian kids at the summer camp or at Saugatuck Elementary School. This turned out to be a good thing. Since there was no one to talk to in Russian, I quickly acquired English through immersion. There was no other choice. Small children pick up new languages quickly if immersed in them.*
>
> *In later years, I couldn't believe that respected educators in California claimed that Hispanic children could only learn English through a laborious process of "bilingual education" in which they would first be taught primarily in Spanish. Whatever validity such theories might have for high school age students, immersion is clearly the best way to teach a new language to younger kids.*
>
> *Ilya Somin, Leningrad, Russia*

Joe DiMauro came with his family from Sicily to New York as a sixth-grade student. His early experiences centered on school and trying to assimilate into a culture where he had no attachments and no ability with English.

> When we got here in late October of 1960 we were living directly across the street from a Catholic elementary school. My father wanted me to go to the Catholic school, but when we went there, they told us they could not take me because I did not speak a word of English. Because of that, we had to go to the public school where, of course, they legally had to take me. I was supposed to go into the 5th grade, but because I didn't speak any English, they put me back in the 4th grade. As you might expect, no one, including the teacher, spoke Italian or Sicilian; I was alone.

> Everything was totally English. In those days, there was no ESL class, so I had to figure things out for myself. For a long time, I just sat in class and looked at other students and the teacher. I tried to pick up what I could from their expressions or body language, but nothing was really understood. As a young person I started by watching my classmates or friends, and I began learning words and phrases relatively quickly. Within three months I was able to have at least a rudimentary conversation in English.

> As math is an international language, I was actually ahead of all my classmates in that subject. Even so, I was put in the lowest level of math as well. But here I could compete. I started making strong progress and my English kept improving. Going into the 6th grade I was put into the best class. Once my English was established, I was able to get back on track and finish both the 7th and 8th

grade in one year. It took over a year, but I could finally at least function in English.

Joseph DiMauro, Sicily

The Lesson:

From these three stories, we learn that one of the most important and influential factors is learning a new language, any new language. As much as possible, speak that language in everyday conversation with native speakers. All of the ESL, formal instruction, grammar lessons, online courses, or any other mode of teaching will not be as effective as daily conversation in the real world. All languages, most assuredly English, include slang, idioms, colloquialisms, and tonal variations that cannot be duplicated in conventional teaching.

One can even learn a great deal of English by watching television. Almost every program includes a closed caption option that displays the English words for you to read as well as hear. In some cases, the closed caption can be shifted to other native languages that could make things even easier. The key to climbing the mountain is not hard to see; to learn any language, you are best served by conversing in that language.

A second common theme to emerge is the importance of continued application. It would have been far easier for each person to have simply lived among those who spoke their own language, but the desire to learn this new language motivated them to use English as often as possible. Not everyone chose the same path. Not everyone had the same experiences. Yet, everyone recognized the necessity of English to succeed in their new country.

The Barrier: Creating Your Personal American Character

As important as it is to learn English in one's transition toward becoming a more integrated American, it is only one step the new immigrant must take. Reshaping the habits and behaviors that were so a part of your character upon arrival, then gradually growing those into a new, more American version of yourself, is a journey only you can take. You will invariably keep much of your past, but living in a new culture will bring about change. Ultimately there is a balance, a compromise that must be struck between the old and the new. Within this newly blended person is the emerging American character; it is that newer adaptation of yourself. It is often during this slow transformation where such things as a lack of approval, unkindness, exclusion, or other unkind events can arise. Biases and stereotyping never seem to go out of business; they remain an aspect of American life that requires continued work by everyone. It was encouraging that most of those interviewed reported that more Americans tried to be helpful and tolerant than bigoted or unkind. Many of the storylines describe how there was a gradual acceptance and greater understanding that took place over time. Common interests and shared experiences were discovered, and friendships emerged. Relationships developed and both parties were changed. The fact remains that we have as much to learn from immigrants as they do from us...perhaps even more.

A Vietnamese immigrant describes how he sees a responsibility for mutual sharing. No one can just take from life what it affords; he must also give back. It is a lesson he has tried to convey to his children so they will ultimately become both teachers and learners.

Well, you know, I believe in sharing and the need to give back to society. Always be an honest person who works hard, and somehow, one day, one way or another, you will be successful. You may not hit the top, but you will definitely be somebody someday. I believe in honesty and loyalty. Those values live in the Vietnamese people naturally. We already have it. Our younger generation should continue and carry on those things, and I believe they will. With all the opportunities, all the education they can get over here, they will be far ahead of me someday.

These ideas I try to live by. I think to be a good teacher is important. You do not only direct your company, but you must also find good ways to deal with your employees; help them when they need it. You need to show that you are a caring person who sees their value. Motivate them and give them opportunities to step up and show them how maybe someday they will be like you...maybe better. I think caring for others and sharing is the right thing to do.

> *It doesn't matter what your position is or how high you are right now.*
>
> Hue Van Lien, Vietnam

The Lesson:

These experiences have shown there is a gradual but inevitable combining of one's own histories and cultural foundations with those of this new homeland. Both parties grow together. Recognize that as your process of Americanization continues to develop; you will find a gradual but noticeable increase in personal acceptance and understanding. More important, whatever occasions of unkindness or personal animosity you encounter, they *will not* determine your destiny; you will be the author of that.

Before we leave this topic of assimilating into our new culture and gradually adopting the personal characteristics of our new American mantle, we need to revisit Marcus Ravage's story regarding his own "Americanization." As it turned out, he ultimately passed his Regents exams and went on to attend the University of Missouri. His first year was complete with nearly every imaginable difficulty. He found himself sometimes ignored, unexplainably excluded, and often misunderstood. He felt entirely on the outside looking in as he tried to understand why others in his freshman class did not fully accept him, include him in their organizations, or have him join their conversations. At times he felt like a man without a country; he no longer fitted into the ghetto of New York from which he came, nor was he a part of this new order at the university where he now tried to co-exist.

Over the course of that first year, however, Marcus gradually became more familiar with his classmates' ways; perhaps, it could be said, their more "American ways." He eventually befriended someone who began to mentor and guide him. His friend explained how to make better connections and helped Marcus understand why others might have behaved as they did. As Marcus began to change, so too did all those around him. Acceptance became more frequent. Barriers began to lower. By year's end, the world had begun to open up, and he returned to New York a completely changed person from the Marcus who had only a year earlier left with fifty dollars, some old clothes, and no idea of what awaited. His old friends and acquaintances were shocked and perplexed by what they witnessed upon Marcus's return. They all commented on how this new Marcus had a totally different demeanor. He had become a new person.

At summer's end, Marcus boarded the train to return to Missouri, now ready to re-establish his place as a second-year student. He felt confident and ready to become a genuine part of university life. What he describes happening upon his arrival back at campus is the remarkable conclusion to one immigrant's gradual evolution into this new world, the world of his new America.

> When I reached the campus, I was surprised to see how many people knew me. Scores of them came up and slapped me on the back and shook hands in their hearty, boisterous fashion, and hoped that I had had a jolly summer. I was asked to join boarding clubs, to become a member in a debating society, to come and see this fellow or that in his room. It took me off my feet, this sudden geniality of my fellows toward me. I had not been aware

how, throughout the previous year, the barriers between us had been gradually and steadily breaking down. It came upon me all at once. I felt my heart going out to my new friends. I had become one of them. I was not a man without a country. I was an American![4]

Marcus Ravage, Romania

The power of Marcus's story is punctuated by the fact that his story is not his alone. There are tens of thousands of such stories. They are the stories of immigrants who have arrived with little understanding of this new country, endured through hardships, faced down adversity, and gradually blended their values and heritage with those of America. They became Americans, and both were changed.

Barriers? Hurdles? Setbacks? No one has ever suggested life would be easy, nor have they intimated that it would be free of disappointments and obstructions. The roads to success are always under construction and subject to detours. Immigrants have forever faced numerous hurdles in the way of that life they so fervently sought. It is of little consequence that those difficulties arose. Everyone faces adversity in life. The importance is how these immigrants dealt with their hardships. What was learned from surmounting them?

No matter what impediment presents itself, there is a fundamental truth that should provide every immigrant the reassurance necessary to continue forward. In America, *"The only limitations a person has are the limitations he places on himself!"* You are not permanently constrained by circumstances. You are not bound by the low expectations of others. Avoid the indecision that comes from self-imposed excuses such as, "I probably can't do that because of my accent, or I'm a foreigner, or I don't have the right background," or whatever other restrictions impede the way. America has *always* rewarded those of positive action and perseverance. Stories offered here confirm that fact. Why should that not be the case for you?

CHAPTER 6

Making It in America

> *"Our attitude towards immigration reflects our faith in the American ideal. We have always believed it possible for men and women who start at the bottom to rise as far as their talent and energy allow. Neither race nor place of birth should affect their chances."*
>
> —ROBERT F. KENNEDY

America has a long list of immigrant success stories; its history is full of people from faraway places who have come and *"made it."* There are millions who are making their way right now...but at what price? What skills and habits of mind are paving the way? What qualities have led to their current accomplishments?

As contemporary immigrants will attest, America boasts tens of thousands of employment openings, training programs, internships, and entrepreneurial opportunities; she has myriad paths toward achieving a successful life. Moreover, all immigrants are free to decide on any path they like to secure that rewarding future. The only question becomes how to best make those decisions and seize those available opportunities? Perhaps there is guidance already that successful immigrants can offer. What might be their advice to a new fellow traveler?

"Making it in America" has never been assured simply by one's arrival. No one attains goals of genuine value without personal sacrifice and diligent pursuit. For immigrants and native-born alike, the true path to success never appeared until that individual took decisive action. It was not until the individual invested hard work and energy into his or her endeavors that progress was made. Immigrant achievements are underpinned by an active participation in pursuing their ambitious dreams. It has required their readjustment to a new culture. It has required the cultivation of essential behaviors to propel that person through hardships and barriers. The good news is, it can be done! It *has been* done.

A recently reported story appeared quoting Adolfo Carrion, Jr., former director of the White House Office of Urban Affairs Policy. Carrion, a first-generation immigrant from Puerto Rico, reflected on his own family's immigration experience, and said this:

> *This may sound cliché to some, but for my family it is not. In one generation we went from parents with little formal education to all four kids graduating from graduate school and going on to successful professions. I have no doubt that my kids will achieve and contribute even more to the American enterprise. This is what keeps me going; that you can go from a sub-basement apartment in a*

1960s Brooklyn ghetto to working for the president of the United States in one generation![1]

Adolfo Carrion, Director of Urban Affairs

There are now more than eight million people living in New York City who are immigrants like Adolfo. Of those, one can only imagine how many might rise up from their current situation to reach highly worthwhile positions in their communities and lives.

The stories and experiences of these immigrants can and should be used to advantage. They should offer an awareness of the human qualities and philosophies that provided for their success. Recognize that there is a time-honored American axiom: "If you want to know how to do something, ask someone who has already done it." In that light, our immigrants have a few ideas worthy of consideration.

The Importance of Envisioning Your Path Forward

One of the more certain ways to delay success is to approach your future with no forethought as to where you might want to go and have no anticipation of what actions you will need to take. This can be especially true when someone comes to a new culture with widely differing employment practices and unfamiliar customs to navigate. No matter how enthusiastic one might be in exploring exciting new opportunities, suddenly finding oneself with no firm vision on how to approach those opportunities almost always insures a poor beginning. This lack of foresight frequently leads to bewilderment, disappointment, and frustration; it can even result in a dislike of the country as one's future becomes increasingly uncertain.

For international students who come looking to complete their university degrees and ultimately find a long-term position in the United States, Bob Mwiti, of Kenya, Africa is adamant about the necessity of thinking things through before you come. It is necessary to have some plan of action before you arrive. He notes how too many arrive in America but never realize their full potential because of this simple oversight. Once admitted to their school, they simply allow events to dictate their futures rather than take charge and act in deliberate ways.

> *Yes, stuff is out there; there actually is something for everyone. You think, OK... America! People have good lives, and perhaps this is a good place where you can come. You get here and you will have a little money. You will live nice. That was the thinking. But, when I got here, I found things to be different. Yes, here in the U.S., there are opportunities and ways to go, but you have to go grab those opportunities. You can't just come, and things will just happen. You can spend money and find jobs and things like that, but there is something even more important; you need to recognize that, with or without a degree, you have to start from somewhere. That's what people don't realize; you actually have to start from the bottom and then work and find ways to go up. But no one tells you how or shows you the way. You have to find it for yourself.*

> *If you are coming as a student, or just coming to look for a good position in a company, you need to think that through first. What kind of job do you want? What type of*

company do you think might offer the best chance of employment? Once you answer questions like this, you can know how to prepare. You can get into a college program or training that will put you in a position to find that right company. In short, you need a plan on how you will do all this, otherwise you will get here and just go from job to job, never really moving forward. I don't believe that is the future people come here dreaming about.

Bob Mwiti, Kenya, Africa

A well-crafted strategy on how you will live and the qualified work you want to pursue will dramatically reduce time lost getting started. Loosely quoting Yogi Berra, one of America's great baseball philosophers, *"If you don't know where you are going, you may eventually wind up someplace else."*

The obvious question this presents is how to do this when you have never even been to America. If someone isn't familiar with what opportunities are available, then how can he or she reasonably expect to plan for one? The answer will be different for every person. It is likely you already possess at least some specific workplace skills, and that is a good place to begin. If specialized skills are limited, then you must take the necessary steps to obtain the ones you want and need. Use the internet, and research where and what job opportunities are available. Find programs and organizations that might help you obtain the kind of position or training you want. As Mwiti wisely observed, it is not enough just to get here; you also need a sense of direction as to where you will go once you arrive.

What is perhaps even more important to your initial vision is your strength of character and conviction. These determine the degree to which you will focus your energy on pursuing opportunities and your willingness to engage in the work required to reach those objectives. No one can see the future. No one can predict what events or personal limitations might arise to impede your progress, but know this...your future *is not* decided or limited by your current place. If you see a job or career you want, but lack the necessary skills, act. There are companies that offer training programs, trade schools, apprenticeships, internships, and a wide variety of agencies all willing to help you attain those required abilities. You simply need to first decide what your passions are, what avenue you would love to pursue, and the kind of future you must have. There are no limitations on this thinking. It is even likely that, after you have been here a while, you will discover possibilities and careers you had never even considered. As you become more familiar with American life, fate may take you in unforeseen directions. Do not be impatient with yourself. On life's road, you may have to "act in the moment," then expand into bigger things later. To exemplify this, here is the experience and advice offered by our Korean immigrant who we met earlier.

> *You cannot always worry about what this job will do or that job will do. For example, you may see an opportunity to work in just a hamburger place. You cannot say, "Well, I don't know anything about hamburgers, so I'm not going to take that opportunity." The most important thing is to just get started. If something is there for you, take it. You can always do more, step up, you know, improve. Just keep moving forward. But for me the most important thing was always to do what was in my heart. I wanted to make true those things in my heart that I really wanted. So, after I am here for a number of years and even had a good job at*

a big company, I saw the success of my other sisters that I had brought to this country. I began thinking about them and realized what I wanted to do. I wanted to be in business for myself. I decided in my heart, I wanted to do business! That was my dream, my passion. Then I began to make plans. I began to look for businesses I thought my husband and I could do. I didn't know what I would find. I didn't worry about that. OK, perhaps I don't know everything about this business or whatever. I just look anyway. Finally, I found a little doughnut shop that we bought and that was a start. That was the beginning of realizing my dream to own a business, and it opened the door to other businesses later. It was a lot of hard work, but it was so worth it! My husband and I, we don't care about hard work. We can do that. What I knew, I was living what I had planned. In America you can do that.

Kim Oksun-Comazzi, Korea

There is an important observation to be made in this short narrative. Kim did not let self-doubt enter the equation. Although she did not come to this country with a fully developed plan for her own business, she ultimately grew into one. The fact is that, upon arrival, it is impossible to know all of the opportunities you might find. As one moves along life's path, things change. You add skills, you become more acclimated to the culture, and you begin to perceive things differently. Positions or avenues you might previously have never considered suddenly become possibilities. Know this! Better opportunities will not come to you; you need to go to them.

As happened for Kim Comazzi, it took her time to fully recognize what opportunities were available; she needed to uncover what she genuinely wanted from life. Once she discovered the desire to be in her own business, she was not to be denied. Naysayers, roadblocks, setbacks, long hours, nothing was allowed to deter her ambition. That is what happens when you actively follow your heart and aspirations to their successful end. What was it Thomas Wolfe said? *"Miracles happen all the time."*

Kim's advice to follow your heart was somewhat echoed by Ilya Somin, our immigrant from Russia who now teaches at George Mason University. As he described his path forward, he was somewhat less than a dedicated student for quite some time. It wasn't until he found an area where he had a sincere interest that he began to make a more serious investment in his studies. He provided the following brief account:

> As far as developing my way forward, I would say that it was greatly helpful when I finally found things in which I was really interested and then tried to focus on that. It was only then that I began to develop a personal educational pathway to a career. I'm not one of those people who have a naturally strong work ethic or general dedication to things if I don't find an interest. For me, it's easier to work hard and be dedicated if I'm actually interested in the work that I'm doing. It absolutely plays to my strength.
>
> *Ilya Somin, Russia*

Here again, we are told how the role of personal interest and development of a specific focus plays an important role in promoting individual success. As Ilya points out, he too did not arrive with those interests in place. He talks in his memoir of a number of years where he did what was required, but never genuinely engaged his studies to his full capacity. Finding what you actually want to do makes dedication and hard work much easier. As revealed by numerous others, achievement may have been limited until they found something where they were willing to apply enthusiastic action but, in the end, it was that dedication and action that made the difference.

The Necessity to Adapt to Your New Country and Language

Ingrid Kliefoth of Germany offers relatively simple advice to new immigrants. To her mind, success in America is essentially up to individuals, and they can help themselves by observing and making every effort to simply become a part of their community and country.

> My best advice is to just look about you and stick to the social rules you see. For me, America was not that different than Germany. Actually, it isn't that different than in most places. In every society, there are rules by which we must live; it's the same way here. You don't come in and everyone has to change for you. You look at how things are done here and do that. You do the best you can. People here are more open and accepting than you might think. Whether we are German or American, we are all struggling just to make life a little better, are we not?

> And too, there are bureaucracies you have to learn. The customs, laws, and requirements you need to understand

in America are different perhaps. Observe those. Learn and try to adjust to them.

And English. That is another thing. When I came, even though I was with the Swedish Embassy in Washington, I didn't speak any English at all. I knew I would have to learn it if I was going to stay in America. I was always pretty fast at learning languages, but English is a hard language in which to be really conversant. I went to ESL classes and studied English, and that made me able to hold simple conversations with people. I did that quickly. But reading technical manuals or legal documents or other more formal texts, that was so hard. Just be patient with yourself. Keep working at it. Eventually you will fit better and find things easier.

Ingrid Kliefoth, Germany

The Importance of Personal Work Habits and Industriousness

Among our immigrants, the term "industriousness" has taken on any number of definitions. It has been described as a strong work ethic, diligence, motivation, passion, solid effort, or a conscientious desire to be better. Whatever the definition, it is the personal quality most often identified by immigrants as having been critical to their personal success. It has also been the characteristic Americans themselves have identified as one of the most admired in its immigrants. A willingness to work hard has been the foundation of almost all achievement, and it would be nearly impossible to underestimate its importance.

Looking through all the writings of the Founders, there was universal agreement that the spirit of hard work in a free society was the preeminent basis of America's future. They were agreed that man's highest potential is best achieved by "steadily improving one's personal worth, securing the safety and well-being of their families, and assiduously working toward the betterment of their communities and country." These American virtues have been echoed throughout the rest of the world. To be sure, work ethic is at the center of these tenets. We are also mindful that it was our past immigrants' almost unlimited capacity for hard work upon which both they and this nation enjoys its place in the world today.

Charles Murray describes how Francis Grund in his 1937 appraisal of our American experiment entitled, *The Americans, in Their Moral, Social, and Political Relations*, opened his comments on this very topic.[2]

> *Active occupation is not only the principal source of [the American's] happiness, and the foundation of their natural greatness, but they are absolutely wretched about it.... [It] is the very soul of an American; he pursues it, not as a means of procuring for himself and his family the necessary comforts of life, but as the fountain of all human felicity.*
>
> Francis Grund, 1837

As Grund observed, this singular quality, coupled with unrestricted liberty, has produced an unending line of success stories. These narratives of success have spread across the world and lured immigrants for more than two centuries. Nothing has been more important to the rise of this nation than the industriousness of its people. Those who embody that virtue almost universally "make it" in America.

In recent years it has been suggested that the willingness to engage in hard work may be in decline. American youth, it is said, are perhaps more interested in their technologies and leisure time than the required work for personal success. This may be true in some cases, but hopefully not in the main. It has *never* been the case with our traditional immigrants. In interview after interview, the "willingness to work hard" was seen by our immigrants as central to any current prosperity.

More recently, there is a rising concern about how loud, misleading voices fail to appreciate the role industriousness and hard work played in this nation's unmatched success. Worse, these voices totally undervalue the importance these qualities hold for our nation's future. Instead, these so-called "voices of concern" speak of victimhood and an "economic system" that exploits the efforts of its immigrants. They would have one believe that the opportunities to succeed that were once so prevalent no longer exist. They disgracefully paint a massive portion of the population as racist, xenophobic, and anti-immigrant (not themselves, of course). Shegitu Kebede, an Ethiopian who experienced tyranny and exploitation firsthand, knows better. She describes her concern about this misguided message and its potential long-term effects.

> *America, over its last fifty years, has seen a growing number of those who don't even understand their own history. They seem ready to take down this nation one brick at a time and have been consistently attempting to do so by destroying today's youth. They have been working to take away our country's work ethic by constantly telling people they are being taken advantage of or they are not*

getting what they are owed. Our people are often not taught to take pride in what they do, or to put out their best effort in every task. Our school system, along with the colleges and universities, constantly diminish the value of America, what it has accomplished, and the sacrifices the Founding Fathers made to even put us here. We need to make everyone, beginning with our young people, aware of how this country has been built on hard work and everyone's participation. We need them to see the lies they are being fed or we are going to end up like everybody else. Millions have risked their lives to come to this country. They saw its value. We desperately need to preserve it.

Shegitu Kebede, Ethiopia

The words of these histories have provided ample indication that every new immigrant must arrive with a great willingness to work hard and actively pursue dreams. Look for solid employment and, when you secure that job, make yourself as valuable an asset as possible. Let no one tell you otherwise. Neither America nor its people ever place limits on what you can attain. All future accomplishment depends upon what you do today. Do it to the best of your ability! Success will follow.

The Role of Self-worth and Tenacity in Success

At a restaurant in Orlando, Florida, a conversation with a young assistant chef in a Mexican restaurant shed additional light on how unwavering persistence and faith can open doors. Because he had family living in the Orlando area, Miguel was able to enter the country in late February of 2016. When he left home to come to the U.S., he assumed his father or brother would find him a good job where they worked as soon as he arrived. Unfortunately, that did not happen. Neither employer was actively hiring, and most certainly they were not hiring someone who did not speak English. Miguel found himself without money and without work. He was willing to try almost anything, but his weak English skills were limiting his chances. Given his personal resolve to be successful, he simply had to find a way to break through. He explains what happened.

Oh, yes, finding that first job was really hard. I mean I went to lots of businesses and just asked the owners if they had any work. The answer was no after no. Even places that had, "Help Wanted" signs were telling me, "No, not right now." One day, however, I went to this Mexican restaurant in the town next door and applied there. There was no sign to say they were hiring, but friends had suggested that, since I'm Mexican, maybe I would have a better chance to be hired in a Mexican business. To me that sounded like a good idea. When the owner came out to see me, I was surprised because he was only a little older than me. Most importantly, he spoke Spanish. Already, I felt relieved. Even so, at first, he didn't look like he was going to take me. I kind of panicked and just began letting everything out, talking about what I could do and how hard I would work for him. Speaking in Spanish, I said, "Listen to me a minute. You won't have anyone here who will work harder than me. I will do any job you need done at any time. I will work in the kitchen, clean tables, do the bathrooms, whatever you need. I'm a good worker. And I will be here every day on time." He was quiet for a minute, then he said ok, he would give me a three-week trial. I thought, finally! I'm working. I'm on my way. You have no idea what a good feeling that was. I did a lot of cooking back in Mexico, so it wasn't long before he put me on the preparation line. It was a little more money and I thought, great, this could lead to something even better. I know, it wasn't much, and it wasn't something that paid real well. But for me, I was happy. It was a good start. Other guys came and went, but I was there...just like I promised. As my father used to tell me, you have to start somewhere and work your way up in life.

Miguel Reyes, Mexico

There is a second element beyond just Miguel's willingness to work hard we should not miss. Perhaps one of the most important employee qualities to a prospective employer is *dependability.* When someone can be depended upon to come every day and be on time as Miguel promised, it is a strong qualification. One's willingness to work hard and be industrious is essential, but consistency in that work ethic is equally important. Convincing his prospective employer of that combination is quite likely what helped Miguel get his opportunity. It is also what will help him advance within any restaurant or organization in the future.

Every immigrants' path to success in America is uniquely his or her own. Yet, the path to success always seems to reward those who have been persistent, those undeterred by setbacks or disappointments. It is always easier to give up in the face of adversity rather than push on through the hardship. However, giving up has never led to personal success, never provided fulfillment to anyone's aspirations. At some point, almost all immigrants have had to rely on their inner belief that success would be theirs in the end. Weak efforts would never be sufficient. They understood that every day would present new opportunities if only they would persist. Shegitu Kebede of Ethiopia again offers her thoughts as to where she derived her inner strength.

I love to study what successful people do. You know, even Abraham Lincoln did not succeed in his first try. People thought that his ability to be in Congress was hopeless; he won't make it. But he believed in himself and that the cause he was standing for was worth trying again. In the same way, our success is up to each one of us. But even so, sometimes we magnify the problems or the challenges we see way beyond what they actually are. I think, though, if we magnify what God has put inside each of us, we can accomplish whatever we set our mind and effort to. Every day, I take an inventory of my life. What did I do with it? Was what I did good? Is there something I could improve? Yes, at this point, I do enjoy success, but it was because I worked so hard. I didn't let things get in my way. I am grateful for everything. Whatever I will pass on to my children and grandchildren didn't come because I was entitled. It came from working hard and was never willing to quit. Because I could take advantage of the opportunities in America, I have been able to reach my promise. I see the results and I'm still driven to be even more. We all have that opportunity, but it is really only available in this land. That's why it's so important for me

*to speak out. I want my children and grandchildren to live
in the same America where I have lived.*

Shegitu Kebede, Ethiopia

Shegitu's determination is obvious in her words. She was
never going to give up and just accept where she was in life.
There was always that determined spirit that pushed her
forward. In the end, it was her faith in God and herself that
kept her going, that gave her the tenacity to just hang in there
until the life she wanted was achieved.

There is another commodity vital to everyone's spirit of determination; it underpins the spirit to persist through all
adversities and setbacks. That quality is called *"attitude."* Events
and circumstances that seem to block the way will inevitably
present themselves. A person's ability to work through these
matters often relies on how they are viewed and addressed. No
one can control all the events of life; they can only control the
manner with which they are dealt. A highly successful
immigrant from Honduras offers the following thoughts:

*First of all, this country opens the door for anybody. If you
are a hard worker and honest, you can do so much.
Everything will depend on you. What you do, and what
you bring to the table, means so much. I'm so glad to be
somewhere where I can find great jobs and feed my kids
and I never have to worry about that for us. To me, it
depends on your attitude. You have to have a good attitude
about yourself and what you are trying to do, believe that
you are at some point going to make it. So what if it takes
more work? It's important; you can't lose your confidence
or ability to stay positive. I try to make every day a good
day. Sometimes things happen that aren't so great. So*

what? You can make your day good or bad. It is your own attitude that will count. So...why not make it good. You can.

Vincent Diaz, Honduras

We know America was a different place at the turn of the twentieth century when it teemed with newly arrived immigrants. In that time, there was a significant bias against recently arrived men who had little understanding of the culture and less understanding of the language. It is here, however, where an interesting experience regarding the value of tenacity, attitude, and setting higher goals are related, again by Marcus Ravage.

After several months of finding no one to hire him, Marcus was given a position as a barman's apprentice. The couple who hired him treated him well, and Marcus slowly learned how things worked in America. He was not unhappy in this newfound position. He finally had a solid job and money in his pocket.

Although already aware of the need to continually move forward in the face of rejection, it was through this new employment where Marcus would further discover the impact of "determination." In life, seemingly mundane occurrences can often turn out to be of significantly meaningful consequence in the longer run. He had been sent on a relatively routine delivery to the wife of a physician in the Bronx, but it turned out to be anything but routine. It was here where, "... *my eyes were first opened to the true meaning of American democracy and my own opportunity in the midst of it.*" Marcus describes the following exchange with the doctor's wife, where he comes to realize the difference between complacency with things as they are and aspirations to higher, more deeply held ambitions. He came to understand how it would be his own determination and larger vision that would overcome the contentment of a comfortable today. Ambition, it seems, is what moves us to those higher planes of accomplishment tomorrow. The doctor's wife admonished Marcus into that reality.

> *"Why, my dear boy, this is no occupation for you. You must look for something better."*

> *I ought to have been flattered, but in my confusion, all I could do was pluck nervously at my cap: "It's all right. I like my work and it pays fine."*

> *"Yes," she replied. "But haven't you any higher ambition?"*

> *"Of course," I blurted out. "I want to be a doctor."*

> *"I thought so," she said in satisfaction. "They all do. Well, you will be," she added with the air of a divinity granting a mortal's wish. "I know. My husband was a poor immigrant boy once, and now he is a doctor. Do you know why?... because he was ambitious and discontented."*

> *These were strange and inspiring words. Hitherto, I had been piously following my parents' injunction to obey my master and to be thankful for whatever God gave me. I had not thought of "discontent" as a virtue. Now suddenly it dawned on me that if I was ever to realize my father's dream, I must follow a course directly opposed to the one he had outlined for me.*

> *What a man did today in no way determined his worth or circumscribed his ambitions. From that night on, my hope*

to get better work turned into determination! Because 'here' was not where I wanted to be, not the kind of work I had dreamed, I began going to evening classes and attending library readings. America was a place where some intelligence was afforded in order to acquire and express ideas![3]

Marcus Ravage, Romania

Ravage was taught the lesson of a lifetime! He was now beginning to understand what might be necessary to succeed in America. For Marcus, he turned a simple conversation into a *revelation*. He now saw this higher version of himself, and it excited him. It energized and motivated him. He became *determined* to make his life better. Even more importantly, he immediately began taking positive steps to expand his education and knowledge in order to get there. He attached himself to like-minded people and grew a higher circle of friends. He purposely read everything he could to make himself conversant when in settings with intelligent people.

One of the more important self-discoveries that emerged from his conversation with the doctor's wife was how he should not be complacent and satisfied in his current position. On the contrary, he should be *dissatisfied!* There is almost nothing more important to an immigrant's future prosperity than to understand that *complacency is the thief of personal growth and future success.* When one is satisfied with the current situation, there is little motivation to do much else. Marcus was shaken into this realization, and in that moment his life took on an entirely different direction.

As has been seen time and again, the greater the effort, the greater the rewards. This has been the experience of one immigrant after another. Success rarely arrived overnight or simply through an epiphany moment. It is always the action *after* such breakthrough moments that matter. Every road forward will be littered with limitations, but it will be this new resolve to provide the higher trajectory. Success worth having relies on our faith, determination, and tenacity. These immigrant accounts lay testament to that reality.

The Importance of Love, Faith, and Religion

Beneath all that man does is a commodity known as *conviction*. There must be faith that the path one has set for himself is the correct one, the one leading most providently to that desired end. In that quest, there is quite often also a reliance on something greater than just oneself. Our immigrants have identified a wide variety of sources to account for the existence of faith in their lives, but they all seem to coalesce into just two central themes: *love and God*. It has often been the love of spouses and families that has provided the motivation to succeed. *"I have a family and if I fail, we all fail. I cannot let that happen."* Where love is present, it seems everything becomes more worthwhile.

The road ahead is full of twists and turns, victories, and disappointments. It can be unimaginably challenging to travel those difficult roads by oneself. That is where such things as family, love, community, and religiosity enter the equation. It is in these realms where individuals find the courage and support necessary to survive the daily forces that may try to take them in unproductive directions.

Immigrants seem to face so much adversity that one might wonder where is it they derive the strength and tenacity to carry on? How do they gather the strength to persevere when they are unable to make themselves understood, find they lack a necessary skill, or encounter someone who offers nothing but discouragement? What provides the doggedness necessary to move forward no matter the setback? There are likely many explanations, but faith and family seem indispensable.

A second element to which many immigrants attribute their success is perhaps something a bit more surprising. When confronted with the question of how they have been able to navigate incredibly difficult circumstances, faith in God has often been their rock. The American immigrant has traditionally possessed a strong religious grounding. From around the world, people of Christian, Jewish, Muslim, or other faiths have found themselves seeking God to guide them through difficult times. It has been rare that any of our interviewees indicated they were atheists or nonbelievers in God. On the contrary, they have almost universally attributed much of their success to God's grace and guidance.

It seems that the stronger their religious faith and trust in God, the less vulnerable they were to the many negative people and events with which they were confronted. Belief that they were not alone in their journey, and that God had a higher purpose for them, provided an inner reservoir of strength from which they could draw. Beyond that, their associations within religious bodies such as mosques, synagogues, or churches provided a community of believers who supported and encouraged them along the way. There is no substitute for the love and encouragement provided by periodic communion with other believers and friends who care.

236

There will always be individuals who will explain why something cannot be done, why a goal is unattainable, or why the current path is unwise. In the face of such negative thinking, it was often the counter-voice of others that made the difference. Such communities can be the difference between a successful transition to a new homeland or a disheartening, unsuccessful journey. Cuban-born Pulitzer Prize-winning journalist Liz Balmaseda provided this quote for the Carnegie Corporation immigration campaign.

> I could say it was by magic that a loving and supportive community emerged around our family. But that village force of good neighbors, church friends, and American-born schoolteachers who took the initiative to visit our home and offer a word of praise and encouragement— that doesn't happen by magic. In response to a life embraced, a life that is often turbulent, painful, and imperfect. This is what I learned from my mother, may she rest in peace...My Cuba is now buried in a Miami cemetery. But my America resounds in all its glory, like a hundred conga drums playing beneath Friday night lights at Hialeah.[4]

> Liz Balmaseda, Havana, Cuba

Liz attributed a large measure of her success to the support and encouragement of her family and the community around her. And no, "It doesn't happen by magic." She and her family shared their collective faith. They shared a faith in their God, faith in one another, and faith in their own dreams. Like Liz, successful immigrants have often surrounded themselves with like-thinking people, positive influencers who encouraged and assisted them in their journey. As noted earlier, there is never a shortage of naysayers, skeptics, and dream killers. The higher an immigrant's aspirations, the more such people seem to abound. It never mattered to Liz Balmaseda. In her America, doors opened, opportunities were seized, and she ultimately found the highest level of attainment...perhaps even beyond what she might have initially envisioned. She did not get there all alone. She did not navigate all the hurdles by herself. She acknowledges that. The important news is that good people still exist. If newly arrived immigrants are to reach their own God-given potential, then faith and community will often be necessary to navigate that path.

In another example, Miguel Reyes talked about how his faith materialized to help him overcome self-doubt and disappointment. Discouragement can often be a dispiriting problem newly arrived immigrants must confront. Experiencing an early lack of success and a string of disappointments can lead to questioning if the right decision has even been made; perhaps they should just go back home. That was Miguel's feeling, and he offers his understanding to help those who might be suffering from this same self-doubt. Take heed, because overcoming such emotions can sometimes be the catalyst to *"making it in America."* (NOTE: Although the following is his story, minor adjustments to some of the wording needed to be made as Miguel was still learning the language when we spoke.)

> *You asked me if I ever questioned my decision to come to America during those early months where I was trying to find my place. Many times. As I said, I had a lot of rejection when I was going for jobs, and I was having a lot of trouble with money and the language. There were lots of times I thought, maybe I should just go back home; this*

isn't what I thought. But I didn't. I would always say to myself, "OK, one more week or one more day and we'll see."

You know, at that time I was not much of a church-type person. My mother, though, she was very religious. When I was growing up, if we were having problems, she would always tell me, "Don't worry, I know God will make a way for us. Have a little faith, Miguely." I think I really didn't buy the idea at the time, but now somehow her voice kept talking to me in my mind. Even I started praying in a strange way. I would be going to talk to someone about a job or thinking about what I was going to do, and I would find myself saying, "Please, God. Help me find something today or help me do good speaking to this boss"; you know, I would just say something like that. I just could always hear Madre's voice in my head. So I would say this little prayer and guess what would happen...nothing. Even one time I went to a store that had a sign, "Now Hiring," I said, "OK, this is a good chance. Help me, God. Get me this job." I thought this could work. It was just a simple clerk-type job. I can do that, I thought. But again, they said no. "They needed a customer service type person, and I wouldn't fit." I knew why. I was so dejected. I just felt all alone, and my hopes were really low. I think I was about at my end that day. But then I thought, well, maybe if I go to church, maybe that would be something. You know, I was running out of ideas. A friend had been telling me about a church that held Spanish masses and said I could go with him and look at it. Think what you like, I really believe God did lead me. It turned out so great. There were lots of Spanish-speaking people there and many of them were so friendly. They would all tell me, "No, don't give up. Have

*faith. God will have something for you. Keep trying."
Suddenly, I didn't feel so alone. These people had
confidence in me. These people had made it. They knew.
You know, why not me? One man, whose name I don't
remember, had become a car salesman and offered to help
get me a job at his dealership as a car-washer. I didn't
really want to do that, but it gave me hope. Then someone
suggested I focus on Mexican businesses. Why that idea
had not crossed my mind before, I don't know. As I already
told you, that was when I happened onto the Mexican
restaurant that took a chance and hired me. I can't help
but believe it was God who led me to that church and that
job. Like my mother always said, "He has a plan, and He
will show you a way." I believe that now.*

*So, you asked what my advice would be to help people
make it in this country? I'm not sure I'm really the right one
to ask, but I would just say, don't get too down on yourself!
Keep your faith, and don't be impatient. Maybe nothing
happens all at once. God will show a way if you trust Him.
I know I am only getting started. My job now is good; I like
it. But I'm not done. I know God has bigger plans for me
than even where I am right now. Who knows, maybe one
day I will even have my own restaurant. I also know that
had I gone back to Mexico, like I almost did so many times,
I would never have the life I have now.*

Miguel Reyes, Mexico

Miguel is making it in America, and he is not done
climbing. That is the good news. His initial isolation, feelings
of discouragement, and lack of success were overcome by the
communion with others in his newly found church. The

spiritual revitalization he found there each week underpinned a new faith. His attitude and spirit were uplifted, and likely that changed his entire direction in life. By simply attending Sunday services, Miguel found himself with others who were supportive and who cared. He was on a better path. It is a near certainty that these differences became evident in his everyday behavior. That affects how others see and relate to you as well. Indeed, it was his mother's words from when he was a little boy that sustained Miguel through difficult days and led him back to his God. Mothers are a powerful force. Faith is a powerful force!

Stories of people "making it" in America abound. Immigrants who have come with next to nothing and gone on to establish honest worthwhile places for themselves populate every city and town. We celebrate them. Many, however, have perhaps not yet "made it" in America. They are continuing to struggle and have not yet fully created that life they so desperately seek. For them, there is hope in these stories. The experiences and positive qualities that have helped their fellow travelers will hopefully provide a roadmap for them to follow. Such accounts can provide much needed optimism.

The choice is yours. In a free society, the choice is *always* yours. We are all ultimately responsible for our decisions in choosing the paths we take. But no individual, no government, no bureaucrat can steal your future. That is America. Every day is ours to do with as we see best. Your future prosperity depends upon the actions of today, and every day is yours to take yet another step forward. Just one concluding thought about making it in America. If you think perhaps your dreams are too big, too unrealistic...think again! This is America. It can happen.

CHAPTER 7

Keeping America Beautiful

> *"Freedom is never more than one generation away
> from extinction. We didn't pass it to our children
> in the bloodstream. It must be fought for, protected,
> and handed on for them to do the same."*
>
> —RONALD REAGAN

K*eeping America Beautiful* is not simply a title. It is a call to arms for the American people; it is a plea for the awakening of our American spirit to confront the forces now seeking to undermine the institutions, liberties, and essential tenets that have made these United States the envy of the world, that shining hope that has literally raised millions of immigrants and native-born citizens to the highest standards of living in history.

The America of its founding has come to a precipice. It now faces existential dangers far greater than any in its previous history, and those dangers are *not* represented by such things as global warming, terror organizations such as ISIS, or even a COVID virus pandemic. Nor is it other major world powers like China or Russia who threaten the existence of our basic fabric. No, the threat to America is crystallizing in the most pernicious arena of all—the halls of American government, through the ever-growing socialist ideologies advocated by politicians who would suggest we materially abandon the precepts laid out in our Constitutional DNA. The threat to America comes from those who suggest we pack the Supreme Court and dismantle the all-important checks and balances system; those who propose upsetting the legislative equation by admitting partisan states on their behalf; those who would abandon the Electoral College and marginalize millions of voters living in heartland states; those who advocate the limiting of free speech and debate should they alone see such speech as "misinformation, antagonistic, or advancing positions with which they disagree." The threat to America comes from those who suggest we forge a new way forward to embrace more globalist ideologies, complete with expansive social programs overseen by a Leviathan government enabled to intrude into every aspect of personal life and property. All of these programs and our entire existence will be regulated and paid for by a staggering array of additional fees, mountainous new taxes, unending enterprise-strangling regulations, and new laws as far as the eye can see—all supposedly "for the good of the people."

Through the summer and fall of 2020, there were literally mobs of anarchists and looters destroying many of our major cities. They burned buildings, defaced property, pulled down statues, and terrorized citizens. Recently, the Capitol itself was overrun by a crowd of citizens contesting the validity of a presidential election. The anarchists have not gone away and will periodically resurface to foment anti-American dissent wherever they may find an opportunity. One might think these people would be confronted by police or other authorities; however, except for the Capitol intruders, that has far too often not been the case. Even worse, numerous governmental officials have not only stood by and done nothing but, on the contrary, many have provided their support for and stood with the rioters under the specious claim, "It is their right to protest." These officials apparently saw no distinction between riots and peaceful protests. In two major cities, "autonomous zones" were established where police and other officials were forbidden to enter under the threat of violent attack. The mob demands defunding the police or, better yet, their elimination. When such mayhem is defended or permitted by mayors or governors, our nation is in trouble. But it goes beyond that. These movements and the actions of their leaders have at times been provided tacit support and encouragement by an entire political party that stood mute! America is in trouble.

> A growing number of Americans want to tear down what it's taken us 250 years to build—and they'll start by canceling our shared history, ideals, and culture.

> Traditional areas of civic agreement are vanishing. We can't agree on what makes America special. We can't even agree that America is special. We're coming to the point that we can't even agree what the word America itself means. "Disintegrationists" say we're stronger together, but their assault on America's history, philosophy, and culture will only tear us apart.

> Disintegrationist attacks on the values that built our nation are insidious because they replace each foundational belief, from the rights to free speech and self-

> *defense to the importance of marriage and faith communities, with nothing more than an increased reliance on the government.*[1]

> Ben Shapiro,
> from How to Destroy America in Three Easy Steps (2020).

This "cancel culture" group, along with its equally dangerous anarchist mobs of Antifa and BLM activists, underlie an insidious effort to discredit and dismantle the America of its founding and vision. They would suggest that our American history is populated by people of unworthy character and personal histories such that their entire presence needs to be expunged from public view. Statues, monuments, and any element of recognition for their contribution to America's past must be torn down and "cancelled." Names of long revered historical founders are being ripped from buildings. Even though the behaviors for which these American icons are accused occurred decades or even centuries ago in a different era, the new, more enlightened view through the prism of 2020 renders the entirety of their lives, contributions, and accomplishments unacceptable. We are not talking about just a few Confederate generals who may have supported or accepted slavery; we are talking about people such as Washington, Jefferson, Madison, Roosevelt, and even Abraham Lincoln. Such misguided behaviors and beliefs are not only dishonest, but they are illogical as well. Viewing events from more than 200 years gone by through the moral optics of today lacks both rationality and validity. Yet this is what today's cancel culture now requires.

Beyond this, there are now claims that the entire nation was founded by racist, white supremacists, based upon immoral ideas. They argue the complete history of America is predicated on corrupted ideals and needs to be rewritten in such a way so as to eliminate and degrade its very existence. Sadly, to date, there has been scant resistance to these radical notions. In fact, if one listens to much of the news media, a growing number of city and state officials, and numerous corporate entities, there is unexplainable *support* for many of these ideas. Yes, America is in trouble.

Today's cancel culture seeks to break down the beautiful history that has bound America together for two and a half centuries. The vilification of historical figures and their ideas is dangerous to the America so many millions continue to love. Douglas Murray, author of *The Madness of Crowds*, made this observation:[2]

> *What kind of future do we have if we destroy our past? Has anyone who has pulled down a statue of Churchill, Lincoln, or Columbus thought to ask themselves this question? I doubt it. The presumption that we could stand in perfect judgment over the lives of historical figures is not merely foolish and unfair; it's dangerous. Consider what the statue destroyers are in effect saying. They are saying that people in history should have known what we know today. That's tantamount to saying they should have known the future. This is of course absurd. Yet more and more people believe it. Why? Simple. It's what they are taught. It is the fruit of an education system that long ago prioritized empathy over facts.*

> Douglas Murray, 2021

In his column, Patrick Buchanan expands on this question one step further and asks just how long can such counterculture behavior be permitted to go on? Is there a purpose? Is there a limit?

> We erect statues to remember, revere and honor those whom we memorialize. And what is the motivation of the people who tear them down and desecrate them?
>
> In a word, it is "hate." A goodly slice of America's young hates this country's history and the men who made it. It hates the discoverers and explorers like Columbus, the conquistadores, and colonists. It hates the Founding Fathers and the first 15 presidents, all of whom either had slaves or coexisted with the injustice of slavery. But hating history and denying history and tearing down the statues of the men who made that history does not change history.[3]

Patrick Buchanan,
How Long Will the Vandals Run Amok?

Of course, Buchanan is right; such behavior and desecration does not change history. But will it change the future is perhaps the better question. The short answer is, "quite possibly." As a prime example, there is currently a sinister movement afoot to install two completely invented (and scandalously erroneous) curriculums into our schools. One is entitled The 1619 Project and the other is Critical Race Theory. Both were totally invented and outgrowths of the Marxist school of communism, "Critical Theory." They seek to supplant the teachings of traditional American history and replace it with a contrived racist viewpoint that denigrates the entire founding and 250 years of history. It is such a drastic, ill-founded misconstruction of our nation's history that it literally attempts to alter the DNA of the nation. These programs will instruct our elementary school children that

248

America actually began when the first slave ships with twenty or so black men arrived in 1619 as opposed to our traditional 1776 signing of the Declaration of Independence. It further teaches that the Revolution was fought simply to "maintain and protect the institution of slavery" as opposed to the search for liberty and national independence. It discredits all of America's founding as based on the racist immorality of white supremacists. And that is only the beginning! Should these preposterous misconceptions and ideologies gain a foothold in our schools, and within the Washington halls of power, there is no telling what direction the future of America might take. Alarmingly, it has already been installed in many thousands of schools all across the nation. Like the many great societies that have failed in the past, they decayed and fell from within. Avoidance of this happening to our own country is the overriding challenge now facing America.

None other than Abraham Lincoln in 1838 in his address to the Young Men's Lyceum of Springfield, Illinois predicted and warned that our fragile Republic was more at risk from within than without. Now, 180 years later, his words have never rung more true.

> At what point shall we expect the approach of danger?....
> Shall we expect some transatlantic military giant, to step
> the Ocean, and crush us at a blow? Never! All the armies
> of Europe, Asia, and Africa combined...with Bonaparte for
> a commander, could not by force, take a drink from the
> Ohio, or make a track on the Blue Ridge, in a trial of a
> thousand years.... If destruction be our lot, we must

ourselves be its author and finisher. As a nation of freemen, we must live through all time, or die by suicide.[4]

Abraham Lincoln, 1838

And so it is that now this American dream faces that threat of political and economic annihilation Lincoln so feared. There exist today powerful individuals who would gladly throw America's founding documents, along with the Founding Fathers themselves, onto the trash heap of history; they are individuals who believe they alone have the innovative and better idea for a new America in a Utopian world they wish to create.

If that is to be the future, then who will be the great thinkers that will guide this nation's reinvention? It *will not* be the likes of John Locke, Edmund Burke, Adam Smith, Benjamin Franklin, George Washington, Thomas Jefferson, James Madison, Alexander Hamilton, et al. It is more likely to be Thomas Hobbes, Karl Marx, Georg Wilhelm Friedrich Hegel, Vladimir Lenin, Saul Alinsky, John Maynard Keynes, and any of a host of modern-day leftist politicians. With our suggested new founding principles relying on this group, could it be even remotely possible that their design would be an "improvement" to America?

Regardless of political stripe, these modern revisionists are the statists who daily exclaim that a massive central government be granted power to oversee every aspect of American business, place ever-increasing boundaries on individual freedom, and be given the authority to regulate almost every facet of free enterprise. This is what they see as necessary to "ensure prosperity for all." It is these new power brokers who will determine which businesses are promoted and which discouraged, how much property a person may keep and how much must be yielded to government, who will receive government distribution of property and who will give up such personal property and, further, which kind of speech is acceptable for public discourse and which is not.

What these statists propose is the total opposite of what our Founders envisioned and set into place. It is contradictory to that magnificent Constitution designed to ensure *everyone's* liberty, freedom, and pursuit of prosperity. For this very reason, the progressive left must dismantle any Constitutional tenets that stand in their way, the America of its founding, and all of the history that has gone before. *All of it must be discredited and replaced* if they are to bring about their new world socialist agenda.

More to the point of this discussion, what the progressive leftist of today promises is *not* what drew the traditional immigrant to America. It is *not* the America that even today beckons across the seas and speaks to our future immigrants. America's greatness and beauty has never been embodied in a higher minimum wage or social handouts. Men and women the world over did not abandon their homelands to reach a country promising an improved base pay for low-tier employment. Neither did they make their trip to live in the impoverished conditions given those who rely on social assistance to support themselves. For so many, they did not risk everything to now live in a socialist nation similar to what they just escaped. NO! Those coming to America's shores sought something far better—*individual liberty and economic mobility*. Prompting their decision has always been the belief that, whatever their financial circumstance when newly arrived, with industriousness and determination, a chance for real prosperity was possible. Marcus Ravage in his petition to America even back in 1909 provided our people an outsider's concern when he observed:

> *Many who were born and raised in America have forgotten what it means to be American. They have ceased to recognize its rich blessings and privileges. Perhaps they are unaware of the lofty message which America wafts across the sea. America speaks to the world!*[5]

Marcus Ravage, Romania

Ravage's words are still alive today, possibly even more so. It is not unusual that young people take for granted the gifts they have received. Perhaps it has always been that the young are less aware of the price paid for them to enjoy their current place in the world. In the society of today, how could it be otherwise? Schools rarely teach much, if anything, about our Constitution. The founding and Revolution are given short shrift at best. Civics classes are gone. Dinner tables rarely engage topics of thankfulness or conversation on our national heritage. In some quarters, patriotism itself has been branded an indicator of "white supremacy." As a result, too few recognize the importance and value of their liberty, nor can they appreciate the danger it is in. The siren's song of progressive policies, such as free everything, open societies, guaranteed incomes, equality of prosperity, and central governments that attend to every need, seduce the unappreciative and ill-informed down a path of tyranny from which, once accepted, they will never recover.

For obvious reasons, it is essential that we illuminate for *every* American the true danger of these mesmerizing lies. Left unchallenged and unchecked, our people may well find themselves slowly handing over their liberties one piece at a time to an ever-expanding government. Make no mistake; the socialists are on the march, and we are *already* allowing them to creep in like thieves in the night to steal the dream that is America!

If we are to survive Lincoln's admonition, it is critical that our youth and our nation understand how these were the very promises historically made by those such as Castro, Maduro, Hitler, Stalin, Lenin, Mussolini, and a frightening list of other socialist despots. It is *the same* message, the *same* Utopian lie! Mark Levin points this out in his book, *Ameritopia*.

> *Yet there is nothing new in deception disguised as hope and nothing original in abstraction framed as progress. A heavenly society is said to be within reach if only the individual surrenders more of his liberty and being for the general good, meaning the good as prescribed by the state.*

And he continues:

> *Utopianism is not new. It has been repackaged countless times—since Plato and before. It is as old as tyranny itself. In democracies, its practitioners legislate without end. In America, law is piled upon law in contravention and contradiction of the governing law—the Constitution.*[6]

> Mark Levin
> *Ameritopia*, 2012

Now is a time when it is essential that every family and every parent establish in their homes the real message of America, the real message of a free society. The only way to inoculate our children and young adults against false narratives is to arm them with values and understandings sufficient to dismantle the self-defeating, anti-American arguments launched at them every day. Our youth must be provided the wisdom and confidence best derived from a faith in their God-given abilities and a commitment to self-determination. Once was the time not long ago in our country's history where there was unity around the idea that America was "a good country; it was a nation based in sound Christian and ethical values." The family units were stronger, and patriotism was preached at nearly every table. It would do this country well to return to those days of family dinner table discussions and the traditions that have historically made us a great country—the traditions of individualism, gainful employment, self-reliance, enterprise, a strong reliance on family values, and a religious founding to provide a virtuous moral compass.

Of late, however, these time-honored Western values—American values—now stand in stark contrast to the deafening message of systemic inequality and personal victimhood that constantly drone on from our media, left wing pundits, and socialist advocates. Today's progressive politician always sees government as the path to universal wellbeing while traditional America has always seen the individual as the author of his own wellbeing. The socialist ideology sees government as the entity best equipped to correct the "ills" of a free market and its associated meritocracy (a chief ill being that of income inequality). Buchanan, in his book *Suicide of a Superpower*, says this about the egalitarian's notion of equality:

> *Today's drive to make us all equal is no fulfillment of the vision of the Founding Fathers.... America is embarked on an ideological crusade to achieve a utopian goal, that we*

will inevitably fail, and that, in the process, we shall ruin our country.[7]

Patrick Buchanan,
Suicide of a Superpower

"Equality," as today's statist attempts to define it, has no resemblance to the concepts outlined in our founding documents. In fact, the word "equality" does not appear in either the Constitution *or* the Declaration of Independence. The leftist of today, however, has taken the phrase, "*...all men are created equal*" to somehow mean that every individual in America should have some preconceived level of "equal prosperity in addition to *an equal right* to a decent living." These vagaries of terminology are completely out of context and are a shameful misconstruction of our Founders' intent.

The full phrase concludes with *...that they are endowed by their Creator with certain unalienable Rights, that among these are Life, Liberty, and the Pursuit of Happiness — That to secure these rights, Governments are instituted among Men, deriving their just Powers from the Consent of the Governed..."*

Nowhere does this phrase suggest equality of incomes, personal prosperity, living standards, basic healthcare, or any other such current modernization of the words. Moreover, are we to assume the confiscation of one individual's property to provide an equal standard of living to another would be something to which "The Governed" of the day might have "consented"? Is that what the Founders intended when they debated these matters at the Constitutional Convention?

Then just what was the vision of the framers as to the proper place of government in the lives of its citizens? How did they see the new nation's promise to its people in regard to their guarantee of life, liberty, and the pursuit of happiness? The key word in this discussion is the word "liberty" ; the freedom to *pursue* one's highest aspiration. To a person, the framers believed this was best accomplished in an atmosphere of *limited* government and, further, where the individual needed *protection from*, not *protection by*, an overreaching state. It must be remembered that the nation had just concluded the almost-impossible struggle to free itself from just such rule. David Limbaugh addresses this very topic in his book, *Guilty by Reason of Insanity*, when he says:

> The framers didn't idealize the state but believed the government's purpose is to protect its citizens from domestic and foreign threats, to enforce the rule of law, and to preserve order to maximize citizens' freedoms. They cherished liberty and considered it a virtuous end in itself. Today, we have lost sight of the value of liberty, as we have increasingly traded it for the illusory promise of economic security. As history has consistently shown, when you engage in this Faustian bargain you end up losing both freedom and security.[8]
>
> David Limbaugh

Today's immigrant is a particular target of the progressives' misleading narrative of victimhood in our so-called "repressive society." The statist would have them believe that, in this new world, equality (meaning their version of utopian prosperity) is unattainable without government support and regulation. Liberty and individual prosperity are attenuated by systemic inequities that unfairly limit an immigrant's ability to compete and succeed. But, as history will attest, nothing could be further from the truth. *Every* immigrant who has ever set foot on American soil has had limitless opportunity to succeed...and millions have! The road has not always been easy, but unbounded personal enterprise and persistence has resulted in countless stories of success; there will be countless more in the future if we can but maintain our Republic.

The words of Maximo Alvarez, the immigrant from Cuba who, starting from nothing, created one of most successful gas distribution companies in Florida, directly confronts the deception, lies, and pathology of the socialist promises and agenda. Viewing it firsthand in his native Cuba, he saw how others were taken in by the empty promises and left to the ruin of a nation. Coming to America was the salvation of Maximo and his entire family, yet he still pains for the destruction of his former homeland. He explained this in his address to the Republican National Convention in August 2020.

I am speaking to you today because I have seen people like this before. I've seen movements like this before. I've seen ideas like this before. I am here to tell you, I cannot let them take over our country. I heard the promises of Fidel Castro, and I can never forget all those who grew up around me, who would play with me, but who suffered, who starved, and who died because they believed those empty promises. They swallowed the communist poison pill. If you have a chance, go visit the Freedom Tower in Miami. Stop and listen. You can still hear the sounds of those broken promises: it is the sound of waves in the ocean that carry families clinging to pieces of wood, families with children who can't swim willing to risk everything to reach this blessed land. It is the sound of tears hitting the paper of an application to become an

American citizen. Most heard and liked the empty promises, but soon after they experienced the reality. Look at them. Listen to them. Learn the truth. Those false promises; spread the wealth, free education, free healthcare...defund the police? Trust a socialist state more than your family and your community? They don't sound radical to my ears...they sound familiar. When Fidel Castro was asked if he was a communist, he said he was a Roman Catholic. He knew he had to hide the truth. So, the country where I was born is gone, totally destroyed. When I watch the news in Seattle, along with Chicago, Portland, and other cities, when I see the history being rewritten, when I hear promises, I hear the echoes; echoes of the former life I never wanted to hear again. I see shadows I thought I had come out of.

My parents only wanted one person to decide my fate: me. Not some party member, not some government official, not some bureaucrat. In America, I would decide my own future. I am so grateful to America, the place where I was able to build my own American dream through hard work, determination. [The President] knows that the American story was written by people just like you and me who love our country and take risks to build our families and our futures. I may be Cuban-born, but I am 100% American. This is the greatest country in the world. I said this before; if they take away everything that I have today, it will not equal 10% of what I was given when I came to this great country of ours. They gave me the gift of freedom. Right now, it is up to us to decide our fate and to choose: freedom over oppression. I choose America. I choose freedom. I still *hear my dad, "Do not lose this place! There is no other place to go." Thank you and may God bless America!*[9]

Maximo Alvarez, Cuba
Republican National Convention Speech

Maximo's father was right. "There is no other place to go." America is the last shining destination of freedom, free enterprise, and hope on this planet. In that respect, it represents the dreams of our fathers as well as those of our nation's founders. It is that dream that demands our renewed spirit and unbending support. Any person, regardless of his ethnicity or place of birth, can rise to attain whatever level of success his skills and industriousness will allow. And, though it is true, those levels of success will differ; governments are incapable of eliminating such variance, nor is such the government's responsibility.

The responsibility for success has always been assigned to the individual. The immigrant understands this and gladly welcomes the opportunity to engage in it. For all the immigrants who ever made their way to this land and all the immigrants who will make their way in the future, it is this lure of liberty that brings them, not the assurances of government intervention. Going all the way back to Bradford's Pilgrims, it was his initial bond with the settlers to allow men the freedom to become whatever "your labours and initiatives would provide" that has brought so many to the doorstep of the United States. It has been that sacred promise, guaranteed by our founding documents, that has endured the test of time. None other than Thomas Jefferson articulated this bond to our people and the world's immigrants for what he hoped would be all time.

> *A wise and frugal government...shall restrain men from injuring one another, shall leave them otherwise free to regulate their own pursuits of industry and improvement, and shall not take from the mouth of labor the bread it has earned.*
>
> *Thomas Jefferson*
> *March 4, 1801*

Still, there are those who now see personal prosperity and family wellbeing as a responsibility for general society; it defines outcomes to be promoted by political intrusion. In fact, prosperity itself is now seen by liberal progressives, pregnant with the ideals of world communism, as a disdainful evil! To achieve their socialist ends, they are willing to ignore and discard the promises of Jefferson, Madison, and all of the nation's founding documents.

Government intervention regarding differences in individual achievement is certainly not a new issue. The Founders assumed there would be unequal distribution of wealth and property. In fact, this debate extends as far back as the Constitutional Convention. One of Madison's most famous essays, in *Federalist 10*, posited:

> *People possess different natural endowments, leading to an unequal distribution of property and conflicts of classes and interests.*

Madison further added that, in a large heterogeneous country, such conflicting interests would ultimately balance one another and check the abuses of power.

Let ambition counteract ambition.[10]

James Madison
Federalist 10, 51

F.A. Hayek, in his classic book, *The Road to Serfdom,* warns about the efforts to attain social equality by governments. He notes that no socialist movement has ever gained complete equality, and that such illusions have at best attained only somewhat more equal distributions among a few, but at what price?

> *While agreement on complete equality would answer all the problems of merit the planner must answer, the formula of the approach to greater equality answers practically none. Its content is hardly more definite than the phrases "common good" or "social welfare." It does not free us from the necessity of deciding in every particular instance between the merits of particular individuals or groups, and it gives us no help in that direction. All it tells us in effect is to take from the rich as much as we can. But, when it comes to the distribution of spoils, the problem is the same as if the formula of "greater equality" had never been conceived.*[11]

Frederick A. Hayek

History has proven both Hayek and Madison right. Governments cannot successfully or rightfully intervene to alleviate whatever ills they perceive might exist in income inequality. No government that has ever existed or ever will exist could socially engineer the equity of results. And still, socialism continues to be advanced as the best way to "level the playing field" and produce more general prosperity, even though, as Hayek observed, one cannot name even a single fully socialist or communist country to have fulfilled such promise.

Indeed, it has been free enterprise, coupled with individual effort, that has produced millions upon millions of prosperous American families, a great many of whom have notably been immigrants. It has been traditional America that has created more millionaires and lifted more people from poverty than any other country in history. These facts fly in the face of the socialist because his ideology cannot tolerate the existence of large populations of individuals who were once in limited circumstances but ultimately found success through personal enterprise and sound work ethic. Individual prosperity based on merit contradicts the statist's insistence that government and social programs offer the best path to a vibrant America. Never has this been more true than as applied to our immigrants, those men and women who arrived with little, sought a better life, *and succeeded!*

The traditional immigrant to America has always rejected the idea of "limited potential" when provided the liberty of a free society and opportunity. Listen to their stories. It is nearly always the opportunity to secure an unfettered road to prosperity that has been the great attraction. *This* was the promise of Franklin, Jefferson, Madison, and 20,000 patriots who gave their lives to give birth to this, our sacred Republic. *This* has been the promise that has made America great!

> *In my experience, almost every person who migrates to United States has come with the same drive and honest hope to succeed. They know this land is so crazy with opportunity and our system will allow them to go as far as they want as long as they will work for it. In the*

American way of life, it doesn't matter where you came from or what kind of background you have. Whatever level where you are, you are always working hard because you know that if you work hard, tomorrow you can make something special! That's the heritage of America. That's the story of America. At the end of the day, it is the real value of the America I know.

Shegitu Kebede, Ethiopia

Shegitu speaks with the voice of almost everyone who has come to call America home. It is *this* America that thousands upon thousands of immigrants have and will come to and take advantage of her unlimited possibilities for success. Like everyone, they come with dreams of a bright future. They come with a vision of what might be. It is important to understand, however, that realizing such visions and dreams, even in America, takes positive action. If there is but one lesson our nation's immigrants have learned, it has been that nothing of value was attained until they actively set and pursued such goals. Bob Mwiti of Meru, Kenya describes this concept when he is speaking about his America to others in his home village:

When I am back home, I love talking about my life here because I want to inspire someone who is maybe in the village just starting. You know, they don't know the actual facts about America, and for them it is still perhaps just a dream. I normally tell them of the real America because the picture they see is that America is a wonderful place with very few real troubles; a place where money seems to be everywhere. They don't realize how America is also somewhere where, like everywhere, you have to desperately want to succeed and work hard to have that life you are dreaming about. I tell them, "Yes, America is a nice place, an amazing country. That's why I like it, and why so many immigrants want to come here. America is a place with its own charm, and I now have things you cannot even imagine." But people need to be careful if they come to America, but have not yet taken the time to think things through. If you think you will come here and then everything will just work out and be great, then you are probably not going to succeed. When you come, you must be ambitious. Think about what you want to do. Have clear ideas on how you intend to achieve those dreams when you get to America. I tell them, "If you do this and are willing to work hard, then yes, you can succeed in America, and probably beyond what you are even imagining."

The great thing about America is this country has a lot of opportunities! You might have to search for the ones that fit you, but once you find them, you need to act. No opportunity stays there forever, so act on it as soon as you can. There are so many opportunities here you can become anything you want! You are free! You can grow as much as you want, so be ambitious. America is the greatest country in the world for this.

Bob Mwiti, Kenya, Africa

Mwiti, in these few paragraphs, captures the essence of why so many from his country have made coming to America such a priority in their lives. There is something else in his message we should not miss; immigrants who have come here and succeeded have added their value to that of America. Mwiti's suggestion to reject the status quo and take full advantage of

America's free enterprise system provides the basis on which immigrants can build a future of prosperity. Immigrant success is the byproduct of full liberty, limited government, and economic initiative for *all* of its citizens. It is this America that must be preserved. It is this America to which the immigrant, past and future, is attracted. *This* is their American dream.

Hue Van Lien is a Vietnamese immigrant who was one of the many thousands who escaped Vietnam by boat after 1975. He came with his eight-month pregnant wife by way of Malaysia when he was but 21 years of age. As he did not speak a word of English when he arrived, he spent almost eight years acclimating himself to the language, culture, and business world. After finally achieving his GED diploma, and then graduating from a technical school with a second diploma from Tools and Die, Hue was hired by Chuck Larsen at Modern Machine. Hue first worked his way up to become a plant manager, and ultimately a partner. In 1998, he was able to buy the business from the retiring Larsen family. These were accomplishments he admits he could not have envisioned happening to him, but glowingly spoke of his thankfulness to have come to this land. He too came to America with a dream.

You know, a lot of people dream about things. But, besides dreaming, I think it takes a lot of hard work and effort; yes, it takes patience and honesty to make your own American dream a success. And, you know, in a lot of other countries, Vietnam for certain, you probably don't ever have this kind of opportunity...the chance for such a dream to come true...an American dream. America is really the

place for any talented or hard-working people...a place
where they can dream of things, and it can happen!

Hue Van Lin, Vietnam

Those who have arrived as immigrants have almost universally come to find their new country more than they had ever hoped. They take pride in being Americans, and Americans they are. They will stand up for America and its great heritage without reservation, and they wonder why those who are born with all these advantages fail to see what they have in their hands.

I don't ever want to hear anything negative about this
country. All of us who came here, it was a privilege. I think
if you were born in the United States that you don't see it.
I don't want to say you take it for granted, but I don't think
you see it.

Gunta Krasts-Voutyras, Liepja, Latvia

After listening to these stories and considering the beauty of America, it is clear her greatness *did not* arise from socialist hand-out policies; it rose from the hard work, creativity, and the entrepreneurship of its people, many of them immigrants. Our freedom to pursue dreams continues to be the blessing of so many. Their voices compellingly speak to this unassailable fact. Hear what another Vietnamese refugee who came here as a boy tells his California audience about the America he found. Even though there were doubters as to how far he might go with his initial limited English-speaking ability, he surmounted the doubters and reached a level of success that surprised even him.

"If you haven't heard lately that this is the greatest country on earth, I am telling you that right now. It was the freedom and the opportunities presented to me that put me here with all of you tonight. I also remember the barriers that I had to overcome every step of the way. My high school counselor told me that I cannot make it to college due to my poor communication skills. I proved him wrong. I finished college. You see, all you have to do is to give this little boy an opportunity and encourage him to take and run with it. Well, I took the opportunity and here I am.

Quang Nguyen, Vietnam

Whatever the starting place of our immigrants, so many have risen to now enjoy a sense of true accomplishment. America's promise extends across all continents to offer the prospect of a better life and the means to pursue it. Many came with nothing but a glimmer of hope for a better future. Their voices provide a small insight as to the value of an opportunity when in the hands of someone determined enough to pursue it to the very end!

On another personal note, I'm grateful to this country for an important thing: its ethos of individualism and recognizing every individual's uniqueness enabled this bookworm and misfit to find her calling: to parlay a life-long love of reading, and of words and ideas into a career of writing and self-expression.

The best part of immigration and assimilation is that you feel like you're at a giant buffet where you get to pick, choose, and retain the best from both worlds. That's the hidden gift of all these years of change and adopting and adapting.

Saritha Prabhu, India

America has a history of more than 200 years of immigration and assimilation. It is even engraved on our currency, *E Pluribus Unum: Out of many, One*. Throughout that time, the immigrant population has ebbed and flowed as the country grew in strength and economic power. There is no question of the positive effect from peoples of other nations; they are results, it might be argued, that otherwise would never have been possible.

John F. Kennedy once said that America is a nation of immigrants, and America was built by immigrants. Whereas this is in great measure true, it is perhaps not entirely accurate. It would be better stated as, *all of us have an "immigrant past."* For many native-born Americans, however, their immigrant history may be six or seven generations ago if they have one at all, and it is unlikely they know much of their own immigration story. Additionally, it would be more appropriate to say, *immigrants were instrumental in "helping" build America.* It is true that, without the great migration during the latter 19th and early 20th centuries, the prodigious economic and industrial expansion of the country might have been significantly slowed, but it was always the combination of the immigrant *and* the native-born American to fuel that revolutionary growth. These early immigrants brought great enthusiasm, special skills, extraordinary work habits, and a strong motivation for success. Coupled with American enterprise, entrepreneurship, and opportunity, their efforts resulted in the greatest economic expansion ever known.

Examine America's history, and you will understand the source of her prominence. It has been the economic system of *free enterprise* that has fueled the engine of her greatness and, in that greatness, the prosperity of millions of immigrants as well. Yet even that foundation is now under assault. Those who would have us embrace a more socialist egalitarian approach have raised fundamental questions regarding the ideologies set out by the Constitution and our historic immigrant past. They acrimoniously question the fundamental value of America's free enterprise system where diligence and merit are rewarded, while indolence goes unrewarded. They argue such systems "unduly punish the underserved (meaning immigrants and minorities) and less fortunate." They allege that such a system is steeped in things like systemic racism and white supremacy.

To those who understand this country's history, however, the undeniable fact is that free enterprise is what most incentivized individuals of *all* ethnicities and backgrounds to work hard, rise to greater prosperity, and add value to both their family and community. Our meritocratic system offered a framework that allowed *all* people to prosper based on their own hard work and personal initiative. Those were the core values that historically provided our nation's greatest hope...and it is precisely those values that must now be preserved, regardless of what socialist politicians or others might allege. Significant others agree.

> *Americans chose a free enterprise system designed to provide a quality of opportunity, not compel a quality of results. And that is why this is the only place in the world*

where you can open up a business in the spare bedroom of your home.

Marco Rubio, Cuba

So that the record of history is absolutely crystal clear. That there is no alternative way, so far discovered, of improving the lot of the ordinary people that can hold a candle to the productive activities that are unleashed by a free enterprise system.

Milton Friedman

Whether we look at capitalism, taxes, business, or government, the data show a clear and consistent pattern: 70 percent of Americans support the free enterprise system and are unsupportive of big government.

Arthur C. Brooks

This is the only country in the world, no other country, where you can start a business in the trunk of your car, and in a very few years, with hard work, commitment, and all the core values that we learn from this very culture of ours, we can become very important to our future. We can become those people who make the next generation better than the one before. Why do you think you had to close the borders? Because everybody in the world wants to come over here. Nobody's ever forced to come over here.

Maximo Alvarez, Havana, Cuba

As these great Americans tell us, the ability to thrive and create a life of prosperity has never been greater. There is a reason for that. Mark Levin, in his book *Liberty and Tyranny*, advances one of the more cogent arguments for the inherent value of our free enterprise system. He suggests that both the native-born American *and* the immigrant are better served by free enterprise than any other system yet devised.

> *The free market is the most transformative of economic systems. It fosters creativity and inventiveness. It produces new industries, products, and services, as it improves upon existing ones. With millions of individuals freely engaged in an infinite number and variety of transactions each day, it is impossible to even conceive all the changes and plans for changes occurring in our economy at any given time. The free market creates more wealth and opportunities for more people than any other economic model.*[12]

Mark Levin

The great Winston Churchill adds his wise insight and wit regarding the superiority of a democracy over other forms of government.

> *Many forms of Government have been tried and will be tried in this world of sin and woe. No one pretends that democracy is perfect or all-wise. Indeed, it has been said that democracy is the worst form of Government except for all those other forms that have been tried from time to time....*[13]

Winston Churchill
November 1947

Let us here and now dispel a commonly advanced misconception: free enterprise based on individual effort *is not* a system that "unduly punishes the underserved." It is quite the opposite. Free markets provide the vehicle for people to rise from their existing circumstances. It allows the individual to take charge of his or her own future rather than wait for the government to cast a few crumbs off the socialist table or institute another tepid handout to further their existence. Democracy and a free market economy offer one of the greatest gifts ever conceived—*personally driven economic mobility!*

Native-born and immigrant Americans must work together to ensure the preservation of these free market values: values such as maximum liberty to allow everyone equal pursuit of personal property, the access to unfettered entrepreneurial enterprise, and America's promise of personal success based on one's God-given gifts. What better way to offer *all* the chance for a better life?

There is another pernicious idea circulating in today's media that suggests that, because so many Americans display a strong sense of national pride and historic reverence, our longstanding history of welcoming immigrants is somehow diminished. Nonsense. Do not mistake this interest in "cultural nationalism" as an indication that America wishes to close its doors to people from other lands. To read or listen to certain media outlets, one might well conclude vast segments of the population are now anti-immigrant and disdainful of opening America's doors to those who "only wish to pursue a better life." This is simply out of step with reality. America is today, and always has been, one of the most open-door, diverse, accepting countries in the world. Its people have been overwhelmingly generous and considerate of those less fortunate or who wish to come better their lot. Legal immigrants with industriousness and the desire to grow are always welcome. This is true now just as it has been throughout our history.

The new left decries our current social fabric as uncaring and insensitive to its newest immigrants. They suggest it promotes an environment where only the privileged or select few can survive and prosper. That *is not* an honest or accurate assessment of today's American culture. There are any number of personal stories here and thousands more that speak to the generosity and support newly arrived immigrants receive. It is unconscionable to permit anyone to use immigrants to divide our country into factions of winners and losers. Americans cannot allow themselves to be painted as unwelcoming xenophobes who fail to recognize the value of human life or who turn their backs on those who want to come add to America's rich legacy. That is a neo-Marxist lie that must not go unchallenged.

The identity politics of class and racial division have become a favorite tool of the progressive neo-Marxist left. Their manipulation of these divisive tactics is intended to create wounds that, left to fester, will lead to unending hatred and competing groups. Today's Marxist politicians will then use these groups to cultivate and exploit ideologies of victimhood while they simultaneously expand their desired governmental control. It is a Marxist tactic that dates all the way back to the 1930's Frankfurt Group and Henry Marcuse. It has now been brought forward into American life under the names of "social justice, political correctness, BLM, and *Critical Race Theory*"; it includes all political agendas designed to divide Americans into separate competing groups. As these political agendas grow, individual rights will inevitably wane. The only means to forestall such plans is to call out such agendas and firmly stand for the liberties granted by our magnificent Constitution and free enterprise system. Anyone who loves

America must as forcefully as their abilities allow insist on a limited government that provides native-born and immigrant alike the fullest range of economic opportunity and liberty possible.

Levin vigorously notes that statists and their dreams of Leviathan governments do not own the "right" to regulate our lives in every aspect, nor do they possess the power to usurp the liberty of the people for what they consider "a higher cause." They do not occupy such elevated moral ground that they alone should dominate the courts, legislative bodies, educational institutions, banks, and all other levers of power. He suggests that a new movement to retain and restore America's traditional values must be *established now*, lest we lose forever the America that once was.

> *This new movement must vigorously and resolutely engage socially, culturally, and politically. From the dinner table, classroom, and workplace to social clubs, churches, and synagogues...from the old media to the new media and social media, the rising generation must make itself known, heard, and felt. It must speak out, challenge, debate, rally, and protest.*[14]
>
> Marc R. Levin

We need to take pride in this America, the one of Jefferson, Washington, Madison, and the other Founders. It is and has been the beacon for our country's immigrants. It is *that* America that has been the cause of the Great Migration and every other immigration movement in our history. How do we know this? The immigrants themselves have told us. So, before we abandon everything in favor of new and empty promises from the socialist left, perhaps we could listen one last time to

Ravage's biographical appreciation of our American heritage. His words might help us more fully understand the value of what we have in our hands.

> Oh, if I could show you in America as we of the oppressed peoples see it! If I could bring home to you even the smallest fraction of this sacrifice and this upheaval, the dreaming and the strife, the agony and the heartache, the endless disappointments, the yearning, and despair—all of which must be ours before we can make a home for our battered spirits in this land of yours.
>
> We have glimpsed a vision of America, and we start out resolved that whatever the cost, we shall make her our own.[15]

> Marcus Ravage, Romania

When hearing such words, can anyone wonder about the greatness of America? Can we not have some appreciation for the wisdom of its Founding Fathers and the Constitutional Republic they gave us? To be sure, Ravage is not the only one to recognize the significance of America's original promise. Other more contemporary voices have added their stories to show us just how this land of ours has fulfilled their dreams as well.

> In 1982, I stood with a thousand new immigrants, reciting the Pledge of Allegiance, and listening to the National Anthem for the first time as an American. To this day, I

can't remember anything sweeter and more patriotic than that moment in my life.

Quang Nguyen, Vietnam 2010

Should you wish to understand how incredibly special America is to its immigrants, you might want to attend a citizenship swearing-in ceremony. You will be more inspired to rekindle your love of this country in that one event than perhaps any other. You will be stirred by these new Americans and recognize how much better we might be when we all are standing together.

Let it be made abundantly clear: America and its people continue to value the addition of new immigrants to the country and its society. Immigrants are a prized resource of new talent, added labor, and social enhancement. At this time, there are more job vacancies than we have people to fill them. American economic growth is at an unprecedented high with new businesses opening every day. Immigrants who come with a true desire to learn, work, and engage in an industrious pursuit of their dreams continue to have unlimited potential. Although in jeopardy, America's promise is still alive and prospering. But we will have to take it upon ourselves to stand against those forces that might undermine our future Republic. We each of us, all of us together, have a responsibility in that effort.

Whether you are native-born or one of the many millions who have come as immigrants and now call this land home, we must *all* act to safeguard this great land and its great institutions. No longer can we simply sit by and allow events to take their course, leaving the leadership to others. If the beauty of America is to be preserved, then the battle for its soul must be fought here and now by its modern-day patriots, we everyday people who believe she is worth preserving. America must depend on men and women with rekindled spirits who refuse to idly stand silent as our country's foundation is chipped away one piece at a time.

We have now seen firsthand what can happen when politicians are provided near unlimited power to govern if they can simply declare "a crisis." We have witnessed the loss of liberty once political leaders declare the authority to sidestep the Constitutional rights of the people. State politicians have been able to determine which businesses could open and which forced to close, which people were "essential" and which were not, what venues could be attended and which avoided. They seized control of almost every aspect of public enterprise. *This* is the level of government the neo-Marxists hope to perpetuate as far into the future as possible. However, this *is not* the government 20,000 patriots gave their lives to secure. It is not the kind of government for which our Founders labored and risked all to provide in 1788. Nor is this the kind of governance Americans of today envision for their future.

You must understand; it is we alone who stand in the way. It is we who must take up arms and man the battlements. Levin is absolutely correct in his observations on the importance of our active involvement. Your voice *can* be heard; your voice *must* be heard! As to the means by which to make your lone voice resonate, here are seven essential steps:

Actions for Modern Day Patriots

1. ***Reject the politics of division en masse.*** The neo-Marxist left would have us believe that there are two Americas, that we are divided between ourselves. There are not! There is one America, and we are *all* a part of that one country. Black or white, native-born or immigrant, man or woman, prosperous or struggling, we are *all still* Americans. We must reject their idea of victimhood and repression. We must totally rebuff the communist narrative of oppressor and oppressed. None of those ideologies represent the promise and opportunity of America. They never have. All of us, right now, have the opportunity to learn, to grow, to improve our station, and grasp hold of the American dream. The false narrative of a system set against minorities or other groups has been proven wrong hundreds of thousands of times by Americans of every stripe and color. The fact remains that, no matter what our situation today, there is always an opportunity to move to a better place tomorrow. Look again at the numerous stories related in this book; it is impossible not to see how they all came from difficult circumstances and rose to far better places today. That is why they came! There is no reason that cannot be true for any of us. In America, it has never been where we started that counted; it has always been where we ended.

On these points, we do not merely need a few voices of dissent; *we need a movement!* Similar to great movements throughout our history, such as we witnessed with civil rights, we need the millions of us who believe in the miracle that has been America to step forward into the streets, the halls of government, the schoolhouses, and every public venue available. We must wrestle back our country from the toxic ideologies and communist narratives being advanced by the neo-Marxist voices of the left. It is we who must now take the initiative to thwart the deconstructionist cancel culture. We cannot stand idle and wait for other so-called leaders or disinterested politicians to step forward in this nation's defense; it must be us! The urgency of this cannot be understated. Our movement must begin today!

2. ***Stand up for America.*** In today's politically charged environment, the voices on the left coupled with loud trumpets from the media have shouted down, marginalized, berated, and done everything in their power to silence any voice of dissent. Conservative speakers have been regularly excluded from our nation's campuses, physically attacked, thrown out of restaurants and public venues, publicly humiliated, intimidated, and shouted down. Social media outlets have banned much of conservative speech on the specious grounds that it peddles misinformation or inflammatory language; this is done as if censorship of contrarian ideas was somehow the intent of our First Amendment free speech rights. Major news network anchors have publicly called for the shutdown and elimination of competing networks who offer a different message. Some corporate cultures have made it dangerous to even voice conservative opinions, support specific ideas, or advocate particular

candidates for fear of losing one's position or living. To be sure, the concept of free speech is under withering attack. Nonetheless, it is essential that those who value traditional America, or who simply hold an opposing view to the progressive message, stand up and refuse to be bullied into silence. Know that you *are not* in the minority when you stand up for long-held American ideals; you are in the majority. Far more people want to preserve our constitutional liberties than overhaul them. It may take resolve and courage to stand strong but, if you make yourself aware of the facts supporting your position, you will be well prepared to confront any progressive ideologue; and you *must* do so! Is America not worth it?

3. ***Make yourself aware of national news and events.*** Unless you know which issues are the "central topics of the day," along with their full range of realities, you will be at a disadvantage. An oft-used practice of many on the political left is to advance simple "talking points" on every subject, then unceasingly repeat them until they become accepted. Their weakness is they often only know the talking points. If you recognize the strengths and weaknesses of important issues, it is you who will be in control of the discussion. Your understanding of "fact-based counterpoints" will embolden you to stand your ground. It may be that the other party will not change, but observant others might be influenced by the clarity of your thoughts. Whatever the outcome, you can be proud of having stood up for what you believe and your refusal to be bullied.

4. ***Make America a part of your home.*** Discuss issues of importance about our country with your family and children. Whether at the dinner table, family gathering, or just casual time, take the opportunity to occasionally discuss the history and values of America. Reinforce the character that makes us America. Call out those (Republican or Democrat) who you see as undermining the best interests of our country. It is abundantly clear that this task cannot be left to government schools, colleges and universities, or mainstream media. If anything, those institutions are more likely to lead in the *wrong* direction. To provide sound American values to our children, parents and family must take up that cause. Rebuilding America's future begins with rebuilding America's promise and virtues at the dinner tables in our homes.

5. ***Take back the education of our children!*** You read correctly, "take back." Of all the action steps, this may well be one of the most important. For the last nearly three decades, the educational agenda for our children has been increasingly dictated by federal and state influences that have led to a steady erosion of our national history, patriotism, and appreciation of core American values. Nothing could be more demonstrative of this fact than the recent introduction of the outrageous *1619 Project, Critical Race Theory,* and any of a number of other social engineering ideologies now so common in our public school curricula. We currently have two generations of children who have too often been rigorously indoctrinated into the belief that America is a fundamentally flawed nation, and we are

an incredibly racist society that preys upon specific minority groups and those of limited financial resources. Deconstructionist teachings are on the attack!

There is a reason for this assault on our national heritage. To advance the neo-Marxist ideologies for their new globalist agenda of big government and national socialism, the planners must first undermine and eradicate allegiance to the old. How better to do this than poison the minds of our youth? *This agenda is already here and accelerating at a frightening pace; it will get worse, and we cannot allow it to continue!* Take the time to examine the history books your son or daughter is studying. Do they provide a sound, positive view of America's founding, or do they take your children in the opposite direction? There are now numerous curricula in circulation that literally teach young learners to hate their own country. Be sure your school's curriculum is not one of them. If it is, you must organize other parents and flood your local Board of Education meetings en masse. You may even identify a slate of candidates who better reflect your values to run in the next BOE election. *You* must make a stand and rise as one voice to take back the education of *your* children!

The first and most fundamental action we must initiate is school choice. We must take to the battleground in numbers and demand that whatever dollars are behind each child's education, such money must follow the child, not be solely directed to state-run government schools. It is your tax money. Whether it is school choice, voucher programs, home schooling initiatives, or some other system, the money must stay with the student so that *every* parent has the opportunity to decide which school offers the education they seek for their children. Demand it and do not take one step backward! The option to select an alternative to government-run schools cannot be limited to only the political class, privileged, and well-off; the same opportunity must be *available to all!* When the marketplace enters the equation, local school boards, teacher unions, and administrators will find themselves forced to be more attentive and responsive. If they are not, you would then have the resources to pursue other possibilities.

Our children and this country are too important. You must ask yourself this question: *If we do not instill in our children the love of our country's heritage and founding principles, then how can our Republic be expected to survive?* Our nation's enduring values must be instilled in our youth, or they will surely be lost forever.

6. ***Take a role in both local and national politics.*** Whether local or national, it is critically important who gets elected to political office. From boards of education to local government, to the statehouse, to national elections; it matters! One need not run for office or be a prominent voice in political campaigns to have a role in our election process. There are many other opportunities such as call-in radio programs, voter registration drives, town hall meetings, get-out-the-vote phone calls, transporting people to voting venues, talking to our neighbors, or even just placing a

sign on our lawns. Choose to participate and understand your role is of vital unimportance.

7. ***VOTE! VOTE! VOTE!*** Whether it is a national, state, or local election, become informed about the candidates and their proposed policies. You must make your vote count in every election. Understandably, there are many, after this last presidential election, who feel that perhaps their vote no longer counts; political operatives and unscrupulous voting precincts have undermined and rendered the entire system unreliable. Progressive statists seeking expanded power would like nothing more than for that perception to take hold and keep you home, keep you away from the ballot box, and keep you quiet. NO! We are not at liberty to allow such thinking, however strong, to govern our actions. We must instead fight to hold our elected legislators and courts responsible to take whatever action necessary to restore faith in our election methods. Require them to make the procedures more transparent, more verifiable, and more accurate so *everyone* can and will have full confidence in the election process. It must be *demanded* of them if they wish to remain in office! This is not a right-left or Democratic-Republican issue. This is an American issue! If there is to be *any* confidence in American government, any chance of maintaining our sacred Republic, then *everyone* must have full confidence in the honesty and fairness of our electoral process. America's promise literally hangs on this central necessity, and it is in serious jeopardy!

Beyond this, take the time to identify the candidates who most promote traditional American values and are worthy of your support. But here must be added an important caveat:

CAUTION: Choose and ascribe your loyalties **not** to one specific individual or party, but rather ground your allegiance on the policies and ideas you think best for America. Choose your candidate based on his or her recorded **actions**, not his or her lofty promises. Do this regardless of political stripe, race, or ethnicity. Choose those who promote values embodied in our founding principles: individual liberty vs. expansionist government; national interest vs. personal power; moral purpose and virtuous ideals vs. secular hegemony and diminished religiosity; meritocracy vs. universal wealth redistribution. If every person who loves America were to employ such standards in a free and accurate election, there would be little way our Constitutional Republic could be undermined.

These steps *are not* optional. It has been argued that America will likely always be here, and perhaps that is so. But if the magnificent America we grew up in is to survive, then its advocates must today, right now, be its defenders. If we are to keep America from committing what Victor Davis Hanson calls "cultural suicide," then *we* must take the necessary steps of renewal. Perhaps, more than ever, we need America's newest citizens, its immigrants, to stand up and proudly declare the kind of America *they* want for *their* children and grandchildren.

Hansen reminds us of historical precedents and underscores the forces capable of bringing down flourishing societies. Rome, Greece and, more recently, the Soviet Union and Venezuela all declined as a result of corruption and disregard for their own history and values. They decayed from within. He describes how institutions such as Hollywood, Big Tech, and the ever-increasing, self-absorbed WOKE countercultures such as Antifa and its "cancel culture" allies are blindly devouring our history, patriotic values, and identity. He summarizes his concerns for the nation should we not rediscover a respect for our rich history.

> At this late date, all that matters is that the country itself learns from these suicidal examples and heals itself. If the U.S. is not to become an extinct Easter Island, it must rediscover a respect for its past, honor for the dead who gave us so much, the desire to invest rather than spend, and the need for some sense of transcendence.
>
> If we do not believe that what we do today has consequences for our children after we are gone, there are ancient existential forces in the world that will intervene.
>
> And it won't be nice.[16]
>
> Victor Davis Hansen, 2020

Ask yourself this question: If we cut ourselves off from our roots, destroy our history, and abandon our economic system, along with all that has nourished our nation's vitality and growth for more than two centuries, how can we expect the America of its founding to have any hope of continued survival? How do we avoid becoming that "extinct Easter Island" of which Hansen forewarns? The sad answer is, we cannot. It is we who must now decide her fate. Half measures and tepid allegiance will not suffice. We, the people, must proudly stand together and yet again boldly chart the road forward ...immigrant and native-born alike.

As our stories and this book draw to a close, we can all take heart in the knowledge that we live in the freest, most vibrant, beautifully crafted nation ever conceived. In spite of its flaws, upon which we still must labor, let us not lose sight of all the good and all the enduring beauty that is America. Regardless of our color, our race, our ethnic background, or whether we are native-born or immigrant, we are Americans. With all our differences, this is still our country, and it is we who must carry her torch, we who hold her destiny in our hands.

America has always been a proud nation, proud of its great history and proud of its place in the world. She is also proud of her long-standing immigrant heritage. She invites others who might also wish to find their own future on her shores. Only two things can be asked of those who come. First, that he or she does so through one of the many legal channels available. They are currently expanding. Yes, it might take a bit longer. Yes, it requires more work. But the benefits of legal immigration to a place such as America is worth the effort. The many comments and stories within these pages attest to that truth. Second, when you arrive, you do so with the *determination* to work, become conversant in the language, and be a credit to your new community. It is through these virtues that both you *and* America will be enhanced. We have much to offer one another. If you do these things, there is no limit to the heights you might climb.

A last question that might be asked is, why are there only stories and features of success in these pages? Why is there no attention paid to the failures as well? The reason is not complicated. *There are no "failures."* Certainly, there are many who have not yet fulfilled their American dream; they have not yet attained that level of success or prosperity for which they had hoped. But their stories are not yet over. Their journeys are still in progress. With continued determination, perseverance, and allegiance to that indomitable immigrant spirit of success, their lives' narratives, too, will one day take their place among the many chronicled here. Ultimately, they will also be counted along with the hundreds of thousands of others who have found a better life for themselves and their families in this great land. Why? Simple. *This is still AMERICA THE BEAUTIFUL!*

CHAPTER 8

America's Immigrant Contributors

> *Hold fast to dreams, for if dreams die,*
> *life is a broken-winged bird that cannot fly.*
>
> —LANGSTON HUGHES

Many immigrants have contributed to the contents of this book. They (along with the many millions of others who have their own experiences and values) are, without exception, great Americans who embody the very spirit and virtues envisioned by our Founders. It was inspiring to hear and share their stories. In order to give greater context to you, the reader, some of them are pictured here along with a short information segment. They are arranged alphabetically. In some cases, no picture was available, or the person indicated they preferred no picture. Those included here, as well as those who are only quoted in the book, represent just a small portion of the numbers I met over the two and a half years of the project but who also provided their experiences or thoughts.

To all of them, I owe my unending "thank you" for their inspiring ideas.

Maximo Alvarez, Havana, Cuba

Maximo escaped Cuba with his family and came to the United States in 1961 at the age of 13. He began his working life as an employee of Cities Service Company (Citgo). After eight years, and against the advice of almost everyone, he convinced Citgo to let him buy four failing service stations in south Florida to form Sunshine Gasoline. He installed his own business model based on honesty, helping others succeed, and establishing business relationships that could be started on a handshake. He was convinced that, between fairness to others and persistent hard work, his businesses would eventually flourish. He became a distributor for his previous employer. His company now supplies 515 gas stations while owning 360 of them. He is president of Sunshine Gasoline Distributors, one of the largest gasoline distributors in Florida.

Kim Oksun-Comazzi, Suwon, Korea

Kim came to America as the wife and American Air Force serviceman. She arrived in New Jersey and initially worked in several jobs including positions with Honeywell Corporation. She ultimately decided she wanted to own her own business and, with her husband, opened a small doughnut shop. The business did well, and when they sold it, she was able to open a restaurant in the western part of New Jersey. Currently, she is retired and living with her husband, Bob, in the Villages, Florida.

Kathryn Court, London, England

Ms. Court came to America following a brief period in the UK publishing industry. After persevering through more than sixty attempts to find a position in the U.S. publishing industry, she was finally hired by Penguin Books. In a relatively short period of time, she rose through the corporate structure, during which time she worked with a number of other outstanding luminaries in the industry. She ultimately rose to become the president of Penguin Books and one of most celebrated women leaders in American publishing. She is now retired.

Victor Diaz, Honduras

NO
PHOTO
AVAILABLE

Victor arrived in the United States and through the help of family found his initial employment in a Chinese restaurant. He quickly moved up to the food preparation line and then on to night manager. His ambition to become a full partner in his own restaurant led him to a later position in a Mexican restaurant. It was here that he worked for 16 years and ultimately realized his ambition to become a partner. Victor now owns two restaurants of his own and is looking to expand to still another location.

Joseph DiMauro, Sortino, Sicily

Joe DiMauro came to America in October 1960 with his older sister. They were met by their aunt at the ship when it arrived in New York City and taken to her home in the Bronx where they lived for the next 14 years. Although he spoke no English, Joe was enrolled in one of New York City's public schools. He made his life working for MetLife Insurance and is currently retired.

Sly Silviu-Christian Dumitru, Bucharest, Romania

Sly immigrated to Florida when he was in his late teens. After moving through several jobs that were not what he considered long-term opportunities, he moved to Colorado. Again, he found employment, but nothing sufficiently interesting to make it a career. He then made the decision to join the Army and served our country in both Iraq and Afghanistan. Upon leaving the Army, he returned to the United States where he went on to attend college and earn both his BA and MA degrees. Upon graduation, Sly worked for a time as a university teacher and then as an Android software development engineer. He is now married and works for the Oak Ridge National Laboratories in Tennessee.

Kirsten Langoy-Epley, Stavanger, Norway

Kirsten was brought by her parents to America when she was only nine years old. The family moved to Chicago, where her father became a tugboat captain on the Great Lakes. Kris, as she is called now, studied accounting for two years, and after marriage became an accountant in Illinois. She and her husband raised their family and are now retired, living in Tennessee.

Said Fadloullah, Morocco

Said came from a large family in Morocco and arrived in America with almost no English-speaking or technical skill. Initially, the only work he could find was in a fast food restaurant and then busboy in a large Orlando hotel. After overcoming numerous roadblocks, he moved from busboy to bellman, where he had improved financial chances. Said saw even more rewarding future prospects and left the hotel industry for real estate sales. His strong record of success in public relations and marketing led to his elevation to Director of Sales VIP at Sheraton Vistana Resorts, where he works still today.

Maria Flores-Guerra, Peru

Maria came at the age of 18 because she had wanted to go to America since early childhood. Once Maria arrived, she took on a wide variety of occupations while continuing to renew her visas until she could obtain her Green Card. Today Maria has become a citizen and lives with her husband in Tennessee, where she is employed by Jewelry TV.

Shegitu Kebede, Ethiopia

After losing her parents at age five and then being placed in a Catholic orphanage, Shegitu grew into her teens under the protection of the missionaries. When the Ethiopian government was overthrown during the civil war, the mission was forced to close. Shegitu and her brother found themselves on their own. Her first goal was to simply escape Ethiopia and reach Kenya, where there were refugee camps. Over the next year, she made her way across dangerous ground until she finally reached a refugee settlement. As part of a United Nations program, she was granted asylum in the West and relocated to North Dakota. Ms. Kebede soon moved to Minneapolis and initially worked in the commercial cleaning industry until she was able to open her own restaurant business. Today, Shegitu operates the humanitarian organization she founded, *Women at the Well International*. This organization's aim is to improve the livelihood of refugees and bring awareness to the plight of refugees around the world.

Hue Van Lien, Vietnam

Hue was one of the many boat people who escaped Vietnam with his family shortly after the Vietnam war and came to the United States. He spent a number of years working, learning English, getting his GED, and then attending machining school. After moving from Iowa to Minnesota, Hue was hired by Modern Machine, where he rose through the company to ultimately become a partner and then its owner. Hue is currently in partial retirement and his daughter Nancy has become president of the company.

Myo Thwe Linn, Myanmar (Burma)

In 2010, at the age of 37, Myo came to the United States as part of the Health and Human Services Refugee Program. Through his contacts in the Burmese militia, he was able to obtain refugee status and immigrated to Michigan. Myo is currently employed in a full-time job, and also drives for Uber. He hopes that one day he might enter college in pursuit of an even better career. For Myo, he has found America to be a country where he has been able to live, work, and find success in safety. He has explained that his new life has only just begun and he is looking forward to "things getting better each year."

Bob Mwiti, Kenya, Africa

After failing numerous times to get a United Kingdom visa, Bob Mwiti came to the United States on a student visa for Indiana University of Pennsylvania. Upon graduation, he went for additional training in the Oracle Systems and worked in this industry as a consultant. He used this knowledge to open his own business, Appstec America, in Tampa, Florida. His company is designed to assist highly qualified foreign students gain entry to the United States and establish successful careers in the technology field.

Ingrid Kunde Kliefoth, Stuttgart, Germany

Ingrid was a child during WWII and, after being separated from her parents, lived with her aunt and uncle in a refugee camp in Germany. After the war, she attended business school and ultimately became an executive secretary. On the advice of a friend, Ingrid moved to Sweden where she eventually accepted a position caring for the children of a Swedish ambassador's family. When the ambassador was assigned to Washington, DC, Ingrid accepted an offer to come to the United States as part of the Swedish Embassy. Although she spoke no English when she arrived, she soon learned the language, married, and became a United States citizen. Currently, she is retired and lives in Tennessee.

Joseph Pell (Yosel Epelbaum), Biala Podlaska, Poland.

Joseph Pell, born Yosel Epelbaum, had an unimaginably dangerous teenage life. His family was Jewish and, during WWII, his father and two brothers were compromised, arrested by the German SS, and later murdered. His entire family became separated in the coming years and he found himself painfully alone. Joseph served as a partisan in the resistance movement, where his specialty was destroying railroads. After the war, he made his living in the black market and by smuggling goods across borders. In time, he was convinced by a friend to come to America where he made his way to California and opened the highly successful Shirley's Ice Cream Store. Sometime later, he began buying and developing properties, which became his passion. Joseph Pell went on to become one of Northern California's most respected and successful developers. His full story can be read in his autobiography, Taking Risks.

Saritha Prabhu, India

Saritha arrived in 1992 at the age of 27. Originally living in Orlando and Dallas, she describes her assimilation into America in how she was able to "...parlay a life-long love of reading, and of words and ideas into a career of writing and self-expression" into a career in journalism. She is currently a USA TODAY NETWORK Tennessee columnist.

Sorin Ranghiuc, Galti, Romania

Born in Romania under communist rule and working in a company producing computer motherboards to be shipped overseas, Sorin came to the conclusion that his future would be better served by living in the West. After making a stressful journey through five different countries to reach the United States, Sorin now works independently as a successful business owner in the construction industry. He has been in the country since 2002 and lives with his wife and children in the Nashville, Tennessee area.

Marcus Ravage, Vaslui, Romania (1909)

Marcus immigrated to the United States near the turn of the 20th century and published his autobiography, The Making of an American, in 1917. Starting with nothing and living in a primarily Romanian ghetto of New York City, Marcus initially found work as a street peddler, then a "sleever" in a shirt manufacturing company, and then as a barman in a saloon. As he gradually gained his English-speaking ability, he began taking classes, going to lectures, and joining discussion groups, which added important qualities necessary to reach success in his new country. With borrowed money and a small scholarship, he was ultimately able to attend the University of Missouri where he earned his bachelor's degree. Marcus went on to become a prolific writer and noted speaker regarding Jewish issues in America and the world.

Miguel Reyes, Mexico

Miguel Reyes was born in Mexico and immigrated to the United States in 2016 to live with his uncle and father. As he spoke no English, he struggled for many weeks to find work in the Orlando, Florida area. On the advice of friends, he began applying to businesses that had Spanish-speaking owners where he finally found employment as a busboy and floor person in a local Mexican restaurant. He has now worked his way up to become a sous-chef in the restaurant where he received his initial job. He continues to work and live in the Orlando area today.

Ilya Somin, Leningrad, Russia

Born in the Soviet Union in 1973, Ilya immigrated from Russia with his parents in 1979. Coming to America by way of such places as Israel, Austria, and Italy, he finally arrived in the United States. His early schooling was marked by very modest progress, with his only real interest being the art of debate. Because he was an insatiable reader and highly competitive, he became one of the United States' best debaters, but did not academically bloom until his later high school years. The turning point came when Ilya decided he wanted to attend one of the better colleges in New England. That aspiration invigorated his educational ambitions and ultimately led him to a B.A. in political science and history from Amherst College, an M.A. in political science from Harvard University, and a J.D. from Yale Law School. Ilya is currently a law professor at George Mason University and an adjunct scholar at the Cato Institute. He is also author of the book, Free to Move: Foot Voting, Migration, and Political Freedom, published by Oxford University Press, 2020.

Yassin Terou, Syria

Coming from Syria in 2011, Yassin came to America with nothing. When he arrived, he spoke no English and had no means of employment. He went to his Imam at the local mosque and asked if there was some employment he could have. Unfortunately, there was nothing for him, so he asked if he would be allowed to make sandwiches and sell them outside the mosque. This was permitted and he set up a small stand. From that humble start, Yassin grew his little sandwich business into a small store front and, ultimately, Yassin's Falafel House, which has gone on to receive numerous national awards. Yassin currently operates two locations and has been voted the 2019 Person of the Year.

Gunta Krasts-Voutyras

Living in a small village in Latvia during the WWII German occupation, Gunta and her family were taken prisoner and shipped to Germany where they were put to work in a war materiels factory. Once the war concluded, she immigrated with her family to the United States and, on a March evening in 1949, they disembarked in Boston, Massachusetts. Her family made their initial home in the Bronx, then moved to Long Island, and eventually her father purchased an older home in Lake Champlain, New York. After living there for a large portion of her life, Gunta moved to Whitehall to take care of her ailing mother. Gunta continues to operate a small online sweater design business, Gunta Collections, LTD. She is proud to display the framed copy of her citizenship certificate in her home.

END NOTES

CHAPTER 1: Becoming America

1. Medved, Michael, The American Miracle: Divine Providence in the Rise of the Republic (New York: Crown Publishing Group, 2016), 360

2. Excerpts from William Bradford's Journal: Of Plymouth Plantation. 20 June 2019. Microsoft Word - EXCERPTS-OF PLYMOUTH PLANTATIONL.docx (quia.com)

3. Limbaugh, Rush (2018). "The true story of Thanksgiving." https://www.rushlimbaugh.com/daily/2018/11/21/the-true-story-of-thanksgiving-2/, retrieved November 24, 2020.

4. Rutman, Darrett B., John Winthrop's Decision for America: 1629 (Philadelphia/New York/Toronto: J. B Lippincott Company, 1975), 3

5. Stedman, Edmund Clarence and Ellen Mackay Hutchinson, John Winthrop, "A Model of Christian Charity," in A Library of American Literature: Early Colonial Literature, 1607-1675, eds. (New York: 1892), 304-307.

6. Medved, Michael, The American Miracle: Divine Providence in the Rise of the Republic (New York: Crown Publishing Group, 2016), 40, 41

7. Medved, Michael, The American Miracle: Divine Providence in the Rise of the Republic (New York: Crown Publishing Group, 2016), 78

8. Lillback, Peter and Jerry Newcombe, George Washington's Sacred Fire (Bryn Mawr, PA: The Providence Forum, 2006), 161, 162

9. Bennett, William J., America: The Last Best Hope (Nashville: Nelson Current, 2006), 63

10. Unger, Harlow Giles, Lion of Liberty: Patrick Henry (Cambridge, MA: Da Capo Press, 2010), 59

11. Peabody, Selim, American Patriotism: Speeches, Letters and Other Papers which Illustrate the Foundation, the Development, the Preservation of the United States of America (New York, New York, John Alden Publishers 1881), 24-28

12. Kidd, Thomas S., Patrick Henry: First Among Patriots, (Philadelphia: Basic Books, 2011), 67, 88

13. Bennett, William J., America: The Last Best Hope (Nashville: Nelson Current, 2006), 77

14. Andrews, Evan. "History Stories." Patrick Henry's Liberty or Death Speech. 22 Mar. 2015. https://www.history.com/news/patrick-henrys-liberty-or-death-speech-240-years-ago

15. Ibid..

16. Unger, Harlow Giles, Lion of Liberty: Patrick Henry (Cambridge, MA: Da Capo Press, 2010), 100, 101

17. Bubis, Dan and Jax, Revolutionary War and Beyond, 2008-2020. George Washington Quotes 1775-1776 (revolutionary-war-and-beyond.com)

18. O'Reilly, Bill and David Fisher, Legends and Lies: The Patriots (New York: Henry Holt and Company, 2016), 55

19. McCullough, David, John Adams (New York: Simon and Schuster, 2001), 109

20. Meacham, Jon, Thomas Jefferson: The Art of Power (New York: Random House , 2012), 99

21. Bennett, William J., America: The Last Best Hope (Nashville: Nelson Current, 2006), 82

22. Meacham, Jon, Thomas Jefferson: The Art of Power (New York: Random House , 2012), 102, 103

23. ibid.

24. Levin, Mark, Ameritopia (New York: Threshold Editions, 2012), 108

25. Rubenstein, David M., The American Story: Conversations with Master Historians (New York: Simon and Schuster, 2019), 108

26. ibid.

27. ibid, 109

28. ibid.

29. Medved, Michael, The American Miracle: Divine Providence in the Rise of the Republic (New York: Crown Publishing Group, 2016), 55

30. ibid.

31. Fitzpatrick, J. C. ed, The Writings of George Washington (Washington, D.C.: U.S. Government Printing Office, 1931 Vol 3), pp 124-125

32. McCullough, David, 1776 (New York: Simon and Schuster, 2005), 243

33. Straub, Steve. Thomas Paine," The American Crisis, No. 1, December 19, 1776," 13 May 2011. Thomas Paine, "The American Crisis, No. 1," December 19, 1776 (thefederalistpapers.org)

34. O'Reilly, Bill and Martin Dugard, Killing England (New York: Henry Holt & Company, 2017), 135

35. McCullough, David, 1776 (New York: Simon and Schuster, 2005), 271, 272

36. ibid.

37. O'Reilly, Bill and Martin Dugard, Killing England (New York: Henry Holt & Company, 2017), 136-139

38. O'Reilly, Bill and David Fisher. Legends and Lies: The Patriots (New York: Henry Holt & Company, 2016), 144,145.

39. Ferling, John, Almost a Miracle, The American Victory in the War of Independence, 9 August 2014, Almost a Miracle | Twistification

40. Bennett, William J., America: The Last Best Hope (Nashville: Nelson Current, 2006), 100, 101

41. O'Reilly, Bill and Martin Dugard, Killing England (New York: Henry Holt & Company, 2017), 272

42. Rackove, Jack, Revolutionaries: A New History of the Invention of America (Boston and New York: Houghton Mifflin Harcourt, 2010), 270

43. Wood, Gordon S., Empire of Liberty: A History of the Early Republic, 1789-1815 (Oxford, England: Oxford University Press, 2009), 7

44. Lillback, Peter and Jerry Newcombe, George Washington's Sacred Fire (Bryn Mawr, PA: The Providence Forum, 2006), 292

45. Ibid.

46. Wood, Gordon S., Empire of Liberty: A History of the Early Republic, 1789-1815 (Oxford, England: Oxford University Press, 2009), 9

47. Chernow, Ron, Alexander Hamilton (New York: Penguin Group, 2004), 226

48. Ibid.

49. Prager, Denis. *Hamilton: The Man Who Invented America.* Prager U, Nov. 2018, PragerU - Hamilton: The Man Who Invented America Accessed 5 Aug 201

50. Unger, Harlow Giles, Lion of Liberty: Patrick Henry (Cambridge, MA: Da Capo Press, 2010), 187-189

51. Ibid.

52. Bennett, William J., America: The Last Best Hope (Nashville: Nelson Current, 2006), 115

53. McClay, Wilfred M., Land of Hope: An Invitation to the Great American Story (New York: Encounter Books, 2019), 71

54. Bennett, William J., America: The Last Best Hope (Nashville: Nelson Current, 2006), 118, 119

55. Medved, Michael, The American Miracle: Divine Providence in the Rise of the Republic (New York: Crown Publishing Group, 2016), 113

56. Ibid.

57. Ibid.

58. Cheney, Lynne, James Madison: A Life Reconsidered (New York: Viking, 2014), 150

59. Ibid, 155

60. Isaacson, Walter, Benjamin Franklin: An American Life (New York: Simon and Schuster, 2003), 458

61. Medved, Michael, The American Miracle: Divine Providence in the Rise of the Republic (New York: Crown Publishing Group, 2016), 116

62. Isaacson, Walter, Benjamin Franklin: An American Life (New York: Simon and Schuster, 2003), 459

63. Bennett, William J., America: The Last Best Hope (Nashville: Nelson Current, 2006), 126, 127

64. Ellis, Joseph J., American Creation: Triumphs and Tragedies at the Founding of the Republic (New York: Alfred A. Knopf, 2007), 114-117

65. Levin, Mark, Ameritopia, (New York: Threshold Editions, 2012), 142-144

66. Cheney, Lynne, James Madison: A Life Reconsidered (New York: Viking, 2014), 175

67. Ibid, 176-177

68. Ibid.

69. Ibid.

70. Medved, Michael, The American Miracle: Divine Providence in the Rise of the Republic (New York: Crown Publishing Group, 2016), 121

71. Kennedy, John F., A Nation of Immigrants (New York: Harper Row, 2008), 68

CHAPTER 2: Coming to America

1. Prabhu, S., (2019 July 15). *My immigration story is personal but it is also universal.* The Knoxville News Sentinel. After immigration comes assimilation. US offers best of both worlds. (usatoday.com)

2. Ravage, M. E., *An American in the Making: The Story of an Immigrant* (Charleston, SC: Nabu Press, 2010), 200

3. Ibid.

4. Ibid.

5. Lhamon, Greg (2015). "Looking at America through the eyes of an immigrant." https://greglhamon.com/looking-at-america-through-the-eyes-of-an-immigrant/, retrieved November 11, 2020.

6. Tingley, Ken (2020). FLASHBACK: An American Journey, FLASHBACK: An American journey | Local | poststar.com. Accessed 22 April 2021

7. Ibid.

8. Downs, Hugh, *My America: What My Country Means to Me* (New York: Scribner, 2002), 135-138

9. Ibid.

10. Alvarez, Maximo (2020). Address to the Republican National Convention. 24 August 2020, https://www.cnn.com/videos/politics/2020/08/25/maximo-alvarez-florida-businessman-rnc-2020-speech-full-vpx.cnn/video/playlists/2020-rnc-night-1/. Accessed 25 August 2020.

11. Somin, Ilya (2010). *A Road to Freedom – Antonin Scalia Law School.* Microsoft Word - HIAS Memoir - Revised Version 2 - November 2010.doc (gmu.edu)

12. Ibid.

13. Ibid.

CHAPTER 3: Journeys In America

1. Kebede, Shegitu, *Visible Strengths, Hidden Scars* (Hennepin House: Minneapolis, 2011), 37-39

2. Harris, Liz, Joseph Pell, 95, Reflects on a Life of Struggle and Triumph. Holocaust survivor Joseph Pell reflects on a life of struggle and triumph (jweekly.com), 24 Jan 2020

3. Ibid.

4. Ibid.

5. Terou, Yassin, Welcoming Refugees Like Me. *Knoxville News Sentinel.* Welcoming refugees like me is what makes America great (knoxnews.com), 20 Jun 2019,

6. Powerful Women in Publishing: Rising to the Top. March 2001, https://www.c-span.org/video/?163841-1/powerful-women-publishing-rising-top, Accessed 19 August 2019

CHAPTER 4: Realities In America

1. Ravage, M.E., *An American in the Making: The Story of an Immigrant* (Charleston, SC: Nabu Press, 2010), 50

2. Prabhu, S., (2019 July 15). My immigration story Is personal but it is also universal. *The Knoxville News Sentinel.* After immigration comes assimilation. US offers best of both worlds. (usatoday.com)

3. Lhamon, Greg (2015). "Looking at America through the eyes an immigrant." https://greglhamon.com/looking-at-america-through-the-eyes-of-an-immigrant/, retrieved November 11, 2020.

4. Ibid.

5. Bennett, Bill. "The Gates Test," *National Review Online.* 9 Nov 2009. The Gates Test|, National Review

6. Ravage, M. E., *An American in the Making: The Story of an Immigrant* (Charleston, SC: Nabu Press, 2010), 78

7. Carpenter, Tabitha and Anne Kosvanec, From the Promised Land: My Country, Chapter XI. (upenn.edu) 15 Aug 2020

8. Ibid.

CHAPTER 5: Confronting Obstacles In America

1. United States Government. US Visa Guide: The Different Types Of US Visas You Should Know About, *US Visa Guide: 10 Different Types Of US Visas You Must Know* (career-guider.com). Accessed 4 December 2020.

2. Haley, Nikki, <u>Can't Is Not an Option,</u> (London: Penguin Books, Ltd., 2012), 16, 17

3. Ravage, M. E., *An American in the making: The story of an immigrant* (Charleston, SC: Nabu Press, 2010), 91-93

4. Ibid, 266

CHAPTER 6: Making It In America

1. Kimbriel, Dean. Our Favorite Inspirational Messages About Immigrants, *Our Favorite Inspirational Messages About Immigrants - Coyote Legal*, 7 Jun 2021

2. Murray Charles, *Coming apart: The state of White America, 1969-2010* (New York: Crown Forum, 2012), 131

3. Ravage, M. E., *An American in the Making: The Story of an Immigrant* (Charleston, SC: Nabu Press, 2010), 130, 131

4. Balmaseda, Liz. Great Immigrants, Great Stories: Three Tales of Becoming an American. Carnegie Corporation of New York, Great Immigrants, Great Stories: Three Tales of Becoming an American | *HuffPost* 19 Jul 2013

CHAPTER 7: Keeping America Beautiful

1. Shapiro, Ben, *How to Destroy America in Three Easy Steps* (New York: Harper Collins and Broadside Books, 2020), back cover.

2. Murray, Douglas (2021). No future: No future: No past, *No Past, No Future | PragerU*, accessed February 7, 2021

3. Buchanan, Patrick A. (2020, June 23). How long will the vandals run amok? Retrieved from https://buchanan.org/blog/how-long-will-the-vandals-run-amok-138741 (2020, August 1).

4. Brewster, Todd, *Lincoln's Gamble: The Tumultuous Six Months That Gave America the Emancipation Proclamation and Changed the Course of the Civil War* (New York: Scribner & Sons, 2014), 4

5. Ravage, M. E., The American Melting Pot. Thoughts — blog — W E R O (werokitchen.com), 7 Feb 2017

6. Levin, Mark, *Ameritopia* (New York: Threshold Editions, 2012), 5, 22

7. Buchanan, Patrick A., *Suicide of a Superpower: Will America Survive to 2025?* (New York: St. Martin's Press, 2011), 191

8. Limbaugh, David, *Guilty by Reason of Insanity* (Washington, DC: Regnery Publishing, 2019), 178

9. Alvarez, Maximo (2020). Address to the Republican National Convention. 24 August 2020, https://www.cnn.com/videos/politics/2020/08/25/maximo-alvarez-florida-businessman-rnc-2020-speech-full-vpx.cnn/video/playlists/2020-rnc-night-1/. Accessed 25 August 2020.

10. Cheney, Lynne, *James Madison: A Life Reconsidered* (New York: Viking, 2014), 176, 177

11. Hayek, F.A., *The Road to Serfdom: The Definitive Edition* (London: The Chicago Press, 2007), 140

12. Levin, Mark, *Liberty and Tyranny: A Conservative Manifesto* (New York: Threshold Editions, 2009), 61

13. International Churchill Society, Quotes on Forms of Government, *The Worst Form of Government - International Churchill Society* (winstonchurchill.org), 2021

14. Levin, Mark, *Plunder and Deceit* (New York: Threshold Editions, 2015), 188

15. Ravage, M. E., The American Melting Pot. Thoughts — blog — W E R O (werokitchen.com), 7 Feb 2017

16. Hansen, Victor Davis. "Our summer of cultural suicide." *National Review Online* July 30, 2020: www.nationalreview.com/2020/07/summer-cultural-suicide-sports-movies-schools-go-woke, 5 August 2020

Made in the USA
Monee, IL
03 January 2022

87766988R00177